经管类课程思政系列教材

中国物流故事 古代辑

（汉英对照）

主　编：易　兵　王丽华

副主编：熊文杰　龙　伟　李　平

中国财富出版社

图书在版编目（CIP）数据

中国物流故事 . 古代辑：汉英对照 / 易兵，王丽华主编 . — 北京：中国财富出版社，2024.9

（经管类课程思政系列教材）

ISBN 978-7-5047-7118-6

Ⅰ . ①中… Ⅱ . ①易… ②王… Ⅲ . ①物流－经济发展－中国－高等学校－教材－汉、英 Ⅳ . ① F259.22

中国版本图书馆 CIP 数据核字（2019）第 294956 号

策划编辑	黄正丽	**责任编辑**	刘 斐 郑泽叶		**版权编辑**	李 洋
责任印制	尚立业	**责任校对**	庞冰心		**责任发行**	敬 东

出版发行	中国财富出版社			
社　　址	北京市丰台区南四环西路 188 号 5 区 20 楼		**邮政编码**	100070
电　　话	010-52227588 转 2098（发行部）		010-52227588 转 321（总编室）	
	010-52227566（24 小时读者服务）		010-52227588 转 305（质检部）	
网　　址	http://www.cfpress.com.cn	**排　　版**	宝蕾元	
经　　销	新华书店	**印　　刷**	北京九州迅驰传媒文化有限公司	
书　　号	ISBN 978-7-5047-7118-6/F · 3702			
开　　本	710mm×1000mm 1/16	**版　　次**	2024 年 9 月第 1 版	
印　　张	20	**印　　次**	2024 年 9 月第 1 次印刷	
字　　数	346 千字	**定　　价**	60.00 元	

《中国物流故事》系列编委会

南京师范大学外国语学院　　　湖北第二师范学院经济与管理学院

湖北经济学院工商管理学院　　湖北省现代物流发展促进会

黄冈师范学院商学院　　　　　湖北省高等教育学会物流教育专业委员会

武汉工商学院物流学院　　　　九州通医药集团股份有限公司

武汉市商业经济学会　　　　　湖北普罗格科技股份有限公司

武汉物流协会　　　　　　　　北京金文天地信息咨询有限公司

武汉维壬科技有限公司　　　　湖北梦想有位来文化传播有限公司

武汉研众科技有限公司

前言

中国物流业历史悠久，对世界流通领域影响深远、贡献卓著。早在西周时期，就出现了物流业的雏形——古代国家仓储制度，用于备灾和备战。《礼记》中记载的"车同轨"是最早的公路运输标准，它通过减少畜力消耗和车轴磨损，不仅降低了运输成本，更方便了物资周转。古代丝绸之路，则开辟了国际物流发展的道路，被联合国教科文组织誉为东西方文明的对话之路。京杭大运河将钱塘江、长江、淮河、海河、黄河五大彼此独立的天然水系打通成网，并形成了水陆运输标准——漕运制度。郑和下西洋访问了30多个西太平洋和印度洋的国家和地区，是有记载的、最早的大规模远洋航海。到了近代，物流业是在丧权辱国的条约中被动发展的。西方列强在中国各处开辟口岸、修筑铁路、架设桥梁，物流业的发展在失去民族独立自主时顿时显得暗淡无光。经过辛亥革命与新民主主义革命艰苦卓绝的英勇奋斗，一个在中国共产党领导下的新中国诞生了！百年奋斗，物流行业发生了翻天覆地的变化。高铁、天宫、蛟龙、天眼、悟空、墨子、大飞机、港珠澳大桥等，上天遁地，无不是让世界惊叹的中国奇迹！

《中国物流故事》是贯彻和落实习近平总书记在全国高校思想政治工作会议上"……其他各门课都要守好一段渠、种好责任田，使各类课程与思想政治理论课同向同行，形成协同效应"讲话精神的教材。本书以重大历史事件、重要历史人物和伟大物流工程为背景，致力于把学科资源、学术资源转化为育人资源，实现"知识传授"和"价值引领"的有机统一。它把理论融入故事，借故事阐述道理，用道理赢得共识，以悟道完成育人。它以社会主义核心价值观为教育指向，坚持"育人为本、德育为先"，把培育和践行社会主义核心价值观有机融入专业课程体系中，全面渗透学生在校教育教学全过程。它为物流管理专业教师的课程思政教育提供了德育案例，也为物流管理专业学生学习学科发展史提供了丰富素材。

本书由《中国物流故事》系列编委会策划编写。感谢武汉商学院领导和师生在编撰过程中给予的关心与指导,感谢社会各界同人给予的帮助与支持。

　　我们在编写的过程中,参考了众多文献资料,在此谨向相关文献作者表示深深的谢意。由于时间仓促、水平有限,敬请各位读者提出宝贵意见,以便我们不断完善,更好地服务于高等教育专业课程思政建设。

2023 年 5 月 6 日于后官湖畔

Introduction

China's logistics industry has a long history, which has a far-reaching influence and an outstanding contribution to the world circulation field. As early as the Western Zhou Dynasty, the embryonic form of the logistics industry—the ancient national warehousing system was born, which was used for disaster and war preparation. According to *The Book of Rites*, "Uniform wheelbase" is the earliest road transportation standard. By reducing animal power consumption and axle wear, it not only reduced transportation costs, but also facilitated material turnover. The ancient Silk Road opened up the road for the development of international logistics and was praised by UNESCO as the road for the dialogue between eastern and western civilizations. The Beijing–Hangzhou Grand Canal connected the five independent natural water systems of Qiantang River, Yangtze River, Huai River, Hai River, and Yellow River into a network, and formed the water and land transportation standard—grain transport. Zheng He visited more than 30 countries and regions in the Western Pacific and the Indian Ocean during his voyages, which is the earliest recorded large–scale ocean navigation. In modern times, the logistics industry developed passively in the treaties of humiliating the country and forfeiting its sovereignty. Western powers opened ports, built railways, and erected bridges everywhere in China, and the development of logistics industry suddenly appeared to be bleak when China lost national independence. After the arduous and heroic struggle of the Revolution of 1911 and the New Democratic Revolution, a new China under the leadership of the Communist Party of China was born! After a hundred years of struggle, the logistics industry has undergone earth-shaking changes. High-speed railway, Tiangong, Jiaolong, Tianyan, Wukong, Mozi, large passenger aircraft, Hong Kong-Zhuhai-Macao Bridge, etc., all of which are Chinese miracles amazing the world!

China Logistics Story is the textbook which implements the spirit of the speech of President Xi Jinping at the National Conference on ideological and political work in colleges and universities that "... All other courses should keep a good canal and plant a good field of responsibility so that all kinds of courses and ideological theory courses can walk in the same direction and form a synergistic effect". With the background of major historical events, important historical figures, and great logistics projects, this book is committed to transforming discipline resources and academic resources into educational resources, and realizing the organic unity of "knowledge-imparting" and "value-leading". It integrates theory into stories, expounds truth by stories, wins consensus with reason, and educates people by enlightenment. It regards the socialist core values as the educational orientation, adheres to the principle of "educating people first and moral education first", organically integrates the cultivation and practice of socialist core values into the professional curriculum system, and fully penetrates the whole process of students' education and teaching in school. It provides moral education cases of ideological and political curriculum education for teachers majoring in logistics management and also provides rich materials for students majoring in logistics management to learn the history of the discipline development.

This book was planned and written by the editorial board of the *"China Logistics Story"* series. We extend our sincere thanks to the leaders, faculty, and students of Wuhan Business University for their care and guidance throughout the compilation process. We are also grateful for the support and assistance provided by colleagues from all walks of life.

In the process of compiling, we have referred to many works of literature, and we would like to express our deep gratitude to the authors of relevant literature. Due to the short time and limited level, we sincerely invite readers to put forward valuable opinions, so that we can constantly improve and better serve the ideological and political construction of the curriculum of higher education.

Yi Bing

May 6th, 2023, Houguan Lake

目录

CONTENTS

中国物流故事 古代辑（汉英对照）

京杭大运河
——人水互动文明的巅峰之作

拱宸桥（汪萍 摄）

春秋时期，中华儿女开始用一土一石开凿京杭大运河。京杭大运河是世界上跨度最长、历史最悠久的运河，既作漕运动脉，又为灌溉之源，京杭大运河流经之处皆为民生。京杭大运河开掘于春秋时期，兴建于隋朝，繁荣于唐宋两朝，取直于元朝，疏通于明清两朝，从北到南奔流约 1797 公里，扮演着南北漕运黄金水道的重要角色。京杭大运河促进了资源的跨地域流动，催化了商品经济的进一步发展，并孕育了市场经济的萌芽，也由此滋养了丰厚的物质文化和非物质文化。

一、功在当代

在古代，陆路运输主要依靠人力和畜力，运载量小、运行速度慢，耗费的时间多、费用高，所以，水路运输是大宗货物运输的首选。中国天然形成的大江大河大多从西往东横向流动，加上黄河流域历经战乱，经济文化环境被破坏，长江流域得以发展，中国就逐渐形成了经济文化中心在南方、政治军事中心在北方的局面。运河可以加强南北两大中心的联系，保证南方的物资能够源源不断地运往北方，因此，开辟并维持一条纵贯南北的运河，对历朝历代来说就变得尤为重要。

中国人开凿运河的历史已经有两千余年。公元前486年，吴王夫差为北上伐齐，修建了自扬州向东北，经射阳湖到淮安入淮河的"邗沟"。邗沟全长约170公里，沟通了淮河与长江，是京杭大运河河道成型最早的一段。此外，战国时期，魏国修建的鸿沟和秦国修建的郑国渠，都是历史上著名的运河工程。

隋朝大运河是运河开凿的一个顶峰。"喜在东南"，隋炀帝杨广开凿运河是为了方便去扬州看琼花美景，这是古代说书人常用的开场白。其实并非如此。"尽道隋亡为此河，至今千里赖通波"，人们更愿意相信，这是一个帝王的魄力与远见，由此，开始了跨越千年、千秋受益的宏大工程。

开皇元年（公元581年），杨广被封为晋王。北御突厥期间，得益于秦朝开辟的陆路交通网，杨广戍边屡建战功。

杨广继位后，迁都洛阳，开始以洛阳为中心开凿运河。一方面，开辟一条纵贯南北的运河有利于通过水路运输将江南稻米供给北方；另一方面，杨广注重疆域的扩大及辖域的稳定，疏凿运河有利于集中皇权，加强控制，将北方政治军事中心与南方经济文化中心联系起来，形成南北统一的整体。

大业元年（公元605年），隋炀帝诏令征调上百万民夫，开挖通济渠，拉开了修建隋朝大运河的序幕。在当今先进的技术和理念的支持下，开辟航道尚且需要很长一段时间。而在1000多年前，隋炀帝依靠人力和最原始的工具，仅用6年时间，就挖掘了全长2000多公里的完整运河网。其中，通济渠、永济渠、邗沟、江南运河，将中原地区、河北平原和江淮地区紧密地联系到一起，形成了一个以洛阳为中心的交通大动脉。加上隋文帝时期修凿的西通大兴城的广通渠，隋朝大运河连接了长江、黄河、淮河、海河、钱塘江五大水系，构成了沟通全国水上交通的完整体系。

唐朝大运河在隋朝大运河的基础上有所发展。史学界把唐朝沿用隋朝的运河，统称为隋唐大运河。隋唐大运河主要分为两支，一支是永济渠，连通东北地区；

另一支是通济渠、邗沟（又名山阳渎）和江南运河，连通东南地区。

隋唐大运河连接了黄河与长江两大经济圈，是隋唐时期的重要经济命脉，它以漕运为主，不仅节省了巨大的物流成本，解决了古代南北大宗货物运输的难题，还带动了运河沿线地区的经济发展。同时，北方有了南方的物资保障，"以东南之粮，养西北之兵"的物流格局逐渐形成。

二、国之命脉

隋唐大运河对沟通南北起到了重要作用，但唐朝灭亡后，进入了混乱割据的五代十国时期。北宋定都汴梁（今开封），粮食供给地也转移到了江南地区。宋金时期，黄河水患频发，屡次决口，冲坏河道，使得永济渠的部分河道基本断航。

元朝定都大都（今北京）后，国家重心转移至北京，仍利用隋唐大运河旧道转运漕粮。此时，受长期战乱及黄河水患的影响，运河河道多有壅塞，水陆转运颇为不便。

水利专家郭守敬向元世祖忽必烈提出了筹划多年的运河治理方案：一是以汶水和泗水为水源，开凿济州河，而后开凿会通河，修建闸坝，以通漕运；二是修建运输能力更大的运河，开凿坝河和通惠河，解决旧有河道通航能力弱的问题。由此将运河改造为直接沟通北京与江南地区的内陆运输水道。

忽必烈下令对隋唐大运河实行局部修凿，京杭大运河登上历史舞台。尽管起止点相同，但是京杭大运河全长约 1797 公里，相比隋唐大运河缩短了约 903 公里。京杭大运河途经京、津、冀、鲁、苏、浙 6 个省市，其主要水源是微山湖、昭阳湖、独山湖、南阳湖组成的"南四湖"。至今，它仍然是重要的航运水道，与长城、坎儿井并称中国古代三大工程。

隋唐大运河南北走向，兼顾东西，是"人"字形的，而京杭大运河纵穿南北，呈"一"字形。为了避免绕道洛阳，裁弯取直，就必须修建新的人工河道，放弃以往取道洛阳、开封的线路，改道山东。把原来的横向运河，修筑成纵向运河，大体上南北呈一条直线。"杭州码头装大米，一纤拉到北京城"，京杭大运河上的俗语，道出了两座城市以河为媒的历史渊源。

在解决运粮问题的同时，京杭大运河作为南北交通大动脉，也促进了南北经济文化的交流。通过商船运输，丝绸、茶叶、竹木、蔗糖等出产于南方的货品与松木、皮毛、煤炭等北方物资交换互通，因此商业繁荣发展。

中国物流故事 STORY 古代辑 汉英对照

京杭大运河航运（朱吉鹏　摄）

　　此外，京杭大运河还是连通陆上丝绸之路与海上丝绸之路的重要枢纽，促进了沿岸地区工商业的发展。京杭大运河北接陆上丝绸之路，南连海上丝绸之路，形成了完整的通道。从京杭大运河北端北京通州向北出发，有成熟的驿道或商道，与陆上丝绸之路相连接，绵延至北方草原，再延伸至欧洲；从京杭大运河南端杭州出发，有浙东运河延伸至宁波，与海上丝绸之路相连接，通向南亚各国。中国文化得以向世界各地传播，在世界范围产生了广泛而深远的影响。

　　京杭大运河的贯通，进一步加强了元朝江南地区与北方草原地区的联系，进而促进了陆上丝绸之路与海上丝绸之路的贯通。据《马可波罗行纪》记载，马可·波罗沿陆上丝绸之路来到元朝的上都，返程的时候沿京杭大运河到镇江，然后到达福建泉州，经海上丝绸之路回到家乡。另一位旅行家鄂多立克，通过海上丝绸之路从意大利来到中国，沿京杭大运河到达大都，回程沿着黄河折向西南，进入河西走廊，穿越中亚回到意大利，恰好经过陆上丝绸之路。

三、淌金之河

　　京杭大运河不纯粹是一条人工运河，更是一个横向可通东西、纵向能连南北的物流运输体系，其对经济和文化的带动作用和辐射作用不容小觑。

京杭大运河北起北京，南抵杭州，从华北平原直达长江三角洲地区。京杭大运河的修建，使政治中心和经济中心更稳定，使北方有了来自南方的物资支援和保障，一个宏伟壮阔的运输网络得以形成，中国的政治经济结构也由此基本固定。

河道的走势决定了城市发展的格局，同时也影响着城市的功能性。京杭大运河对沿岸城市的经济发展起到了巨大的推动作用，使南北贸易兴盛。物资流动催化了财富积累，运河沿岸的一座座城市逐渐丰饶，大片的街区随着商业的发展繁荣兴起，城市的格局随之改变，城市的烙印逐渐凸显，形成以扬州、苏州、济宁等为代表的全国性商业中心。

这些工商业发达的运河城市，倚运河而建，以物流为特色传承运河精神，逐渐吸引世界瞩目。

崔溥所著的《漂海录》记录了当时南来北往的商贩以及运河的沿岸风貌和交通情形。

明清两朝维系了京杭大运河的基本格局。因地制宜，通过多次大规模修缮，京杭大运河能够长期发挥运输漕粮、维系国家协同发展的重要功能。

进入近代，海运的发展和津浦铁路的通车，使京杭大运河陷入萧条，但京杭大运河依然保有着非同寻常的交通运输价值。新中国成立后，京杭大运河成为北煤南运的主要通道，也成为南水北调东线工程的重要组成部分。逐水而居，至今仍有约 3 亿中国人生活在运河河畔。

尽管现代化交通已经非常发达，但像苏州这样的现代化城市，每天有超过 6000 艘船只从京杭大运河通过，运河水网承担着近乎一半的货运量。

波光粼粼的大运河，承载着厚重的历史。联合国教科文组织归结，京杭大运河代表了人类的迁徙和流动，代表了多维度的商品、思想、知识和价值的互惠和持续不断的交流，并代表了因此产生的文化在时间和空间上的交流与相互滋养，这些滋养长期以来通过物质和非物质遗产不断得到体现。

京杭大运河全程行经大量湖泊和水渠。为何历朝历代的君主，宁可动用大量人力物力来挖掘维护，也没想过利用现成的湖泊？

这是因为京杭大运河扛起的是中国历代南北地区物资输送的大任。运输就得讲求效率，航线上的每个地点，都是位置极佳的物资中转地，整条航线的距离设定，更要起到高效的作用。此外，湖泊上搞运输，最怕的就是"不可抗力"。尽管整条航线上的湖泊水量充沛，但季节气候不对，哪怕只有一处枯水，整条航线都要瘫痪。茫茫湖泊还是"水匪"的最爱。加上古代造船技术有限，遇上大风大浪，船毁人亡的悲剧时有发生。所以，"傍着湖"走，看似"笨办法"，却是古人极其智慧的选择，也由此诞生了最早的水陆联运物流系统设计。

四、利在千秋

1. 从逐粮而居到分段运输的物流思想

唐初实行府兵制，士兵平时为耕种土地的农民，战时便从军打仗，粮食基本自给自足。即便运输困难，航行缓慢，粮食供给仍可维持，运河运输劣势没有显现。随着中央集权的加重，唐玄宗李隆基统治时期，府兵制逐渐转为募兵制，兵农分离使得朝廷对粮食的需求进一步增加。然而关中土地狭窄，粮食产量无法满足京师所需。从粮食产量高的江南地区调运粮食，货船又受阻于三门砥柱一带，不能直接水运，粮食运输问题逐渐突显。粮食供不应求，中央政权受阻，皇帝开始了逐粮而居的生活。洛阳位居中原地区，农业发达、交通便利、粮食储备丰富，每当粮食不足，皇帝便率文武百官一同迁往洛阳，"就食东都"有效缓解了朝廷的压力。

开元十八年（公元 730 年），裴耀卿建议改变以前漕粮直运的方式，初步提出分段运输。他建议在入黄河口处建造仓库，将江南地区的粮米布帛运到这里并卸入库中，漕船即行返航，待黄河适于航行时，再将货物送抵目的地。

分段运输减少了漕运损耗，节约了开支。分段运输可使江南地区的漕船不入黄河，节省了因水位高低不一致而等候的时间，同时也规避了三门天险，运输成本大幅度降低的同时，运输效率也大幅度提高了。

分设转般仓再换船转运的"转般法"，也体现了分段运输的物流思想，对漕运乃至中国物流的发展都产生了积极而深远的影响。

2. 从分段运输到水路直达的物流思想

三门天险在黄河漕运的咽喉之地，是整个黄河漕运的关键所在。三门天险河段特殊的地理环境给过往船只带来极大威胁，稍有不慎就会发生船毁人亡的悲剧。历代黄河漕运治理均围绕三门天险展开，但治理结果并不理想。后大多采用迂回战术，在三门天险河段停船登陆，舟车上下，要倒腾很多次，造成了巨大的运输损耗。由于难以克服的天然障碍，黄河漕运时断时续。

为了克服这个障碍，公元 741 年，李齐物效仿前人凿山为栈道，纤夫在栈道上助力拉纤，协助船只通过三门天险。虽然修凿栈道对船只通行有所帮助，但并未彻底解决航行难题，甚至纤夫坠河死亡事故频发，加重了人民的疾苦。

后又实施水路直达的运输方案，于三门峡附近开凿开元新河，用人工开河的办法，避开三门天险，使船只直达长安。

仅三个月左右，与黄河平行的开元新河就通航了。船只在开元新河上航行，可避开激流，航行较为安全。水路直达，这与分段运输异曲同工，且更为先进。采用分段运输，船只装卸太过麻烦，开元新河开通后，过往船只不再从集津仓卸转陆运，而是直接从河阴仓通过开元新河，到达渭口的永丰仓，运输效率大幅提升。

3. 从水路直达再到分段运输的物流思想

安史之乱后，北方经济遭到了严重破坏，农业生产荒废，民生凋敝，常年饥荒。从唐肃宗时期开始，各朝皇帝都在绞尽脑汁思考，如何把江南地区的物资运到长安。当时的漕运因为战乱而中断，运河渠道年久失修，尤其是汴渠，早已被泥土淤塞，根本无法通行。直到公元 764 年，刘晏临危受命，负责整顿漕运。

刘晏把裴耀卿的漕运分段运输推而广之施行于运河的各个河段，使"江船不入汴，汴船不入河，河船不入渭"，采取分段运输的方法，解决了各个河段因水势不同而难以连续通行的问题。

为了配合这一方案，实施"置仓储、近转运"的方法，即在运河南部的扬州设立船运码头，在河道沿岸设置转运仓。江南漕船运粮至扬州，交官入库，船即返回，再由官船将漕粮分段转运。每段水路都有专属的船只负责运输，船只在特定河段往返，船工对所属河段行船的情况更为熟悉，知道如何避开航行中的险滩，减少了路途中的损耗，节省了航运时间，缓解了船只倾覆之忧。

经刘晏改革，河道疏浚，大运河恢复了往日的繁荣，满足了长安粮食之需。

4. 标准化管理的物流思想

刘晏在扬州建成 10 个大型造船厂，根据淮河、汴河、黄河及渭河四段水路不同的水位特点，分别打造标准船只，每艘都是吃重一千石粮食的大船，每艘船固定船工 35 名。

在过三门砥柱一带时，规定以 10 艘船为一纲，将 10 艘船绑到一起。每纲标配 50 名撑篙的船工，负责稳住船体；岸上标配 300 名纤夫，负责拖动船只。并且纤绳位置、队伍阵型、间距全部标准化管理，在统一的号子下，所有人一鼓作气，同时发力，船队冲破天险势不可挡。

经刘晏改革之后的漕运，相比唐玄宗时期，运输时间缩短了，每石粮食的运输成本也降低了，更重要的是，它不再消耗民间巨大的人力、物力。

5. 发明水闸改进设备的物流思想

随着运河的迅速发展，宋朝的运河工程建设也有了较大提高，在唐朝单闸节制用水的基础上，创造了复闸和澳闸。

雍熙元年（公元 984 年），乔维岳任淮南转运使时，开始建造我国第一个规范的船闸，由船闸代替堰埭，克服运河地形上的限制。船闸的工作是利用"水涨船高"的原理，虽然比堰埭更具优越性，但在过船时，水量损耗仍然无法避免，这就要求采取一定的措施来减少水量的损失。

北宋中期出现的澳闸，就是用来解决蓄水行船的问题的。将闸室放出的水储入水澳中，当水量不足时，利用水澳的水回闸室。澳闸能有效节省用水，解决水源问题，加上水澳修建简便，在淮南运河、江南运河中得到广泛推广。

宋朝是运河水闸技术发展的高峰期，这种依托湖泊储水，以水闸操控运河流量的技术，结束了大运河"靠天吃饭"的历史，是人类运河工程史上的重大突破。

6. 开凿通惠河形成内河与海运联运的物流思想

元大都人口众多，粮食供应上依赖南方。元世祖忽必烈时，开凿了从山东东平到临清的会通河，又开凿了从通州到大都的通惠河。另外还开辟了海运，海运比河运省钱，还可以免去陆路辗转之劳和搁浅之患。

元世祖不仅打通内河直达大都，还将海运船只与内河运输船只在直沽统一集货，通过通惠河直达大都，每年输运京城的粮食增加 300 多万石，这成了元、明、清三朝繁荣的关键。这一伟大壮举，使江海湖泊全线相连，实现内河与海运联运的局面，对今天实现海上"丝绸之路"与内河运输联运，推进"一带一路"倡议起到了至关重要的作用。

五、焕发新生

船舶运输从古至今都是在运量和成本方面最有优势的运输形式，一直以低能耗著称①。纵观世界区域经济，从美国密西西比河对沿岸工农业发展的促进作用，到莱茵河对德国乃至整个欧盟的经济可持续发展的助推，再到京杭大运河对运河经济带的催化功能，都说明了大江大河是重要的经济增长轴。

京杭大运河从北到南，流经千里，虽为人工开凿，却改变了中国的地理格局，是古代交通文明成果和现代内河航运成果的历史见证。2017 年 6 月，习近平总书记指出，"大运河是祖先留给我们的宝贵遗产，是流动的文化，要统筹保护好、传承好、利用好。"

时间并没有让京杭大运河成为冰冷的遗迹，今天，京杭大运河还继续在国家经济、社会和文化发展中发挥着巨大作用。它是中国人心中值得敬畏的历史，也激励着我们敢为人先、追求卓越的民族情怀。

故事一 京杭大运河——人水互动文明的巅峰之作

---

① 船舶运输的平均运输成本只有铁路的 1/2、公路的 1/8；单位能耗仅为铁路的 1/4、公路的 1/9。

丝绸之路
——东西方文明交汇的千年之约

1871 年春季的一天，中国西部的戈壁黄沙中，一位金发碧眼的外国人正骑在骆驼上，由向导带领一步一步跋涉着。骆驼队伍拉得老长，一箱箱行李里装着的是地质勘探的工具、矿产图纸以及描绘风土人情的资料。

这个外国人便是李希霍芬，一位德国地理学家和地质学家。他说服了北洋大臣李鸿章允许他来中国内陆考察。从 1868 年到 1872 年，他先后七次沿着不同的路线考察，从沿海到内陆，从东北到西南，在中国留下了他的脚印。

李希霍芬有一个习惯，每次调研，除了记载当地物产外，还尤其注意运送这些物产的道路。他每到一个地方，必先在调研报告上叙述各地的

《李希霍芬——"丝绸之路"的命名者》雕塑（项金国作品）

水陆交通状况，记录在此交通基础上形成的市镇和商业路线，由此形成了报告主线。渐渐地，他发现中国古代的商贸道路，与西方关于"丝绸之国"的记载之间有着紧密的联系，历史的大脉络已然被他抓在了手中。

李希霍芬1872年归国后，担任柏林大学校长，他晚年的绝大多数时间都在写《中国——亲身旅行和据此所作研究的成果》（以下简称《中国》）。李希霍芬在《中国》第一卷中，首次明确提出了"丝绸之路"的定义。

1936年，李希霍芬的学生斯文·赫定以《丝绸之路》之名出版了一本书，此后，"丝绸之路"一词慢慢被大众接纳并快速传播。

从此，一个闪闪发光的名词走进了中国人，乃至世界各国人民的心目中。那条被滚滚黄沙掩盖的经贸文化之路，也重新鲜活起来，向人们讲述着传奇的历史故事。

一、凿空之旅

公元前2世纪初，西汉王朝经过文景之治国力渐盛，踌躇满志的青年帝王汉武帝刘彻，决定向威胁西汉边境安全80余年的匈奴宣战，希望将多年来的耻辱洗刷掉。

《张骞》凿空西域（邮票）（高云设计）

建元二年（公元前139年），刘彻决定联合西域诸国打击匈奴，于是派遣特使张骞去联络被匈奴逐出河西走廊的大月氏[①]。

当时的大月氏，为躲避匈奴追杀，已经迁居到了中亚阿姆河流域一带。要联络大月氏，就得穿越匈奴控制的河西地区。然而，要越过西域7000多公里的荒漠与流沙绝非易事，更何况还是穿越敌人的领地去联合敌人的敌人。这是一片汉人之前从未涉足的地区，遍布沙漠、雪山，时而长风漫卷、飞沙走石，时而

---

① 公元前2世纪中亚地区的游牧部族。

万里寂静、杳无人烟。

　　然而，张骞果断地踏上了征程。由堂邑父做向导，张骞率领一百多人组成的使团，一路簧野火、逐水草，远离一切可疑的乱蹄踪迹，从陇西出发前往大月氏所在地。但是张骞一行在河西走廊不幸碰上匈奴的骑兵队，除他和堂邑父被俘外，其他人全部被杀。

　　匈奴不想杀死张骞，而是试图劝降他，但是未果，于是就将张骞等人软禁了起来。后来单于将一名匈奴女子许配给张骞做妻子，张骞不得已成了婚。整整过了 11 个春秋，张骞和向导堂邑父才摆脱了匈奴的软禁。大惊初定，张骞没有回汉朝，而是继续向西，初衷不改，誓要完成出使西域的使命。

　　张骞一行向西越过葱岭，经过几十天长途跋涉后抵达大宛，即今中亚乌兹别克斯坦费尔干纳盆地。随后大宛王派人护送张骞抵达康居（中亚阿姆河与锡尔河之间），张骞再由康居到达大月氏所在地。然而大月氏已立新王，并越过阿姆河吞并了当地部族的大片土地。大月氏的人民已然安居乐业，加之当时的大月氏距中原王朝太远，已不想联合汉朝再向匈奴复仇了。

　　张骞在大月氏住了一年多，依然无法劝服大月氏攻打匈奴，不得已而东返。返回途中，张骞选择沿塔里木盆地南麓进到柴达木盆地，绕路青海地区归国，主要是为了更好地避开匈奴的阻拦，但运气不好，还是被抓住了。所幸一年后，匈奴因单于去世而发生内乱，张骞才得以逃脱，最终经过千辛万苦在汉武帝元朔三年（公元前 126 年）回到长安。

　　张骞第一次出使西域历时 13 年，虽然没有达到同大月氏结成联盟的政治目的，却了解了西域地区的政治、经济、地理、文化风俗等情况，为以后加强中原同西域的联系奠定了基础。不久，张骞就在参与卫青出击匈奴的战争中利用到了他的西域知识。因其知水草所处，为此次军事行动立下大功，被封为博望侯。

　　张骞出使西域时，西汉王朝也对匈奴展开了一系列打击，肃清了匈奴在漠南及河西走廊的势力。

　　但是，西域各国仍为匈奴控制，依然威胁着西汉王朝西北边境的安全。于是，汉武帝再度派遣张骞出使西域，目的是设法联络乌孙等西域各国，建立抗击匈奴的联盟。这一次出访随员三百，团队宏伟，携带钱币、丝帛数千巨万。张骞到达乌孙（伊犁河、楚河流域）时，正值乌孙因王位之争而政局不稳，乌孙方面无意与汉朝结盟抗击匈奴。在这期间，张骞派遣副使分别到中亚、西亚和南亚的大宛、康居、大月氏、安息、身毒（今印度）等国联络交涉。公元前 115 年，张骞回到汉朝，乌孙派了翻译和使者各一名随行来到长安。使者见到汉朝人众富厚，回到乌孙后广加宣扬，使得汉朝的威望在西域大大提高。很快，被张骞派去的副使们也陆续回国，并从他们访问的国家带回了许多使节。从此，中西之间的交往正式开启，西汉王朝与西域及中亚、西亚、南亚地区的友好关系迅速发展，西来使者相望于道。

据称自西汉起，向西方出使的使团一年之中少则五六个，多则十几个，他们去访问的地方很远，有时出访一次甚至需要八九年。使团人数多的时候有几百人，少的时候也有一百多人。"日款于塞下"，与使团相得益彰的是一群群胡商贩客。在这之后，中国与西方之间的陆路交通继续向西延伸。

张骞的征程打通了被匈奴长期封锁的东西方陆路交通，促进了东西方的经济文化交流，建立了中原与西北边疆地区的友好关系，开启了中国与西方各国直接交流的新纪元。张骞出使西域的开创性意义重大，司马迁在《史记·大宛列传》中给予其极高的赞誉，称其功绩为"凿空"①。

二、震撼西方

张骞的出访之旅使中国通向欧洲和非洲的陆运安全通道连通。这条路线以汉都长安为起点，经过河套平原，随后分成两路。一条路以阳关为起点，经过鄯善，沿昆仑山北边山脉往西，历经莎车、葱岭，出大月氏，到安息，西到犁靬，或者是从大月氏南进入身毒。另一条路从玉门关出发，经车师前国，沿天山南边的山脚往西走，出疏勒，西经葱岭，过大宛，抵达康居、奄蔡。

汉朝的使商陆续西行，西域的使商也陆续东来。中国的丝绸和其他纺织产品从洛阳和长安经河套平原、今新疆维吾尔自治区运送到阿拉瓦，随后装运到欧洲，又把西方世界各国的稀世珍宝运往中国境内。

公元前五十年左右，罗马执政官率领四万人进攻东方的安息（位于伊朗高原东北部），结果被安息人包围。双方鏖战很久不分胜负。这时安息人忽然挥舞起颜色鲜艳夺目的军旗，罗马人一下子乱了阵脚，他们认为这是安息人得到了上帝的帮助，立刻失去了斗志，在混乱中丧生无数。

---

① 意思是开通道路。

这是罗马军队历史上输得最惨的一次战役，可悲的是，他们是被吓输的，而不是被打输的。而那些忽然间出现的鲜艳夺目的军旗，其原材料就是中国的丝绸。

当时的罗马人主宰着地中海，上流人士将丝绸衣服看作富裕的象征。凯撒大帝十分钟爱丝绸，总是穿着进入元老院，丝绸成为罗马人狂热追求的对象。

即使不缺钱，罗马人要想购买丝绸也并不容易。因为丝绸的运输是个艰难而漫长的过程，要经过罗布泊、塔克拉玛干沙漠、帕米尔高原，再经过中亚的撒马尔罕，到达波斯后才能转运到罗马。因为波斯征收过境关税，使得一些商人望而却步，而罗马人要得到丝绸就只能高价从波斯购买了。为了满足对丝绸的需要，无奈的罗马人只能拆了丝绸，在里面添入羊毛等廉价材料。

尽管罗马人已经与安息、贵霜和阿克苏姆王国进行贸易，丝绸却始终供不应求。对丝绸的渴求，刺激商贩们积极开拓商路。根据很多考古新发现，在北纬50度线周边，在尼罗河流域、两河流域、印度河流域和渭河流域往北的辽阔草原，有一条由很多断断续续的小商路相互连接的大草原经济带，它就是丝绸之路的原型。

西汉末年，匈奴封禁了丝绸之路。公元73年，东汉班超又再次连通阻隔了约58年的西域，并第一次将这条路拓展到了欧洲。罗马帝国的使臣也第一次顺着丝绸之路到达东汉都城洛阳，这次出使是有记载的欧洲和中国的第一次"触碰"。

沿着这条连接亚欧的路，中国的锦、缎产品源源不绝地运往东亚和欧洲。因而，古希腊和罗马称中国为赛里斯国，称中国人为赛里斯人[①]。

这条丝路成为当时世界上路程最远、意义最重大的国际商道。罗马作家老普林尼曾讲道，遥远的东方丝国在山林中获得丝制品原料，历经浸泡等流程，出口到罗马，促使罗马逐渐尊崇丝制服装。他还说，保守估计，印尼、赛里斯和阿拉伯半岛每年能够通过贸易从罗马帝国挣取一亿银币的盈利，这就是罗马帝国的女性每年在奢侈品上的花销。

丝绸之路就像丝绸，有时，它是千万条丝线，有的断断续续，有的清晰；有时，它是一张浩瀚的网，不时展现绚丽的色泽。

三、千年兴衰

各国大批官员、商人、学者和旅行家常年在丝绸之路上来来往往，他们中的

---

① 古希腊语中"赛里斯"意为丝绸。

部分人在沿途的城镇停下来，在当地居住、通婚。他们的生活方式与当地的生活方式相互影响，促进了民族的融合，也促进了沿途各国的繁荣和昌盛。

丝绸之路在西汉、东汉时期的起点分别位于长安和洛阳，这两个城市均是当时中国的经济文化中心。无论丝绸之路从哪里出发，一般都在张掖、武威一带会合，接着沿河西走廊，直达敦煌一带。

丝绸之路由敦煌开始分成若干支线。因为到达了这里再往前就是塔克拉玛干沙漠，商队要穿越大沙漠往西行进是不现实的事情。所以商队只能沿着沙漠的边缘行走。

如果沿着沙漠的南线行走，出古时的阳关，绕过塔克拉玛干沙漠，经过鄯善、和田、莎车等国家，最后可抵达葱岭。汉朝时人们到达了这里，看到葱岭高7000多米，岭顶直插云霄，便以为抵达了神话传说中的不周山。

如果沿着沙漠的北线行走，会经过楼兰、车师、高昌、尉犁、龟兹、姑墨、疏勒，最后抵达大宛。另外，再往北还有一条路线，那条路线从安西出发，经过伊吾、庭州、伊犁等地。

葱岭是古代丝绸之路的一个中转站，从这里开始，便可经过中东地区抵达欧洲。同样，从葱岭往西也有三条路线，分别和葱岭以东的三条路线对应。

第一条路线是沿咸海、里海和黑海的北海岸，经过碎叶、怛罗斯、伊蒂尔等地到达君士坦丁堡。第二条路线是从喀什开始，穿越费尔干纳盆地，经过撒马尔罕、布哈拉等到马什哈德，并在此处与第三条路线会合。第三条路线从葱岭起步，经过克什米尔抵达巴基斯坦等国，也可以经过白沙瓦、喀布尔、马什哈德、巴格达、大马士革等前往欧洲。

综上所述，丝绸之路经过哪些国家，主要视商队的性质和目的地而定，不同的路线经过的国家也有所不同。但丝绸之路就像一条辐射线，延伸至当时的中东地区和欧洲地区的各国。

丝绸之路是一条"活"的通道。因而，在不一样的历史时期，因为政治、自然、宗教信仰等要素的影响，丝绸之路会不时变换方向。比如南北朝时期，占据北方的鲜卑统治者，不仅与南朝处于敌对状态，而且与其北面的柔然也经常兵戎相向。新疆吐鲁番出土文书中有一份公元474—475年阚氏高昌王国护送各国使者出境的记录。短短数行文字说明，当时来自子合国、塔里木盆地的焉耆、西北印度的乌苌国和中印度的婆罗门国的使者们，要前往蒙古高原的柔然，都要经过高昌。这份文书，勾勒出公元 5 世纪下半叶南北、东西交往的路线，也就是说，虽然当时兵荒马乱，但连通东亚、北亚、中亚以及南亚的丝绸之路，仍然通畅无阻。

从汉朝到隋朝，丝绸之路迅猛发展。在唐朝，朝廷击败了东、西突厥，中西部领土到达了阿姆河周边。经济文化的繁荣，加上与西部地区联系的广泛和便利，让古代丝绸之路的贸易达到了一个高峰时期。中国向西方出口了精美的丝绸、瓷器、茶叶等，而波斯的丝织品、各国的金银器和其他商品也进入了中国。

除此之外，中西方宗教信仰、文化艺术也跟随丝绸之路而散播。公元 627 年，玄奘法师从长安出发，沿着丝绸之路的传统北道西进，最后到达印度。18 年后，玄奘法师带着他精心搜集的佛经，又一次踏上丝绸之路，返回故土。记录丝绸之路的珍贵史料《大唐西域记》，就是他根据自身一路的见闻写出的。

四、重焕生机

明朝之后，丝绸之路逐渐没落。15 世纪后奥斯曼帝国[①]发展起来，建立了一个横跨亚洲、非洲和欧洲的庞大帝国。这个帝国把控着丝绸之路的重要节点，征收高额关税，垄断丝绸贸易，这使得西方国家通过丝绸之路进行贸易变得十分困难。

欧洲商人都不愿意再走这条路，转而进行技术革新，提高造船业水平和海上航行能力。终于，欧洲开发出绕过奥斯曼帝国，从海上抵达中国东南沿海的航海路线，从此大航海时代来临，东西方贸易迎来全新的时代。可以说，丝绸之路没落并不是因为丝绸之路更难走了，而是因为有了更好的物流方式。

16 世纪以后，这条形成于汉朝的中西方之间的主要通道，渐渐人烟稀少，商旅断绝，繁华的往事随着漫天起舞的黄沙，渐渐淹没在时间的长河中。世界正在逐步进入由海洋贸易主导的经济发展时期。

进入 19 世纪后，西方完成工业革命，列强崛起，西方各国开始疯狂向外扩张，丝绸之路沿线国家与地区纷纷陷入被掠夺和欺压的境地，中东被英法势力控制，中亚被沙皇俄国吞入囊中，中国则被列强屡次欺辱，进入半殖民地半封建社会。丝绸之路上的国家与地区基本处在贫穷落后的境地。

日月如梭，斗转星移，时间的指针指向了 21 世纪。

---

① 奥斯曼帝国是奥斯曼土耳其人建立的军事封建帝国。

因为地缘政治、油气资源、民族与宗教的纠葛，大国势力频繁在丝绸之路中西段的中亚和中东地区"拉锯"，使得这里的局势变得错综复杂。对于此事，有的西方国家专家学者表明，它是一块期待与失落的共存之地，也是一块风采与排斥并行相交的地方。

不过，亚欧大陆的东方，丝绸之路的起点，却出现了改变该地区状况的曙光。中国这条东方巨龙重焕雄威，走出了自己的强国之路。

2001年，中国提倡创立"上海合作组织"，初期以严厉打击恐怖主义、分裂主义和极端主义为目的，各国共同致力于中亚地区的反恐事务管理。之后，该组织将合作内容、合作范畴扩展到对外经济贸易、环境保护、高新科技、文化艺术、文化教育、金融业、交通出行、电力能源等行业，目标是促进创建公平、民主、有效的国际性政治经济新方向。

2013年，中国国家领导人习近平在哈萨克斯坦首都阿斯塔纳发表演说，明确提出了中国与中亚世界各国共创丝绸之路经济带的提议。中亚各国积极响应"一带一路"倡议，致力于共同建立平等、务实、互利的友好合作关系。在"一带一路"的实施过程中，中国既投资中亚石油开发，又给当地带来许多基础建设的发展资金和经济贸易发展的机遇。美国历史学家阿尔弗雷德·麦考伊说，随着亚欧非经济一体化进程加快，开始形成一个以中国为中心的统一"世界岛"。

中欧班列（邹竞一 摄）

往事已矣，凿空西域的张骞，投笔从戎的班超，西天取经的玄奘，还有那伴着驼铃西去东来的粟特商人，都成为我们的历史记忆。但是，丝绸之路的荣光不会随着时间的推移而消散，反而愈发显露着它无尽的魅力。

丝绸之路不仅是连接东西方贸易的通道，也是促进人类文明和世界历史发展的伟大之路。通过这条古径，历史悠久的中国文化、印度文化、阿拉伯文化、古希腊文化、罗马帝国文化相互连接了起来，推动了中西方文明的沟通。丝绸之路呈现了中国的多元性和创新性。

进入 21 世纪，合作共赢已变成国际性多边合作的主基调。中国明确提出搭建丝绸之路经济带，获得了很多丝绸之路沿线国家与地区的迅速响应。呈现了中国和亚欧国家与地区深入交流合作的开放情结，展现了中国和亚欧国家与地区合作发展的使命感和责任感。

油井、电站、中欧班列，一条新丝绸之路正在亚欧大陆展开绚丽画卷，新时期的丝绸之路焕发着无尽的时代魅力。

含嘉仓
——天下第一粮仓

含嘉仓遗址保护区大门（石蕴璞　摄）

作为人口大国，粮食安全是关系中国国计民生的重要工作，一直受到政府的高度重视。在当今社会，中国仍须以庞大的粮食储备来满足人民群众的生产生活需要，支持国家的各项开支，并应对随时可能出现的战争供给、灾荒救援以及国际市场的突变等问题。如何解决粮食的存储和流通问题，使粮食的存储和流通能够更安全、更高效，天下第一粮仓——含嘉仓，或许能给我们一些启示。

一、广建

"仓"是中国古代粮食仓库的统称。《说文·仓部》中记载："仓，谷藏也，仓黄取而藏之，故谓之仓。"

中国粮仓由于建筑形态各异、存储形式多样，所以名称不同。地面上的粮仓称为廪、困、庾，古人最早以露天堆积和简易房屋的形式存储粮食，后来演化成为形式多样、功能齐备的筒形仓、方形仓和仓屋。地上粮仓建造便利、方便存取，且通风、防潮性能较好，但也受限于粮食的存储时间不宜过长，须应对火灾、虫害、鼠患等问题。

地面以下的粮仓则称为窖和窦，从起初的袋型、矩形、椭圆形，逐步发展成为容量更大、储存技术更完善、力学结构更合理的大型仓窖。地下仓窖虽然对建造地区的要求较高，不易存取，但其存储量大，减少了自然原因对粮食的破坏，且建造成本更低，能满足长时间贮存粮食的需求，因此成为隋唐时期重要的国家粮仓形式。

隋炀帝时代，由于关中物资贫乏、漕运不畅，为满足粮食需要，将都城迁往洛阳，并以洛阳为中心，开凿京杭大运河，并在洛河边建立含嘉城、洛口仓、回洛仓等大型仓城，作为漕运的目的地和中转站。

含嘉仓修建于隋大业元年（公元 605 年），在隋末才正式投入使用，主要目的是储藏京都东边州县的粮食。这项修建工程阵仗十分浩大，高峰时曾动用数万人，历时十多年才得以完成。直到贞观年间，这座隋朝粮仓仍然在为唐朝中央政府服务。

隋唐广建粮仓，形成了以都城大兴（今西安）和洛阳为主的两个仓储中心。这个时期有朝廷直接管理的太仓和国家级转运仓，包括西京太仓和洛阳含嘉仓；有地方政府管理、朝廷监管的正仓；有民间自己置办的义仓；有储放粮食、盐和古钱币的子罗仓；有平抑粮价的常平仓[①]。此外还有储藏军械物资的军仓等不同类型的粮仓。

伴随着粮仓的发展，产生了相对独立的地区——仓城，外场以墙为界线，储存以仓为单元。仓城的问世，不但意味着中国古代粮仓走向成熟，更提高了粮食储存的安全性，产生了系统性的粮食储存与管理方案。

随着大运河的修建，隋朝漕运工作取得快速发展，人工修建的河流高效地把粮食从南方地区运到北方首都。隋朝在永济渠、通济渠沿线修建了大量转运仓，

---

① 谷价低时由国家出资增其价而籴以利民，谷价高时国家减价而粜以便民的粮仓。

有效提高了运输效率。

延续隋朝的态势，唐朝经济兴旺发达，粮食生产量极大。含嘉仓代替了回洛仓，变成我国最大的粮仓，被称为唐朝的"天下第一粮仓"。

出土于十九号仓窖的铭砖（张斌 摄）

在我国的每个历史时期，北方地区因为天气寒冷干燥，谷物存储时间一般都比较长，所以修建了很多仓窖。而南方地区因气候潮湿温暖，地下水位高，土壤潮湿，且粮食生产量大，谷物储存时间较短等因素，多用仓屋存粮。

古代粮仓经过了长期的经验总结，形成了一套完整的建造体系和管理方法，其中关于粮食保存的技术，如今看来也是非常实用的。宋元两朝，粮仓仍沿用地面上与地面下共存的方法；到明清两朝，仓城基本建设进入了新的时期，地面上的粮仓占据绝大多数的比例。

二、承接

含嘉仓不是一个仓库，而是一座仓城，储粮量巨大，城内不仅利用地势合理布局了400余座粮仓，而且结合水道实现了水运陆运的中转与储存。整个仓城分为生活管理区与粮仓区，生活管理区位于仓城内的西北部，南面与东面有隔墙使之与粮仓区分开，用以安置管理人员与守护仓城的重兵。

在这之前的含嘉仓，是隋炀帝时期修建的东都洛阳城内的含嘉城。随着隋朝末年的局势动荡，洛阳城陷入混乱的状态，其城外粮仓均被各股不同势力占据，著名的洛口仓和回洛仓，成为瓦岗军的囊中之物；黎阳仓变成窦建德的家产；而永丰仓是唐高祖李渊取天下的关键基石。洛阳地区的粮食存储格局发生了巨大改变，城外的粮仓容易遭遇洗劫，粮食安全岌岌可危。这些粮满仓的优势，非但没有助隋朝一臂之力，反而成了亡国的火药桶。

唐太宗李世民享用着打败隋朝胜利果实的同时，敏锐地感知到粮仓设在城外的弊端，他认为将大量粮食堆积于城中，不失为最保险的方式。他决定在洛阳城内修建粮仓，以保证任何时期洛阳城内的粮食供应，避免重蹈隋朝的覆辙。而这个由李世民精心谋划的囤粮位置，就是洛阳城东北角的含嘉仓。

"含嘉仓"这三个字很考究，将盛唐气象和皇家粮仓的富贵之气表现得淋漓尽致。

含嘉仓的选址十分科学考究。坐落于洛阳城内的含嘉城，紧挨中心城区的宫皇城和东部城区。从地理条件来看，这里属于洛阳城内东北部地势最高的区域，其南部有洛阳四大水系之一的谷水河道穿过。洛阳城以北地区的地下水位比较低，对修建大中型仓窖而言是个关键要素。同时，由于洛阳北部地区黄土的直立性特点，仓窖的稳定性增强，非常适合向下挖掘仓窖。

含嘉仓仓窖分布示意（图片来源：央视《探索·发现》节目）

作为交通网络的重要节点，含嘉仓不仅供粮食给洛阳城，还要向西为长安输送粮食，起着关东和关中之间漕米转运站的作用，兼有贮存和转运的职责。粮食通过人工渠道由船只运送到仓城内，再换成陆路交通运往洛阳城内。而且，仓城东南部有漕运码头的遗迹，谷水向东与瀍河和漕渠相连通，水运交通同样便捷畅通，对来往船只来说非常方便。

结合考古挖掘与文献记载可知，含嘉城有四座城门：分别是北面德猷门、南面含嘉门、西面仓中门和东面仓东门。含嘉城修有敦实高大的城墙，城墙底宽约17米，上阔11.3米。城体向上收分，城墙剖面呈梯形，材质为夯土，安全性非常高。

三、标配

唐中期以后，由于长安地区人口不断增加，形成了极大的人口压力，且这一时期，长安附近水旱灾害频繁，对长安地区百万人口的吃饭问题产生了严重威胁，粮食供应日益紧张。

此时长安的交通形式仍以陆路运输为主，依靠马车运送，而每辆马车只能运送约600斤粮食，运输能力极为有限。暴涨的人口和环境的恶化导致了唐朝政权东移，助推洛阳成为新的政治经济中心。

洛阳距离长安并不远，但旱灾对洛阳的威胁却远低于长安。由于洛阳有着优良的水路交通网络——大运河，而大运河是连接陆上丝绸之路与海上丝绸之路的桥梁，也是古代中国运送物资的命脉。洛阳是陆上丝绸之路与大运河唯一的交汇点，它将南北地区牵在一起，江南生产的粮食通过水路可以运达洛阳。而唐朝的造船技术可以使每艘漕船运粮五十万石以上，这样的运输能力更是让马车望尘莫及。

所以，从唐朝武则天时期开始，含嘉仓便成为真正意义上的"太仓"，来自全国的粮食源源不断地通过大运河汇集到这里。

含嘉仓储存粮食的种类，主要是粟和米。史载唐玄宗天宝八年（公元749年），全国主要大型粮仓储粮总量为12656620石，而含嘉仓就占5833400石，占总量的近1/2，因此被誉为"天下第一粮仓"。

含嘉仓布局很整齐，类似矩形框，四面院墙，古城墙南北长615米，东西长725米，墙宽15~17米，墙高1~6.5米，仓城总面积约为43万平方米。仓城内东西成行，南北成列，密集排列着400多个仓窖，仓窖之间留有一定距离，排布较为规律，占到了仓城面积的一半以上。其中的小路纵横交错，在约两米宽的路面上，当年双轮车、独轮车留下的车辙，如今还历历在目。最小的仓窖口径 8 米左右，深 6 米，最大的仓窖口径可达 18 米左右，深 12 米，平面呈圆形，剖面结构也呈上大下小。仓窖规模不一，最小者可储粮数千石，最大者可储粮数千乃至一万石。

建造仓窖的第一步工序是挖土窖，先从地面向下挖一个环形基槽，再对基槽进行夯打，从而形成一个坚实的窖口，再向深处继续挖一个口大底小的圆缸状土窖。上大下小的剖面形状，不但有利于挖掘，也使仓窖更为牢固。在中后期开展防水防潮工作时，操作起来也更为便捷。

仓窖底面多为平底，有一条紧靠窖壁的弧形沟，沟的一头高一头低，高的一端与窖底持平，可以使窖顶渗入的少量雨水流至窖底后进入弧形沟，从而保证仓窖的干燥。

土窖挖成后，在窖底垫一层干燥的土①，然后夯实窖底，这样做既可增加牢固性，又可使土质密度加大，潮气不易上升。此外，还要用火烧硬窖底，再铺一层由红烧土碎块和黑灰等拌成的混合物，作为防潮层，其上还须铺木板或木板和草卷混合的重叠板。在这个基础上，含嘉仓的仓窖中还擦抹了一层由碎土渣、碎煤渣、烘窖点燃后的余烬及调和剂混合而成的混合物。

从含嘉仓窖底遗留的木质遗迹可以观察到，铺设木板防潮是常规做法，但在木板的排列组合上，并没有使用相同形式，铺设方式和木板尺寸都有所差别。

根据《天圣令·仓库令》可以得知，仓窖底部还要铺设草秆，厚度要求五尺（约 167 厘米）。草秆之上铺设两层扎成捆的秸秆，并在仓窖周壁也铺上秸秆。但凡必须用大捆秸秆的部位，均要以几小捆秸秆封堵间隙。铺设双层秸秆后，再用草席遮盖一层，然后才能够储存粮食。

放进粮食后，还须将粮食的总数、储存的日期和操作人员的姓名等信息刻录在铭砖上，并用草席遮盖。草席上再铺五尺厚的草秆，其上再铺双层秸秆。结束以后，挖填七尺（约 233 厘米）高的土将其封闭，并竖起木牌记述相对应的信息，以便仓吏等随时随地搜索，评定其状况。

---

① 据考古记载，含嘉仓各窖垫土厚度不一，一般厚度为 2~4 厘米。

四、优化

在发掘含嘉仓时，于 19、50、182 号三座仓窖出土了铭砖八方，该砖呈方形，正面磨光，砖上有仓名、仓窖位置、粮食来源、粮食品种、粮食数量、入窖日期、运输方式、经手官吏姓名等的记载。铭砖的发现，结合文献记录，揭示了含嘉仓的粮食储存已经达到制度化、科学化的程度。

铭砖的作用类似账簿，提取粮食时，将铭砖一道取出并进行审核，如果仓窖中贮积的粮食与铭砖上数字差距较大，将追究仓吏等管理人员的责任。

已发掘的铭砖都出现于仓窖底端或近底端的回填土中。这些铭砖是在粮食入窖时投入仓窖，粮食出窖后就作废遗弃的。这种埋铭砖立碑的制度，是隋唐时期地下储粮大发展的产物，也是人们不断总结过去地下储粮管理中的利弊而发明的一种新的行之有效的管理制度，在现代仓储中也有很大的借鉴作用。

从含嘉仓出土的铭砖可以看出，含嘉仓是分区管理的。这种分区管理便于仓窖的编号识别和位置查对，从而方便粮食进出管理。

在做好窖藏的基础上，含嘉仓对不同储存环境、不同种类的粮食的贮藏期限作了明确规定，如《新唐书》记载"下湿之地，粟藏五年，米藏三年，皆著于令"；甚至还考虑到运输距离不同导致的实际储存时间的差异，"同时者，先远后近"，即结合粮食的贮存期限要求，优化粮仓的保存时间。

含嘉仓仓窖结构示意（王旭）

此外，含嘉仓还考虑到以新换陈，保存粮食久藏不朽。《唐六典》就有记载，"凡粟支九年，米及杂种三年"。

五、洗礼

由于仓窖是全封闭的储存方式，一经储存，下一次使用会破坏全部储存步骤。由此可以看出，仓窖内的粮食并非经常使用，而是作为长期储备，所有粮食一经储存，短时期内基本维持该状态。

这种方法在《唐六典》中得到了证实。仓窖输出粮食时，每一窖粮食完全耗尽以后，才可以开启使用另一窖。纳粮进仓时，也是尽早放满一窖并将其封闭以后，再启装下一窖。

为了延长粮食的保存时间，仓窖顶部采取的密封方式是装满粮食后必须夯实、压紧，以减少谷物颗粒间的空气残留，并在粮食上面盖席，席上垫谷糠，谷糠厚 40~60 厘米，谷糠上再加席子。席子夹糠的方法能够隔湿保温，防止粮食发热、发芽、腐烂。最后再用黄土将其密封成圆锥形顶，整体看上去像一个个小山包。

在没有先进除虫剂及防腐剂的古代，正是这些有效措施，一方面让细菌和虫类无法在仓窖内生存繁殖，让种子基本不进行新陈代谢而处于休眠状态；另一方面没有了种子新陈代谢散发的热量，窖内也能持续保持低温，保证了仓窖干燥、低温、缺氧的储存环境，形成良性循环。

仓窖四壁与窖顶采用的是不可燃材料，正常情况下不会起火。窖顶完全依靠粮食本身自封，其全封闭状态有助于防治虫患。在建设时含嘉仓遵循低成本、高效率、重实用的原则，拆卸下来的各种材料还可以重复利用。

含嘉仓 160 号仓窖在被发掘时仍然保持着密封状态，其内还有约 50 万斤的粮食，经历了 1400 多年时间的洗礼，窖内一半左右的谷子已发霉变质而碳化，但碳化程度不同。谷子按堆积层深度分为三种颜色，上层呈淡褐色，中层呈褐色，底层呈黑色。

1969 年，一个偶然的机会，在焦枝铁路的施工过程中于洛阳老城区北侧发现了十五个"墓葬建筑"，考古人员一致认定这是西周时期的八角墓葬，直到接近底部时发现铭砖，上面的文字才让人们恍然大悟——这里就是历史上赫赫有名的含嘉仓。

含嘉仓 160 号仓窖遗址（张斌　摄）

　　考古队员小心翼翼地掘开表层泥土，利用仪器对这些碳化谷物进行检测，发现稻谷中仍含有大量有机物。更让人觉得不可思议的是，在仓窖板壁中发现的一些颗粒在取出后的第三天竟然发芽了，后将其送到洛阳市农业科学研究院培养，第二年竟然长到膝盖高，还结出了果实。

　　用窖穴储存粮食、掘地为坑是我国古代劳动者在长期生产制造的社会实践中造就的办法。远在仰韶文化时期，人们就用口小底大的袋状窖穴来贮存粮食，并知道要用火把窖底烘干。

　　到隋唐时期，人们持续总结先人的工作经验，改善了仓窖构造，造就出大中型仓窖储存粮食的方式。这时候的仓窖，早就不是口小底大的袋状窖，也不是上下尺寸略等的立井形窖，而是口大底小的缸形窖。这类仓窖能够使窖内所储谷物的重量产生的压力根据木板分散在土窖的周边，从而缓解下一层木板的负荷。

六、尾语

　　民以食为天，食以粮为安。粮食作为特殊商品，无论在中国古代社会还是现代社会，都是国之根本。

　　作为战争物资储备和国力强盛的证明，含嘉仓为盛世唐朝的繁荣稳定贡献了十分重要的作用。然而，唐朝鼎盛之下也危机四伏，安史之乱后，随着大运河的流量减小、漕运管理不善，含嘉仓也迎来巨大的转折。失去了重要政治地位的洛阳城，在唐后期逐渐衰败，而见证过盛唐繁华的含嘉仓，也逐渐失去了重要地位，难以重现往昔的兴盛。

宋朝定都汴京（今河南开封）之后，经由汴河每年漕运江、淮、湖、浙粮米到开封，洛阳的漕运影响力逐渐降低，含嘉仓也因而慢慢被忽视，最后终于淡出历史的舞台。古代人民在含嘉仓的建造、管理和使用中总结的很多经验一直沿用至今。其中的文明与智慧，值得我们更深入地学习与思考。

如今，含嘉仓作为大运河的关键遗址，进入了全球历史文化遗产的名录。抚今追昔，含嘉仓奇迹一般的规模和储存效果，书写着一个民族的辉煌，流露出古代王朝的底蕴，其所存储的不仅是凝聚国民汗水的粮食，更是一个国家的雄心。

粮食作为国家经济发展、社会稳定、国泰民安的物质条件，其物流仓储管理方式与规章制度，在中国这一人口大国、农业大国中，从古到今一直受到高度重视。

在全球化的今天，各国都可以通过国际贸易从他国取得本国短缺的物资。但是，由于各种不确定因素，我国粮食进口也受到一定程度的影响，粮食仓储管理的应急性特征更加明显。这就要求管理人员加强重视程度，对原有模式中存在的问题进行深入思考，结合实际工作进行优化创新，从而提高粮食仓储管理的效率。

"车同轨"
——践行千年的物流标准化

《三才图会》中的秦始皇画像

　　繁忙的城市街道上车水马龙，道路、高架桥交错纵横，公交车、出租车、私家车、校车交织穿梭，自行车、三轮车、电动车慢悠悠行驶，车辆各行其道，交通繁忙有序。而这一切的有条不紊正是得益于科学的交通规则、现代化的交通指示设备。在古代，没有现代化的交通指挥系统和智能化导航，道路如何有效地发挥作用呢？

一、认知

　　据《史记·夏本纪》记载，距今 4000 多年前，我国就已经有古人乘车的记载，即夏朝车辆行驶的道路就已初具雏形。到了周朝时期，开始专门修建道路供人们使用，《诗经》中"周道如砥，其直如矢""有栈之车，行彼周道"，描述了周朝道路平坦、笔直的情况。这个时期我国辐射状的交通网络已初显规模，周朝修建了宽阔平坦的"周道"，用以沟通国都镐京与各诸侯城邑的交通，同时设置官员"野庐氏"负责管理从国都通往各处的道路，组织检修车辆、平整道路，保证道路畅通安全。周朝时期还对交通工具设定了严格的等级标准，天子乘坐六匹马的马车，诸侯只能乘坐五匹马的马车，等级越低，马匹越少。这也是世界道路史上最早的完善的道路制度。

在这个古老的道路制度中，不仅配备了完善的国道通往主要城市，保障了道路基础设施，而且设置了专门的交通管理机构，配备了专业管理人员和管理制度。交通管理机构各部门、各人员各司其职，对运输工具（马匹、车辆）的采购、车辆制造、车辆运输和交通统筹等事宜进行管理与实施。然而，周朝对交通工具、文字和道德规范的统一标准，历经春秋战国时期的分裂与混战后，变成了一种理想状态，各地域的发展都有所偏离。

春秋战国时期，每个诸侯国的车辆大小不同，两道车辙之间的距离也不同。也就是说，一个诸侯国的车辆只适合在该诸侯国内行驶。当发生跨诸侯国的远距离行驶时，由于外来车辆与当地车辆规格不同，很难行驶在当地经久形成的车辙上。比如，一个秦国人驾车去赵国，一到赵国地界，就得换成赵国的车，因为秦国车辆的车轮无法套进赵国的车辙。

产生这种情况的原因有两点，一是各国技术交流不密集，二是七国争雄期间，战车是军队中最常见的军备，各国在制造车辆时都有一套独有的车距标准，在本国境内形成固定的轨道，方便本国车辆行驶，防止异国的战车驶入。"车途异轨"，当敌国车辆进入本国时，会因为车轮不适应车辙而产生行车障碍，这也是各国有意用车辙防御，以阻挡其他国家的进攻的一个方法。

车辙不统一导致行车障碍

这一切在秦始皇统一六国后发生了改变。秦始皇统一六国之后，想要建立一个统一的帝国，各国不同的轨道标准，严重影响交通运输的发展，更阻碍着国家的经济发展。

彼时，秦始皇刚刚扫灭六国，天下初定，长达 515 年的分裂局面刚刚结束。他废弃六国原有的防御工事，收缴各国的军事武器，开始统一全国不一样的车轮间距，即"车同轨"。《史记·秦始皇本纪》中记载："数以六为纪，符、法冠皆六寸，而舆六尺，六尺为步，乘六马。"

秦始皇废分封而行郡县[①]，连同周朝施行的乘车等级制度也一并废止，进而对天下马车进行统一规范，"而舆六尺，六尺为步"，也就是说，车辆上两个轮子的距离一律改为六尺，使车轮的距离相同。

全国车辆尺寸规格都一样了，不管是六匹马拉的，还是四匹马拉的，车子宽度一致，所以车轴、车轮等组件的标准也都是相同的，任何零件损坏后更换起来方便快捷。"车同轨"的运用，使得军队和商队的运输效率得到了极大的提升。"车同轨"让秦国拥有一支高效的军队，在经济和军事上保证了大一统帝国的安全和运转。

铜马车正面（图片来源：秦始皇帝陵博物院）

秦始皇用"车同轨"促使天下的马车标准化，此举保证了国家经济和军事的有效运转，从而为长治久安打下了坚实基础。各地交通由防御功能为主转为贸易、文化交流为主，全国范围的"车同轨"推动了国家物流的发展。

二、推动

早在周朝时期我国就已经有"车同轨"的认知，但这作为一种标准真正推广

---

① 以郡统县的两级地方管理行政制度（类似于现在的行政区划），几乎盛行整个封建时代。

和落实是在秦朝。《史记·秦始皇本纪》中记载，"一法度衡石丈尺，车同轨，书同文字"，秦始皇开始在全国实行"车同轨"的法令，这对保障政治稳定、推动经济发展和文化繁荣意义重大。

古代的车轮都是木制的，十分坚硬笨重。车轮和地面的摩擦，使得木制的车轮急剧磨损，使用寿命不长。为了减小车轮和地面的摩擦力，让车轮更加经久耐用，造车人将车轮做得更窄一些，同时在木制车轮的周围箍上一层铁皮，史书称之为铁笼。这样一来，车轮不仅经久耐用，而且行驶得非常轻快。

包有铁皮的车轮

经年累月，来来往往的车轮在泥路和石板路上碾压，由于重力和摩擦力的作用，路上形成了两道深深的车轮沟痕，这便是车辙。

车辆在崎岖不平的路面上行驶，如果将车轮压套在两道车辙中，马车、牛车在远距离运输时会更省力、更快、更平稳。进行长途运输时，车轮行驶在质地较硬的车辙上便能使车辆移动得更加稳定，能够显著减少畜力的消耗和车轴磨损，从而降低运输成本。反之，如果车轮不压套进车辙，就会行驶颠簸，既费力又缓慢。

如果车辆脱离车辙行驶，那么就面临着很大的风险。一旦"出轨"，会有一个再次"入轨"的过程，轻者只是颠簸一下，重者可能发生车身倾斜甚至翻车等事故。当路面上有着与车轴标准相配套的车辙之后，车辆沿着车辙行驶，车轮被限制在车辙中，车辆能够行驶得既平稳又高效。当道路上车辙的沟痕深到一定程度的时候，就形成了一道车辙沟壑，这对行驶的车轮有一定的固定作用，这就是"车同轨"中的"轨"。"车同轨"对于古代运输的意义在于，全国的车辙都是统一的，就意味着全国的车辆轧出来的都是六尺宽的车辙，车马和相关资源可以随意调动。其影响一直到 20 世纪，直至橡胶轮胎出现，传统的铁皮包木头的车轮才逐渐淡出人们的视野。

为了保护路面，提高道路的使用效率，秦始皇除颁布"车同轨"法令之外还对车子的规格进行了限定，他要求车宽六尺（约 1.4 米）、车轮的轮辐为 30 根，同时对全国的马车尺寸、用车标准都做了统一的规范。

古驿道车辙（单昕 摄）

车轨相同则车辙等宽，"车同轨"其实是一个道路标准化的措施。这种标准化，使得秦朝耗时十年，形成了以咸阳为中心、以驰道为主、向四方辐射的全国交通干线，满足了其全国范围内军队调动、情报传送、土木工程材料运输等的需求。

全国车轨统一不仅实现了车辆在四通八达的交通网上的便利通行，更实现了车辆的标准化。我国秦始皇陵俑坑出土的战车，整体和零部件显示出高度的规格化、标准化和系统化。铜车马坑出土的铜车马有 3000 多个零部件，同类零件结构相同、尺寸一致，可以通用。其车轮的轮辐均为 30 根，与兵马俑坑出土的木质车轮的轮辐数量相同，符合《考工记》所载"轮辐三十，以象日月也"。严格按照生产工艺标准制作的车辆，其规格一致，零部件加工尺寸精确，数值接近现代优先数系。全国的车马运输、零部件配置效率提高，实现了车辆的批量生产，有利于车辆零部件维修和替换，也形成了秦朝时期的"标准体系"。

路修到哪里，战略威力就能到达哪里。无论是战争还是贸易，一切之源，始于交通。秦始皇在 2000 多年前就把这个道理想明白了。

"车同轨"是秦国统一后的重要战略举措,对全国的基础设施,尤其是道路建设进行了统一标准化的规划。秦始皇之所以要求"车同轨",其实与秦朝的另一项规模宏大的建设工程有着极为密切的关系,那就是驰道①。

畅通无阻、四通八达的交通的实现,除了需要规范的交通工具,还需要发达的道路网。以交通工具标准化为前提,秦始皇在整修已有的错综杂乱的交通路线的基础上,修建了四通八达的道路网,极大地促进了陆路交通的发展和各地区政治经济文化的交流。

秦朝统一的第二年,秦始皇下令修筑以咸阳为中心,辐射四方的驰道。驰道即快速行驶的道路,秦始皇在已有旧道路的基础上以咸阳为中心,"决通川防,修筑驰道",修筑连通各大城市的主干线,形成中央一级的交通网络,再以各中心城市为原点向周围所辖地区辐射,修筑完成全国性的交通网络。驰道及其支线路网将全国各地连接在一起,使各地区的往来更加便利,促进了经济的交流发展。

驰道两旁进行了绿化,统一种植树木,路面形成两侧百姓行走、中间皇帝专用的三车道。这个交通网络成为汉朝和隋唐时期物流道路和节点的基础,部分线路沿用至今。

驰道既可以奔马,又拥有大量的车辙供车辆行驶,它是秦国的"铁路网",车轮距离的统一是"铁路网"建设的基础。大秦帝国的"车同轨"举措,形成了以咸阳为中心、以驰道为主、向四方辐射的全国主要交通干线。此外,其北通九原的直道,也是当时颇有成效的国防工程。

三、现代物流知识

1.道路制度

我国古代道路制度的发展是由政治、军事、经济和文化需求推动的。春秋时期道路交通网络开始萌芽,至秦汉建成便捷、高效的交通路网,并形成邮驿通信、交通运输事务统筹管理等制度;汉朝沿用秦朝的车马路政制度,并将站点扩大到更广阔的区域。此后,经济贸易的繁荣发展催生了各种物流运输方式,也为民间运输的发展奠定了基础。中国历史上不同的朝代受其政治背景、交通制度、

---

① 驰道是中国历史上最早的"国道",始于秦朝。

经济发展水平不同的影响，交通运输网络规模不同，但总体来看我国的公路运力不断提高，运输规模不断增大，道路制度逐渐成熟、系统化。"十二五"期末，我国综合交通网络总里程达到近 500 万公里，高速铁路营业里程、高速公路通车里程、城市轨道交通运营里程及港口泊位数量均居世界第一。

2. 铁路的"车同轨"

19 世纪时，由于各地区铁路技术不一，地形地势各异，同时为了防止其他地区工农业品的流入，北美的铁路至少有 9 种轨道，火车难以在不同轨道上行驶。

1937 年，国际铁路联盟规定 1435 毫米为标准轨距，这一措施促进了铁路的整体发展，使既有铁路实现最大限度的应用，发挥了铁路运输的连续性优点。目前，中国与欧洲大部分国家都采用标准轨距，日本、非洲各国采用窄轨，俄罗斯和部分中亚地区采用宽轨。中国以标准轨距为主，但是云南至今还有在运营的米轨[①]。我国矿产企业都有自己的铁路，而大部分矿产企业都使用标准轨距以外的轨距。日本在我国台湾修的铁路轨宽为 1067 毫米，台湾的糖业铁路和阿里山的森林铁路更窄，为 762 毫米。

国际铁路货物运输是一种仅次于海洋运输的运输方式，海洋运输的进出口货物大多依赖铁路运输进行集散。近年来，我国也开设了连云港至荷兰鹿特丹的新亚欧大陆桥的国际铁路联运业务。由于轨距不一样，国际铁路联运时货物必须在两国边境重置后才能完成跨国运输。比如从中国开往俄罗斯的列车，每次出境均须在中国的二连浩特站换轮库更换转向架。

20 世纪二三十年代，阎锡山[②]在山西自筹资金修建同蒲铁路。该段铁路北起大同，南至永济市蒲州镇以南的风陵渡，全长 800 多公里，堪称一条贯穿山西中部的南北铁路干线。当时的山西经济落后，修建铁路自然有利民生，然而由于同蒲铁路采用窄轨设计，导致外省火车无法进入山西。后人对于窄轨铁路的说法不一，闭关自守有之，精打细算有之，但不管如何，窄轨铁路限制了当时山西铁路的货运能力以及其与外省的经济往来。从这个故事能够看出，统一的"标准"对于推动文化、经济，乃至整个社会的发展，功莫大焉。

---

① 米轨是轨距为 1 米（1000 毫米）的窄轨，目前世界上还在使用米轨的国家和地区有法国、越南、缅甸、马来西亚等。

② 阎锡山（1883—1960），山西五台人，民国时期重要政治、军事人物。

3. 物流标准化

秦朝制定"车同轨"法令，使得全国各地的车辆统一化、规范化，标准化的道路交通为运输提供保障。道路适合车辆通行，降低了货物运输、军用补给的运输成本，同时极大地提高了军队和商队的物资运输效率和政令传达速度。"车同轨"是我国古代的第一个交通工具方面的国家技术标准，与我国现代物流标准类似。它规定了马车的尺寸、规格等基础性标准；规定了轮轴等零部件的"舆六尺""闭门造车，出门合辙"等尺寸、材质方面的技术标准；规定了"六尺为步，乘六马"等作业标准，以及道路使用、道路管理标准。道路、车轨的标准化对于秦朝发展交通事业、促进全国经济的形成与共同发展具有重要意义。

"车同轨"对我国现代物流标准化的发展意义重大。物流标准化，简而言之，即制定物流行业各个环节的统一标准供行业参考，从而改善目前物流业存在的"车不同轨、书不同文"的情况。现代物流标准同样对道路、交通工具与设备进行了规定。此外，基础通用类物流标准对集装箱、托盘等设备进行了规定；公共类物流标准对物流设施设备、物流技术、作业与管理以及物流信息等做了详细规范；还有农副产品、食品冷链物流、汽车物流等专业类物流标准。

可以说，现代物流行业发展的基础就是物流标准化，成熟的物流标准化制度保障了物流行业的高效发展。一方面，物流标准化可以提高行业工作效率、节约资源。另一方面，我国物流标准与国际标准接轨，可提升我国物流企业在国际物流市场的竞争力。频繁的国际贸易与交流加速了物流业的发展，高效国际物流的实现依赖物流标准的国际性。本国物流标准与国际物流标准的一致性有利于货物运输的衔接，有利于促进国际经济技术交流与合作，提高物流服务的质量和效率。特别在"一带一路"的背景下，物流标准化将是其中的重要环节及基础保障。

现代的物流标准更为全面、科学、规范，它以物流为一个大系统，制定系统内部运输、仓储、配送、流通加工、包装、装卸搬运与信息管理等分系统、分领域的工作、技术标准，并形成全国、国际范围的标准化体系，实现物流系统与其他相关系统的配合。

四、结语

2016 年，第 39 届国际标准化组织大会开幕时，习近平总书记贺信："标准是人类文明进步的成果。从中国古代的'车同轨、书同文'，到现代工业规模化生产，都是标准化的生动实践。伴随着经济全球化深入发展，标准化在便利经贸往来、支撑产业发展、促进科技进步、规范社会治理中的作用日益凸显。标准已成为世界'通用语言'。世界需要标准协同发展，标准促进世界互联互通"。

习近平总书记"车同轨、书同文"的引用，旨在阐释标准化的重要作用，体现在推进经贸往来、支撑产业发展、促进科技进步、规范社会治理各个方面。当然这种"标准化"对现代物流行业的持续、高效发展尤为重要。

改革开放以来，中国标准化工作伴随着时代的进步而快速发展。近年来，我国综合国力显著增强，标准化事业快速发展，中国在全球经济制度建设中不断贡献中国智慧、给出中国方案，为"人类命运共同体"竭尽心力。

郑和下西洋
——大航海时代人类文明的里程碑

《郑和下西洋 600 周年》纪念邮票（小型张）（崔彦伟设计邮票，王虎鸣设计版张边饰）

大海，神秘莫测，喜怒无常，让人恐惧又让人向往。自古以来，中国人对海洋的探索从未停止。一代又一代先民一次次出海远航，惊涛骇浪，折戟沉沙。但是，对蔚蓝的向往岂是危险就能阻断的。六百多年前的中国，一支船队正在远航，它即将创造世界航海史上的奇迹。这只庞大船队的领导者，名叫郑和。

一、缘起

1398 年，明太祖朱元璋去世，皇位传给了他的长孙朱允炆，年号建文，史称建文帝、明惠宗。朱元璋生前，曾因"加强边防，藩屏皇室"，将诸皇子分封到各地，藩王势力日渐庞大。为削弱藩王势力、巩固皇权，建文帝与齐泰、黄子澄等亲信大臣开始密谋削藩。建文元年（1399 年），周王、代王、齐王被贬为庶人，湘王被杀。

燕王（朱元璋第四子朱棣）镇守北平，势力最强，建文帝以边防为名调离燕王的精兵，削弱燕王势力。燕王自知在劫难逃，遂以"清君侧，靖内难"的名义起兵，皇权争夺战自此爆发，史称靖难之役。朱棣亲率燕军占领京师，江山易主。朱棣继位，称明成祖，年号永乐。建文帝在宫城大火中失踪后，其下落成谜。

据史料记载，郑和祖上是中亚布哈拉的贵族，明初曾任云南行省平章，后被追封为咸阳王，其曾祖父曾任中书平章，父亲封滇阳侯。

郑和对海洋和远行的向往，源于其祖父和父亲的经历，其祖父和父亲信仰伊斯兰教，去过麦加（伊斯兰教圣地）等很多国家和城市，对异域城市和国家都非常熟悉，将所见所闻所感讲于郑和，由此在其心里埋下了一颗渴望远行的种子。

洪武十五年（1382 年），明朝大军对云南梁王势力发动统一战争，明朝大军势如破竹，梁王败亡，十一岁的郑和作为俘虏被带到南京，受宫刑做了宦官。洪武十七年，郑和被安排到燕王府服役。期间，因为聪明勤快、勤奋好学、谨言慎行等优秀的品质，深受燕王喜爱，留作贴身侍卫。此后，随着其才能和领导力逐渐显露，郑和崭露头角，并成为燕王信任之人。靖难之役，郑和跟随朱棣出生入死，南征北战，屡建功绩。尤其在郑村坝一战中，郑和随朱棣连破建文帝大将李景隆所部七营兵马，使得该战役成为赢得靖难之役的关键一战。

1402 年，朱棣登基，郑和被提拔为内官监太监。据说，为纪念当年郑村坝一战的功绩，朱棣赐郑和"郑"姓。郑和成为朱棣最信任的宦官之一。

洪武末年，励精图治数十年，明朝已经变得仓廪充实，天下太平。待到朱棣即位后，这位雄才大略的皇帝更为明朝定下了明亮的基调，经济继续增长，文化持续繁荣。在天生喜欢宏大计划的朱棣的统治下，大部头的古代百科全书《永乐大典》被编撰出来，沟通南北的大运河得以疏浚，世界上最大的宫殿群——紫禁城建造成型，文治武功达到极致。《明史》记载："雄武之略，同符高祖。六师屡出，漠北尘清。至其季年，威德遐被，四方宾服，受朝命入贡者殆三十国。幅员之广，远迈汉唐。成功骏烈，卓乎盛矣。"

而郑和下西洋，正是朱棣宏大计划中的重要部分。

关于下西洋的原因，《明史》中记载："成祖疑惠帝亡海外，欲踪迹之，且欲耀兵异域，示中国富强。"在史学家看来，赴海外寻找疑似失踪的建文帝是永乐皇帝派遣郑和多次下西洋的一个不可忽视的理由。但是，对自诩永乐大帝的明成祖朱棣而言，雄才大略的他更在乎的可能是"耀兵异域，示中国富强"。

在当时，明成祖交给郑和的一封敕书中说，要把我（明成祖）的意图向普天下讲清楚，我的意图是什么呢，是人民老幼皆欲使其遂其生业。也就是说，明成祖要让普天之下所有的人都过上好日子。由此看来，通过郑和船队开展海外贸易，展示明朝的富足、传播明朝文明、彰显皇帝威严，或许是朱棣的真实目的所在。

二、盛况

1405 年 6 月 15 日，苏州府太仓的刘家港热闹非凡，浏河与长江汇合处，彩旗飘扬，锣鼓喧天。人们从四面八方涌到这里，争相目睹郑和船队首航西洋的盛况。

郑和船队选择从刘家港出发，是经过深思熟虑的。洪武二十六年（1393 年），朱元璋兴建运仓，在太仓南码头修建 919 间仓房，用于屯粮。《太仓府志》记载："永乐贮米数百万石，浙江等处秋粮皆赴焉，故天下之仓，此为最盛。"明朝初期，苏州贡献了全国赋税的 12%，而其中的 12% 由太仓负担。富余的钱财和充足的物资准备就绪，郑和下西洋势在必行。在祭拜过天妃宫的妈祖神之后，郑和率队登上大船。这支由 200 多艘大小船只，27800 余人组成的船队，满载丝绸、棉布、瓷器、粮食、淡水、燃料、蔬果、药材、茶叶等，离开刘家港，沿海岸南行，至闽江口，入冬后，乘东北季风，驶向茫茫大海。因这些船只满载珍品，被称作"运宝之船"。

有幸目睹这只庞大船队经过的沿海居民，对其惊叹不已。因为在中国南方的广阔海域上，他们从来没有见过如此壮观的海上景象。几百艘船只在海面上排开，风帆遮天蔽日。白天，旌旗猎猎、鼓声阵阵，放眼望去，蔚蓝色的海面上犹如突然出现一片春天里开满鲜花的原野。待到入夜时，号声此伏彼起，海面上灯火点点，大海中倒映的灯光与夜空中的星光交相辉映，恰似天上的街市。只有一个强大的帝国，才能支持这样盛大的远航，才能在海上导演出这样云帆高张、昼夜星驰的旷世美景。

郑和船队离开了明帝国的版图后，首先到达了占城（今越南中南部），又访问了爪哇、旧港、满剌加、苏门答腊，紧接着穿过今天的马六甲海峡，进入印度洋，到达翠蓝屿、锡兰、柯枝等地区和国家，随后，继续沿印度海岸北上。在访问了甘巴里等国后，船队开始返航。

经过两年多的远航，郑和率队凯旋，并带回各国使者向明王朝献上的奇珍异宝，振奋了整个帝国。

随后明朝皇帝再次派郑和出使西洋各国，自 1407 年到 1421 年，郑和舰队又五次下西洋。

当时的中国处在永乐盛世，郑和船队途经的亚非诸国相对落后，大多处于原始部落状态或奴隶制社会时期，有的甚至尚未开化。比如古里国明显还留有母系氏族社会的残余。这些国家大多没有完备的政治制度和法律制度，仍留有原始性的部落习俗。从风俗习惯上来说，这些国家基本上没有"礼"这个概念，衣不蔽体的情况很普遍，以至于男女皆裸形入池沐浴等情况很常见。

郑和出使亚非各国，每到一地，总要"开榜赏赐"进行贸易，将金银珠宝、丝绸瓷器等中国特产倾囊而出。这些东西做工精细，充分展现了中国人民娴熟的手工技巧和高超的工艺技术，是凝聚着中国人民智慧和汗水的劳动成果，是饱含中华文化韵味的器物。对于这些从未耳闻目睹过的东西，亚非诸国人民自然是叹为观止，热烈欢迎，并且产生极其强烈的欣赏、占有欲望。

这些国家从了解中国的器物文化开始，继而饥渴地追求和吸收制度文化，从而产生了"变其夷习"的强烈愿望。郑和使团所到之处，充分展现了强国外交的礼仪与风范，与到访各地民俗粗鄙、举止粗鲁的民风形成了鲜明的对比，从而给当地人带来了很大的震撼。他们发现郑和使团带来的不仅是物美，使团的风范、言行更美。郑和下西洋过程中，往往代皇命敕封各国国王、酋长或头目，并给赐冠服。这种物质上的赏赐和精神上荣誉的授予不仅满足了他们获得尊重的需求，更使他们感受到中国的礼乐之美，于是他们纷纷来华，主动请赐冠服，实现其"愿比内郡依华风"的要求。当下中国"礼乐文明，赫赫异域，使光天之下，无不沾德化焉"。永乐六年（1408 年），浡泥（今文莱国附近地区）国王来华访问，不幸病逝，留下的遗言却是"体魄托葬中华"。可见，郑和下西洋对中华文化的传播具有非常重要的意义，同时也对所到之国经济、政治、文化的发展产生了深远的影响。

三、落幕

永乐二十年（1422 年），第六次下西洋归来的郑和，遭到了文官的批驳。彼时，朱棣醉心于四处用兵，国库入不敷出，本就对皇帝出海扬威政策不满的士大夫阶层，以下西洋花费甚多为由，劝谏皇帝。朱棣开始犹豫了。至此，郑和下西洋暂时退出了历史的舞台。

两年后,朱棣在北征蒙古草原的途中病死。太子朱高炽即位,改年号洪熙,史称明仁宗。朱高炽上台伊始,即要革除父亲的弊政,下西洋作为弊政的重要组成部分,被加以罢黜,诏令西洋宝船全部停办。1425 年,明仁宗病逝,太子朱瞻基即位,史称明宣宗。郑和被贬为南京镇守太监,修理大报恩寺。

宣德六年(1431 年),明宣宗发觉前来朝贡的国家越来越少,遥想祖父时期万国来朝的盛况,感慨不已。于是不顾大臣反对,决定重启下西洋活动。

60 岁的郑和被起用,再次登上了熟悉的宝船,开始他人生中第七次也是最后一次下西洋。宣德八年(1433 年),船队返航,经古里国(今印度西南一带),郑和因疾病逝,享年 62 岁。船队副使、宦官王景弘接管船队指挥权,扶柩返航。彼时,西洋十余国派使臣随船队,到北京朝贡。

宣德十年(1435 年),明宣宗朱瞻基病逝,8 岁的太子朱祁镇登基,称明英宗。正统元年(1436 年),明英宗朱祁镇下诏,"一切造作悉皆停罢",正式宣告从永乐年间开始的下西洋活动就此落幕。

郑和病逝 40 年后,大明帝国由年轻的成化皇帝朱见深掌舵,这天,宫中一位曾目睹郑和下西洋风采的老宦官为皇帝讲起了当年的盛景。成化帝激动不已,命人去兵部取当年郑和绘制的海图一看。消息传到兵部,兵部官员刘大夏立刻将海图藏匿起来,并痛斥三宝(郑和)下西洋,费钱粮数十万,军民死且万计,纵得奇宝而回,于国家何益!此特一时弊政,大臣所当切谏者。旧案虽有,亦当毁之以拔其根。后传说,刘大夏为绝皇帝心思,将海图焚毁殆尽。

至此,轰轰烈烈的下西洋活动彻底退出了历史的舞台。

四、影响

回看郑和下西洋,波澜壮阔的史诗画卷已经远去,但它却给各行各业都留下了恒久的意义。比如船舶行业通过研究郑和宝船可以加深对中国船舶历史的了解,历史研究人员则持续探讨下西洋活动后东南亚各国与中国之间的联系。

对于物流行业而言,郑和下西洋目的之一是与海外诸国开展贸易活动,而贸易活动离不开物流系统的支持。它为我们分析物流的意义提供了借鉴。

从物流的角度来看,郑和下西洋的历史贡献在于,它不仅开拓了新的近洋航线,进一步促进了明朝国际贸易活动,还建立了沿线的物流节点,建立了国际物流系统的基础。其影响具体可从三个方面定义。

（一）开辟了新的航海线路

郑和船队开辟了一条世界航海历史上的新路线，实现了太平洋西部与印度洋等大洋的直达航行。开辟主要航线达 42 条之多，其航线最西到达赤道南面，航线西端延伸到比剌、孙剌两个国家，这可能是郑和船队抵达的最远的两个非洲国家，最南到达印尼爪哇，最北到达红海的天方（今沙特阿拉伯的麦加），总计航程 16 万海里，相当于绕地球三周有余。由苏门答腊经马尔代夫、摩加迪沙横渡印度洋直达东非，这条新航线的开辟是郑和下西洋的最大意义。

（二）建立了合适的物流节点

《明史》记载郑和七次下西洋所经过的国家和地区多达 36 个。每一次出航短则数月，长则几年，漫漫航程若没有中转站补给和休整，如何能够继续。于是，在漫长辽阔的"海上丝绸之路"上，郑和船队建立了四大海洋交通中心站、两大航海贸易基地和两个东西方贸易的大本营。

郑和在这些节点的选择上，不仅考虑地理位置和经济条件，同时还考虑了人文环境。如占城、苏门答腊、满剌加、古里国这些交通中心站，一方面是交通要道，另一方面也是商人集聚的地方。11 世纪以来，泉州商船远航印度洋也多选择这几个地方作为贸易中心和寄泊港，每年航行至此的泉州人不在少数。可以想象，当郑和船队登陆时，迎接他们的多是中国同胞和对中国非常熟悉的土著人，沟通交流自然是顺畅很多。

郑和船队到海外进行贸易时，虽然"厚往薄来"，但仍讲求经济效益。为了实施对海外各国的贸易与经济计划，除了利用各交通中心站和航海贸易基地外，还把东西方贸易的辐辏之地——古里国作为一个大本营。据马欢《瀛涯胜览》记载，在古里国有二大头目，受中国朝廷升赏，在明朝政府的委任下，专门负责协助郑和船队处理其在古里国的外贸事务。以古里国作为东西方贸易的纽带，一方面郑和船队可以在此与南亚各国开展贸易活动，另一方面也方便郑和船队在东南亚和西亚、东非沿岸的贸易运转，有利于促进东西方贸易连接。

郑和带领船队在海洋交通运输方面不断获得发展，不但为发展中国与亚非国家间的经济交流作出重大的贡献，而且大大推动了明初海洋经济的发展，使中国成为当时世界上最强大的海洋大国。所以，郑和下西洋无疑是 15—16 世纪世界大航海时代中人类文明的璀璨成果。

（三）应用和发扬了最先进的海洋导航技术

郑和下西洋的航线，如今仍被称为黄金水道，连接着太平洋与印度洋，每年大约有 10 万艘船航行在这个水道上。船队依靠先进的通信工具和航海技术保证航运安全。如使用全球定位系统（GPS）设备，输入起点和终点后系统就会指引着船队驶往目的港，且每一条船在海上都是沿着既定的航线独立航行的。当年没有先进的信息技术和通信技术，郑和是如何保证船队安全航行并到达目的地的呢？

在记载郑和船队有关航海技术的《郑和航海图》中，保存了大量关于航海路线与历程，沿途海流、水深、礁石分布、停泊地点以及包括指南针、天文导航在内的丰富资料，成为前人留给我们的一份珍贵的文化遗产。根据《郑和航海图》可知，他们在航行中使用了当时最先进的航海导航技术，即过洋牵星术和海道针经。

牵星板复原（陈飚　摄）　　　　牵星板测量原理（图片来源：吴春明）

据史料记载，古人的天文导航主要依赖过洋牵星术测定船舶航行方向与方位。元明时期，开始用过洋牵星术测量航行船舶所在的地理纬度。过洋牵星术主要是通过利用牵星板测量星辰与船舶所在水平面的角度来确定船舶所在的地理纬度的，这种工具和测定原理虽然简易，却凝聚了古人千百年来的智慧，代表着那个时期世界最先进的天文导航水准。据文献记载，古人取乌木制牵星板，一副牵星板由十二块大小不一的正四边形木板和一块约 6 厘米长、四角留有缺口的象牙方块组成，模板按其大小进行排组。象牙方块缺口四边的长度也是不同的。使用者左手持牵星板一端的中心，调整手臂姿势使视线与牵星板的下部边缘处在一条水平线上，牵星板的上部边缘对准所测的星体，此时便可测得船舶所在水平面与星斗的夹角，将夹角代入已有的公式中便可计算出船舶所在的地理纬度了。

由此可见当时的航海技术已经非常先进了。明末学者茅元仪所著的《武备志》①保存有 20 页郑和的航海图，其中有 4 幅有关过洋牵星术的图。早在《淮南子》中就有记载，阿拉伯航海者擅长一种技术，即通过观测星辰来确定船舶纬度位置。阿拉伯航海者在唐朝就已登陆泉州，中世纪时泉州人在与阿拉伯人的频繁往来中，向阿拉伯人学习了这门技术，成为直接应用者，并对此驾轻就熟。

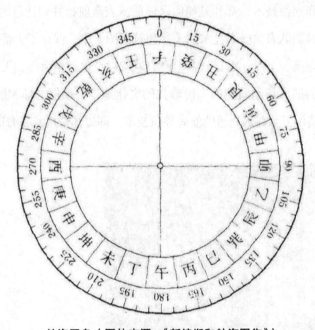

航海罗盘（图片来源：《新编郑和航海图集》）

元、明、清时期的航海罗盘是海道针经。它以 8 个天干②、12 个地支及 4 个八卦方位将航海罗盘圆周 24 等分来指示方向，准确度较高。另外，当时先进的航海技术还有计程仪、测深仪等航海仪器和海图、针路簿等航海地图。

五、尾声

尽管郑和下西洋没有实现地理大发现的历史使命，但毫无疑问的是，它是中国航海史上的壮举，它构建了纵横各个国家和地区的海上通道，加强了沿线各国的紧密联系，不仅对航海事业影响深远，对世界文明的发展也做出了突出的贡献。

郑和船队对加强东西方贸易发挥了重要作用，有力地推动了海上丝绸之路全线国际贸易的发展。

---

① 《武备志》是明朝重要的军事著作，是中国古代字数最多的一部综合性兵书。

② 10 个天干减去"戊"和"己"。

秦直道
——世界上最早的高速公路

（图片来源：鄂尔多斯市博物院）

在黄土高原丘陵地带，数百公里的秦直道为军队的紧急需求做好了准备。秦直道是堪与长城比肩的世界工程史上的奇迹。如果将万里长城比作阻挡匈奴进攻的盾牌，那秦直道就是刺穿匈奴腹地的利剑。

一、插入匈奴腹地的利剑

秦始皇灭六国实现大一统，第一个专制主义中央集权制度的封建王朝由此建立。但雄踞朔漠的匈奴成了秦国的最大威胁，他们民风彪悍、举族为兵，逐水草而居，骑术精湛，极难防御。

为了更好地保护北方地区的安全，秦始皇对燕、赵两国长城的遗迹进行修缮，并使之与秦国长城连接起来，从而形成今天的万里长城。

长城这条防线，可攻可守，能够起到很好的预警作用，但是仅靠长城远远不够。为了进一步抵御匈奴侵扰，秦始皇召集了上万人的精锐部队来保卫边界。一支如此庞大的队伍驻扎在这里，每月仅粮食和草料的消耗就很多，另外还有武器、盔甲等战略物资的运输。要想把长城的作用最大化，就要修建一条从关中平原到北部地区的快速通道，从而更便于部队的物资供应和北方边界地区的基础设施建设。

秦始皇统一全国之后，解散了六国原有军队。但偌大的疆土，一面要防止旧贵族复辟，另一面还要抵御侵扰不断的匈奴，若把秦国原有军队分派防守，则兵力分散，一旦事变，还是不够应对。

为了更好地处理军事力量的"分裂"与"结合"，秦始皇统一规划了各国的道路，称其为"驰道"，然后将它们彼此连接起来，创造了一个以都城咸阳为中心的驰道网，以此来通向四面八方并加强相互联系。目的就是无论哪里发生什么战事，秦国的军队都可以迅速赶到并应对。也是基于这样的战略考虑，秦始皇决定修筑一条可以快速到达北疆的道路，即秦直道。这便是本节要详述的宏大工程。

公元前 212 年，秦国变本加厉地征发民夫进行一系列建设活动和新一轮的扩张战争，并委派大将军蒙恬为统帅，正式修建秦直道。据说这条道路的终点在九原，位于北部地区边境防线的最前沿；而它的起点位于甘泉宫，有安全通道与都城咸阳紧密相连。

秦直道打通了中原与塞北间的大动脉，成为内地与边疆经济文化往来的桥梁。在多年来与北方匈奴的激烈战争中，秦朝所建设的秦直道始终都是举足轻重的，成千上万吨的军需物资的运输都依赖这条大动脉才能完成。秦直道的修造，使关中地区与北方地区的联系更紧密，世界物流史上的奇迹也由此诞生。

道路是一个国家最主要的基础工程，也是国家防御体系的重要组成部分。依靠秦国故地与六国境内的道路基础，驰道网很快修建完成。秦直道是由咸阳通往北境阴山最近的道路，大体南北相直，工程之浩大，远非驰道所能比。

秦直道上寸草不生，这不仅是由于频繁使用，还与建造工艺有着直接关系，建造道路所使用的是经过高温处理的土壤，不仅水分很少，而且没有植物种子和其他有机物；建造路面时，建造者将路基夯实，杂草很难扎根其上。在之后的两千多年时间里，这条秦直道一直是交通主干道，使用率极高，即便偶有草生长，经过人和车的碾压，也会被踏平。此外，秦朝实行极为残酷的刑法，工程建造方面，每一级都有监督人，无论哪里出了问题都可以追究责任，而且出错惩戒力度极重，这使得秦直道的质量无可指摘。

秦直道走向示意（图片来源：鄂尔多斯市博物院）

秦直道路面既坚实，又开阔平坦。宽度一般为 30~60 米，最宽的地方甚至可以作为现今中型飞机的降落跑道。

因秦直道南半程修筑于子午岭，建造者克服了许多困难：逢山劈岭、遇石凿道、临沟填谷。工程之大、工期之短，前所未有。其壮阔之势，堪称空前绝后。据估算，修建秦直道所使用和挪动的土石方，如果用来堆砌成宽、高均为 1 米的墙垣，可绕地球赤道半圈以上。

秦直道距今已有 2000 多年，世界上最早的高速公路——德国波恩至科隆的高速公路于 1931 年才完工。秦直道比著名的罗马大道还要宽，可以称作世界公路的鼻祖。秦直道不仅是全世界公路建筑工程领域的奇迹，同时也是战争时期物资流通发展史上的壮举。它是我国古代劳动人民智慧的结晶，也为战时物流系统的设计与开发提供了极为重要的经验借鉴。

二、战时物流系统设计与开发的经典之作

1.路线选择巧夺天工

据《史记·蒙恬列传》记载："始皇欲游天下，道九原，直抵甘泉，乃使蒙恬通道。"从九原到甘泉宫沿途有草原、荒漠等不同地貌，修建大道何其艰难，况且还要求道路短、平、宽，并保持通畅，否则就失去了修建一条快速机动的战时补给大道的作用，这可谓难上加难。因此，必须找到一条连接两点间的最短的可行线路。

甘泉段秦直道（白腾 摄）

秦直道线路的选择，主要从自然和人力两个维度考虑。自然维度考虑的是尊重自然法则，合理利用自然规律，减少物质成本的投入。这个思维在秦直道的设计和开发中占主导地位。例如，选择在昭君墓所在位置附近南渡黄河直达九原，是因为该处黄河渡口较宽，水流较缓，这样一来就解决了由黄河险滩和汛期、断流等产生的问题，保证物资可以不受季节、地理条件的影响而及时运往前线。

再如，秦直道的南段选择建在子午岭的山脊上，看似不可思议，其实这是最佳的路线选择，这样的筑路方案能够尽量避免被河谷切割。两块相邻的土地，为什么会被分割成两个独立的地理单元，原因在于它们的地形地貌自成体系，直接映射出不同的水系结构。在陇东高原和陕北高原南部，有泾河与洛水两个独立的水系，找到它们的分水岭，就能找到两大高原的分界线，同时也能找到一条不被河谷分割的天然路基。然而，并不是所有的分水岭都可以承担这项任务，

只有海拔不是太高的分水岭才能够做到。子午岭就是这条分割线，其海拔只有1300~1800米，地势起伏较小，地形亦相对平坦，宜于修筑道路，如此才能够最终实现秦直道这项宏伟的工程。

此外，还须考虑军事安全方面的因素。秦朝子午岭地区森林植被覆盖率极高，这利于进行特定环境下的隐蔽作战，而沿着山路行军，可以减少军队在中途被敌人伏击的可能性，既相当安全，又可提高军队的行进速度。而且，居高临下的地理优势，让两侧的河谷道路可以为人所控。这些河谷大道地势平坦、植被茂盛，也是匈奴骑兵入侵的唯一途径，而开通运行后的秦直道使匈奴在河谷大道中行进的压力陡增，进而确保了都城的安全。

秦直道的修建占尽天时地利，为了保证路程最短，且道路宽、平，只能人为堑山堙谷、逢山劈岭、遇石凿道、临沟填谷、遇林开道，其壮阔之势堪称空前绝后。从空中俯瞰秦直道，它就像一条巨龙时而在蜿蜒的山峦中爬行，时而在低矮的丛林中默默行走。

秦直道全长700多公里。而九原到咸阳，即今包头到西安的直线距离才700公里左右。秦朝在条件落后、资源不足的情况下，仅用两年半时间就完成了如此高质量的工程，让人肃然起敬、至为叹服。

历史学家司马迁曾走过秦直道，当其踏入秦直道的时候，北方地区匈奴和南方地区农耕民族的攻防之势早已完全转换。汉人不但凭借着阴山的地理优势修筑起了长城，还翻越了阴山，在茫茫草原和广袤戈壁上建起了大量的城墙和烽火台。

2. 通信系统厥功至伟

为秦直道与秦长城配套修建的预警系统，其功能相当于冷兵器时代的"雷达"。烽燧建在高处，值勤的士兵可以及早发现入侵者的动向，并将其运行的关键信息以烟或光的形式（白天发出烟气，夜间发出火光）传递给附近的驻军，连续传递速度可以达到一天几千里。到了秦直道上，则利用烽燧和驿站，继续将战报传至上一级军事指挥中心直至中央政府。有了这套预警系统，军队的发展水平得到了明显提升，为确保边境安全而部署的士兵数量也大为减少。因此，人力、财力、物力的耗费也会相对减少。

此外，秦直道的预警系统将30万秦军部署在咸阳附近，而非长城之上，这样就可以有机地统一指挥京卫与戍卫，仅此一点，就可以减少没有预警系统时必须负担的相应的赋税、兵役和劳役，节省了何其多的物流成本。

3. 完备的"攻守兼备"体系

除秦直道路面遗址，考古人员还挖掘到与秦直道关联的各类遗址，包含关卡（富县秦直道遗址）、驿站（甘泉安家沟遗址）、烽燧（旬邑大店村遗址、黄陵县五里墩遗址）、宫殿（志丹任窑子行宫遗址）和保护设施（排水沟、护坡）等。不难看出，秦直道并不仅是一条路面，还是一套健全的物流管理系统，对现代物流行业的网络设计与开发设计有非常好的启发作用。

（1）秦直道与万里长城形成合围，对外侵者"一箭穿心"。

秦直道的修建效仿长城，坚持"因地形，用险制塞"的原则，起到"一夫当关，万夫莫开"的效果。游牧民族的马匹由军事行动的利器变成了负担，不但迟滞了其入侵中原的速度，还为其安全撤回草原增加了障碍。秦直道沿途兵站可以快速集合部队，实现人马辎重的快速机动。

秦长城是一个纯粹的国防安全工程，秦直道则是一个迎合国防安全的交通出行运输线。秦直道完工后，汉朝的装甲骑兵军队从陕西驻扎地出发，三天三夜的时间就可抵达阴山脚下。而在 20 世纪 90 年代，从西安乘汽车到榆林也需要几天时间。所以，在这样的情况下，秦直道可以强化守卫长城的武装力量，还可以使一部分增援部队从其他障碍中撤出，并立即越过敌人以实施侧翼包围的攻击战略。长城守军在秦直道援军的配合下，转守为攻，对越过长城的敌军实施"包饺子"战术，这就使得入侵者始终面临一种很难消除的风险，从而出现"乃使蒙恬北筑长城而守藩篱，却匈奴七百余里，胡人不敢南下而牧马"的十年边关安定的局面。

（2）秦直道扼守两河流域，用农耕文化击退游牧民族。

秦直道修建在鄂尔多斯草原和子午岭主脉上，尤其是子午岭一段，拥有居高临下的地形优势，对洛河河段和泾河支流马莲河河段的河谷大道都有十分显著的监管作用。秦始皇充分利用优越的地质资源，将 3 万户人口迁徙到两河平原开展农耕活动，老百姓可以安全耕作定居，既拓展了中原农耕文明的范围，又对身为游牧民族的匈奴造成了挤压感。

有了农耕，就有了粮草，也就有了人丁兴旺。秦直道沿途兴建关卡、烽燧、宫殿、驿站等，战时可临时储备各类物资。平时，秦直道用于通商，不断繁荣两河经济；战时，军民一心，共同完成军用物资的快速集结和运输。

秦直道因依据地形走势而建，宽窄不一。窄道选择小车，灵活机动，行至关隘大道，改装大车前行，小车折返，成为物资集聚的"搬运工"。秦直道后半程建在鄂尔多斯草原上，道路十分宽敞，便于大车运输，保证大批物资直达黄河渡口。

有了秦直道及其沿线配套设施的布局，在战略上可以威慑匈奴，在战术上又可以做到快速反应，才出现了"是后匈奴远遁，而漠南无王庭""建塞徼、起亭燧、筑外城，设屯戍以守之，然后边境得用少安"的局面。

秦直道旅游文化产业园区（图片来源：鄂尔多斯市博物院）

三、新时代篇章

历史总在不断重复，当军事产品或技术转变成平民使用的产品或技术时，它的潜力将得到更加充分的展示。

特别是在昭君出使塞外以后，秦直道也从原来的军事交通设施转变为民用商业交通设施。中部地区的茶叶、丝绸、器皿和北方的牛羊作为主要商品进行交易，不仅丰富了双方地区间的商贸活动，而且拉近了它们彼此的距离，并增强了不同民族之间的情感。伴随着汉族和匈奴长期和平共处时代的开始，在秦直道上运输的物资量成倍地增长。也是从那以后，秦直道沿线成了商贾云集、贸易交往不断的繁华地区，而这样的繁荣一直延续到了唐朝。

唐朝以后，伴随着政治中心的东移，秦直道在甘、陕、宁及内蒙古等地区的经济和文化艺术的沟通交流层面起到了十分明显的作用，中原的先进技术和生产工具被迅速传播到长城以北。而当丝绸之路在河西走廊受阻时，秦直道也是商旅车辆的绕行选择。

据乾隆《正宁县志》记载："此路一往康庄，修整之则可通车辙。明时以其道直抵银、夏，故商贾经行。"由此可见，一直到明朝，秦直道仍是一条重要通途。根据史料，秦直道的日趋沉寂是自清朝初期才开始的。

伴随着北方地区形势的平稳，秦直道也走入了低迷阶段。清朝，北方地区的蒙古部落彻底归附，塞外也已无兵能用。以前人头攒动的闹市区，已然呈现"千里无鸡鸣"的状态。洗净历史的铅华，秦直道已经没有了当初的风采，在延绵数百公里的沿途，所到之处人烟稀少、尽是荒芜，至今已没有一处完整的遗迹。

经历两千多年的喧闹和幽寂、纷争与融合，万里长城仍然横亘于阴山之下，秦直道则串联起了中华民族的历史浮沉和社会转型，在历史的漫漫长路中，留下浓墨重彩的印记。

以史为镜可以知兴替，秦直道的兴衰对其沿线地域发展的影响对现今城市交通产生了重要的启迪。秦直道蕴含着深刻的物流思想，其给现代物流的启示概括起来主要有四个方面。

其一，"货通天下"，无论是历史还是现代，以丝绸之路、秦直道为代表的物流运输网不仅承载着战事、贸易的需要，更是地缘政治、区域经济文化交融的纽带。也正因如此，物流业基础设施建设水平的高低与一个国家经济社会的发展程度紧密相关，必须引起高度重视。

秦直道保护标志碑（图片来源：鄂尔多斯市博物院）

其二，物流是对运输、储存、装卸、搬运、包装、流通加工、配送、信息处理等环节的有机结合。应急物流快速响应的核心是信息的有效传递，如今，一旦出现断电断网甚至是战争的特殊情况，沿袭古代信息传递的思想，并不断推陈出新，不失为一个有效的备选方案。

其三，"书同文、车同轨"，标准化建设是解决物流问题的"量变"，积累物流技术与理论则是物流业高质量发展的"质变"，加强物流专业教育培训和理论研究势在必行。如今，全国数百家高等学府已针对物流这门学科开设了物流管理、物流工程等专业，为我国物流业输送着专业化的中坚力量，同时也为物流企业的基层实际操作设立了专业化的训练科目，为我国物流业的有序发展奠定基础。

其四，历史经验教育我们，文化不仅要传承，更要创新。物流文化在促进物流技术发展上起到了举足轻重的作用。昨天应该被了解，今天应该被把握，明天则更须开拓创新。物流业的发展是每一个物流人的责任，物流文化的发扬更是每一个物流人的使命与担当。

从修建万里长城到建造秦直道，如此快的建造速度，源自劳动人民的百倍努力、千倍坚持，用实干创造辉煌。那些灵光一闪的光环背后，那些动人心弦的创造背后，饱含着劳动人民难以想象的艰辛。

从两弹一星到"嫦娥"奔月，从第一艘潜艇下水到"蛟龙"入海，从第一代巨型计算机银河到如今的互联网大数据，火神山、雷神山两所应急医院的建成速度更为人们津津乐道……造就着世界奇迹的中国速度，映现出中国一往无前的拼搏精神。中国速度与力量，震撼全球，托起各族人民对平安美好生活的憧憬，驱动着中国速度再次加大马力，向中华民族伟大复兴全速前进。

平虏渠与泉州渠

——运河在军事上的应用

（无人机照片）

隋大业十年（公元614年），第三次东征高丽失败的隋炀帝杨广，从辽东前线班师回朝。随行人马垂头丧气，护驾军士也毫无斗志。

踌躇满志的杨广曾亲率百万大军进攻高丽，车辚辚马萧萧，前锋已过辽河，后队仍在涿郡，旌旗猎猎，人马纵横，那是何等豪气干云。但三次亲征三次失败，损失数十万人马，粮草辎重丢弃无数，国内更是因东征而民不聊生，各路反叛四起。这些都沉重打击了这位好大喜功的皇帝，他意图超越亘古帝王宏图霸业的梦想也就此熄灭。

当銮驾经过辽西走廊的碣石，杨广下车伫立良久。在他踏足的高崖之下，海浪拍涌，这里正是四百多年前曹操写下《观沧海》的地方。那年，曹操率军北征乌桓①，大胜而归，途径碣石时心潮澎湃，留下了这首千古名篇。

杨广也是一位文采斐然的帝王。他似乎不怎么喜欢曹操，在他的诗句中，几乎没有赞誉甚至提及曹操。而今，同样是东征，同样的出兵路线，四百多年前曹操能创立丰功伟绩，而他只能饮恨而归，这令杨广叹息不已。

千年之后，当人们复盘杨广东征高丽和曹操北征乌桓的成败得失时，发现后勤成为决定战争成败的重要因素。曹操能赢得那场经典战役，关键在于运河的作用。

一、消失的运河

"物流"原为日语舶来词，本意为"物的流通"。在人类历史上，水运因其运输量大、损耗低等原因，一直是大规模物资运输的首选，因此，修建勾连各大水系之间的运河成了世界各国都热衷的事情。

从广义上讲，运河是用来沟通地区或水域之间水运的人工水道，通常与自然水道或其他运河相连。从狭义上讲，运河是人工开凿的通航河道。除航运外，运河还可用于灌溉、分洪、排涝、给水等。

我国运河建设历史悠久，如公元前514年开凿的胥溪（又称胥河），是世界上最古老的人工运河，也是中国有记载的最早的和世界上开凿最早的运河，因它是吴国伍子胥开凿的，故取名胥河。还有公元前219年，为沟通湘江和漓江而开挖的灵渠，因为是最早沟通两大水系的工程，而得以写入历史教科书。不过，知名度最高的还是京杭大运河。

在人们的普遍印象中，中国的运河多半建设在水系发达、水流丰沛的南方地区，而对北方物流的印象，仍停留在陆路运输上。而事实并非如此，中国北方的气候在很长一段时间内都是比较湿润的。比如，在明朝的嘉峪关长城附近，大量夯土里都有水草的痕迹，这说明在普遍认知里西北缺水的固有概念存在偏差。西北地区在古代尚且湿润，尤其是长期受季风气候影响的华北地区，降水量更大。所以，在古代中国，华北地区河流众多，湖泊沼泽密布。

而今天我们所探究的，就是消失了一千多年的古运河——平虏渠和泉州渠。

---

① 亦作乌丸，是中国古代民族之一。

泉州渠是在如今的福建泉州吗？似乎跟曹操一直在北方活动的范围不搭边？沟河、潞河好像现代也有，和古代是一个位置吗？

所幸，中国古人爱记载的习惯为如今解开这些谜团留下了依据。

《三国志》中有记载："邺既定，以昭为谏议大夫。后袁尚依乌丸蹋顿，太祖将征之。患军粮难致，凿平虏、泉州二渠入海通运。"

大美滹沱（任鹏 摄）

滹沱河，当地人俗称糊涂河。滹沱河发源于山西省五台山，东流至河北省献县，与滏阳河汇合形成子牙河。滹沱河全长 587 千米，流域面积 2.73 万平方千米。

沟河，发源于河北省兴隆县，流经北京市平谷区、河北省三河市，东南进入天津市宝坻区，流入蓟运河。

潞河，今北运河，海河的支流之一，其通州区至天津市的干流也是京杭大运河的北段，在通州区以北的上游称为温榆河。流经河北省香河县、天津市武清区，在天津市与永定河相汇。

邺，即邺城，现在是河北省临漳县，它是魏晋南北朝时期北方的重要城市。漳河流经的邺城，长期以来是北方政权的都城之一。

泉州县，古县名。始建于西汉，现天津市武清区西南，在北魏太平真君七年（公元 446 年）并入雍奴县。

如此，一副宏大而庞杂的曹操擘画的大手笔，就跃然纸上了。

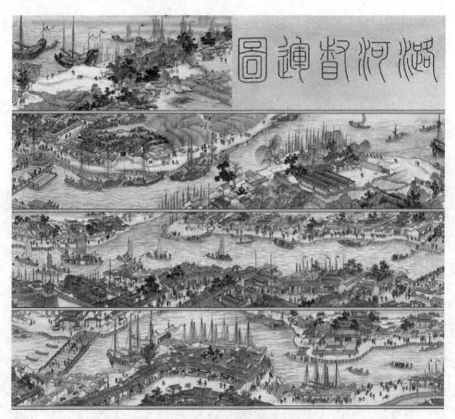

《潞河督运图》（清江萱画，原件现藏于国家博物馆）

平虏渠与泉州渠的修凿，可以使邺城来的船舶直抵塞外。那么，这条运河在当时起到了多大的作用，后来又为何消失了呢？也许，回顾曹操北征乌桓的这段历史，这个谜底就能揭晓了。

二、一切为了战争

由于《三国演义》被广泛阅读，今天的读者对三国的故事都很熟悉，对曹操与袁绍的争斗更是如数家珍，十常侍之乱、十八路诸侯讨董卓、官渡之战都不用赘述。这段关于运河的故事，不得不从官渡之战后说起。

建安五年（公元 200 年）的官渡之战，袁绍败北，退回自己的老窝冀州，休养生息，以图再战。但此时，冀州发生了一些叛乱，这令袁绍十分恼怒，于是开始了扫平冀州内乱的战斗。

人们对袁绍的印象，大多符合曹操与刘备青梅煮酒时的话："吾知绍之为人，志大而智小，色厉而胆薄，忌克而少威，兵多而分画不明，将骄而政令不一。土地虽广，粮食虽丰，适足以为吾奉也！"曹操此话字里行间透露出对袁绍的轻蔑，但是在《三国志》中，曹操在说完上述这段话后，话锋一转，表现出对袁绍的客观看法："袁绍据河北，兵势强盛。孤自度势，实不敌之。"

所以，尽管袁绍在官渡之战中大败，但曹操在袁绍回到冀州大本营四处平乱的一年中，却没有大的行动。毕竟，战败的袁绍实力依然十分强大。

袁绍有多强呢？举例为证，袁绍曾经灭掉了盘踞幽燕之地的军阀公孙瓒，公孙瓒人送外号"白马银枪"，长期镇守塞北，他主政期间，率领手下骑兵部队"白马义从"横扫塞北乌桓、鲜卑、契丹等少数民族。尤其是"白马义从"中有一员小将，原本在公孙瓒手下并不突出，但后来在《三国演义》长坂坡一战中大放异彩，他就是赵子龙。手下猛将如云、猛士如雨的公孙瓒如此厉害，却依旧败于袁绍。

袁绍攻击公孙瓒时，表现出非凡的军事素养。他手下军队先与公孙瓒骑兵正面交锋，佯装不敌，将公孙瓒骑兵部队引诱到骑兵不容易发挥战斗力的沼泽之地作战。公孙瓒被这种战法击败多次后，便采取龟缩防守的战法，长期对峙。公孙瓒部队挖壕沟、筑土山、建高楼、粮草充足。袁绍采取截断公孙瓒的内外联络，消灭公孙瓒援军友军的打法，围点打援，以逸待劳。在历经多年征战后，袁绍发起总攻，袁绍军队将地道挖到公孙瓒城下，最后把用来支撑地道的木柱点燃，使城墙塌陷，《后汉书》中描述"袁氏之攻，状若鬼神，梯冲舞吾楼上，鼓角鸣于地中"。

所以，曹操能够在官渡击败袁绍，充分证明了自己出色的军事谋略。但是，袁绍手下依旧大军云集、谋士众多，且因为袁绍主政冀州时，为政宽仁，百姓都十分感佩他的恩德。这些因素都使曹操压制住了自己那颗乘胜北进冀州的心。

建安七年（公元 202 年），冀州起义平息后，袁绍于家中病逝。袁绍的小儿子袁尚在谋士审配等的拥立下继承了袁绍的政权。这引起了袁绍长子袁谭的不满，袁绍次子袁熙加入袁尚阵营，三人开始了争权夺利的内斗。为击败袁尚，袁谭向曹操求助，最终"引狼入室"。曹操把握机会，大举进军河北，很快击败袁尚、袁熙，并回军诛杀了袁谭。建安十年（公元 205 年）袁尚、袁熙兄弟不敌曹操，仓皇北逃，进入乌桓的地盘，寻求庇护。

乌桓远离中原，乌桓首领蹋顿的王帐更是设在柳城，曹操要从河北进军柳城，既没有今天的公路，也没有当时所谓"驿道"。仅有山中小路能够到达那里，而且还需要穿过长城。在当时，只有商贩为寻求利益，才冒险走这些小路，曹操大军要想进攻乌桓，困难重重。

在交通工具落后的古代，要出兵远征并非一件简单的事情，尤其是军粮的运输。为此，曹操曾与幕下文武官员多次商议此事，多数人认为大军深入塞外，不仅军粮运输困难重重，而且在南面荆州的刘备必然会劝说刘表乘机出兵袭击许都，到时候恐将两头吃亏，因此暂时不宜远征乌桓。

此时，谋士郭嘉力排众议，主张立即出兵远征乌桓：乌桓远离中原，并不知道曹军的厉害，防守必然松懈，可以趁其不备，奇袭乌桓，必能成功。而且袁绍对乌桓素来有恩，如果放任袁尚兄弟与之结盟，其休养生息后定会南下夺取冀州，后患无穷。而刘表此人，素爱清谈，对刘备的才能又有防备，所以刘备的建议他多半不会听取。曹操接纳了郭嘉的建议，决定乘胜追击。考虑到这次远征需要较长时间，军需物资的运输是头等大事。因此，在建安十一年（公元 206 年），曹操命令董昭开凿平虏渠、泉州渠。

三、胜利的底气

就在曹操命人开凿运河的同时，郭嘉的预言很快实现了。建安十一年，乌桓侵扰幽州地区，夺掠百姓十余万户，社会动荡不安。

面对北方的严峻形势，曹操加快了开凿运河的进程。不久，开凿平虏渠和泉州渠的任务取得成功。人马辎重得以快速从邺城转运，曹操大军迅速通过这两条运河集结在了泉州渠北口。

但新的问题出现了，曹操大军的军需物资囤积在泉州渠北口，而乌桓王帐设立在燕山山脉深处的大凌河流域。曹军依然面临着千里行军的窘境。于是，曹操又下令开凿了一条名为"新河"的人工渠连通泉州渠和濡水（今河北省滦河），以求尽可能接近乌桓。

曹操在建安十二年（公元 207 年）四月到达无终县，七月遇到大雨，许多河流都泛滥了，处处积水，曹操本想沿着海岸绕到今辽宁省一带，再向北转往柳城，但河水泛滥，这条"傍海道"不通。

这时，曹操面前突然出现一位叫田畴的隐士。为躲避战火，田畴和一些百姓在山里隐居，他本不想管曹操与袁绍之间的事。但因为乌桓长期欺压汉族百姓，他觉得这是自卫问题，便出山入世，向曹操毛遂自荐，成为曹军的向导带领曹军由一条叫作"卢龙道"的小路穿行，穿过喜峰口，直抵柳城之西，全长五百多里。这条"卢龙道"其实并不是小路，而是卢龙塞直通柳城的大道，但从东汉光武帝以后，这条路破败断绝近二百年，竟成了无人知晓的小道。

曹军在柳城附近的白狼山，遭遇蹋顿的兵将。战斗开始后，曹军先锋部队在指挥官张辽的带领下，士气高昂，奋勇冲杀，斩杀了蹋顿。随后，曹操主力部队赶到，收降了胡人、汉人二十几万，此战大获全胜。袁尚兄弟俩逃到辽东太守公孙康处寻求保护，结果公孙康杀了他们，并把他们的人头送给了曹操。

至此，曹操统一河北之地，将整个中国北方纳入自己的统治范畴，完成了其扫平天下的关键一步。

复盘曹操征伐乌桓，我们发现，曹操自始至终都在关注军队后勤，只有解决了粮草补给问题，他才会大胆用兵。在面对千里奔袭，后勤接济不上的关键时刻，他采取速战速决的方式打败对手，避免因长期对战陷入后勤不继的危险境地。而四百年后，隋炀帝东征高丽，作战距离比曹操更远，但后勤却依赖涿郡转运，再强大的战力也被打了折扣，为失败埋下了伏笔。

那么新的问题来了，历来开凿运河都是费时费力的事情，为何曹操的属下仅仅用了一年，就能开通平虏渠、泉州渠两条运河，并又临时开凿新河呢？答案或许出乎意料，因为曹操可是开凿运河的老手了。

事实上，平虏渠与泉州渠并不是曹操第一次开凿的运河。曹操最初的根据地，地盘小人口少，"白骨露于野，千里无鸡鸣"。所以精打细算的曹操十分注意解决粮食生产和运输问题，他采用屯田的办法解决了生产问题，而开挖运河，疏通荒废的河道，连接长江、淮河、黄河、海河各大水域，则是他解决运输问题的重要手段。

在黄河改道之后，由于原来黄河故道的灌溉需要，产生了白沟。因为黄河改道，白沟水源缺乏，经常处于干涸的状态。建安八年（公元203年），曹操进攻邺城时，他先指挥部队攻下了黎阳，随后率领大军从许昌渡河。为了解决军粮的运输难题，曹操命令军队将淇水河中的水引入白沟，成功地解决了军粮运输问题。

曹操不仅是开凿运河的老手，更是熟悉山川地理的达人。东西走向的滹沱河，在黄河北流形成的高大沙堤前，形成了不少巨大的泊淀。由于山洪的爆发，滹沱河多次改道决口，在华北平原上形成了无数纵横如渔网的古河道。曹操选择在饶阳，沿原来滹沱河北支故道凿渠通泒水北上，到达蠡县，过白洋淀到易州，接着沿永定河北上幽州，继而夺回幽州，这是一条精准计划的路线。为了减少损耗，他又开通了泉州渠，将大军转运路线连通到了大海边，因为沿海取近路可以直捣乌桓老巢。

大运河卫河浚县段（解静怡 摄）

所以，尽管最后曹操攻灭乌桓的战斗是通过翻越燕山山脉，以奇袭的方式取得胜利的，但是，将军粮送抵距离前线最近的新河口，却是曹军大胆进攻的底气。后勤为军队撑起腰杆子，运河是后勤的保障。

天津海河三岔口——曹操开通泉州渠的重要节点（孙凡越 摄）

四、历史的余晖

曹操征服乌桓后，将乌桓骑兵收入囊中，从此，乌桓骑兵成了曹操手下又一支战斗力极强的部队。曹操回到中原后，他的军师郭嘉在易州因病去世。这次战斗，因为千古名篇《观沧海》的流传被世人牢记，但立下大功的运河，却淡出了人们的视野。

由于平虏渠的北口与泉州渠的南口在现在的海河上相通，平虏渠和泉州渠成为河北省贯穿南北、连接黄河及海河和蓟运河的水运通道。然而，虽然平虏渠和泉州渠是在同一时期同一地区开凿的，但它们的历史命运却大相径庭。平虏渠自开通以来，已成为河南通往河北的重要航道，后来又成为魏晋南北朝白沟与清河、隋唐永济渠、宋元御河、明清卫河以及近代南运河的重要组成部分。它在交通运输中起着重要的作用。而泉州渠则完全不同。郦道元在《水经注》中记述道："故渎上承滹沱水于泉州县，故以泉州为名。"这表明泉州渠在北魏时代郦道元写作《水经注》时，已经成为湮废的遗迹了。

但是，平虏渠与泉州渠的历史意义，依然震古烁今。

它们完善了北方的运河网络。平虏渠与泉州渠是一条具有军事、经济、地理、工程、水利多重巨大意义的运河，比隋炀帝借运河运输远征塞上还要早几百年，也是我国北方运河网络的重要组成部分。要知道一千八百多年前的中国，幅员辽阔，地理情况多变，陆路运输成本高，效率低，而海路还没有开通，内河航运则成为一种省钱、省时、省力的运输方式。水运还使北方的粮食生产、经济交流、物资流通都得到了加强。

平虏渠和泉州渠更是进一步促成了全国水系一盘棋的格局形成，为中国大一统奠定了基础。在曹操的统治下，白沟、平虏渠、泉州渠和新河的开通使得黄河以北的漳河、滦河、滹沱河等成功地连接至济水、淮河、长江、钱塘江诸水系。自此，江淮河海之间的水运得到了连通，东至吴越，西及巴蜀、汉中，南尽五岭、珠海，北达幽州、滦河，华夏各地域的百姓均可乘船往来无间，并进行亲密的经济和人文交流。这种交流客观上促进了中国的统一，也为隋唐时期京杭大运河的形成奠定了基础。

丰图义仓
——平战结合的物流思想

（邵瑞 摄）

坐落于陕西省大荔县朝邑镇粮站大院里的丰图义仓，是一座历经风霜的古老民办地上仓库，至今仍保存完好，并发挥着储存国粮、赈济灾荒的作用。其布局之奇巧，展现了中华民族高度的智慧和周密合理的技术，对于我国古代仓储管理研究具有重要的价值和历史意义。

一、底气与担当

谈到丰图义仓，就不得不提阎敬铭[①]这个人。他做官有一个特点，无论官至何处，他都会在衙署内放置一架纺机。他在前堂处理公务，夫人在后堂缫丝织布，纺机吱吱呀呀的声响时刻警示着他心系民生、廉洁勤勉。

[①] 阎敬铭（1817–1892），字丹初，陕西朝邑赵渡镇（今陕西省大荔县朝邑镇）人，道光二十五年进士，理财有道，为官清廉，有"救时宰相"之称。

中国物流
故事 STORY
古代辑
汉英对照

▲阎敬铭雕像（田锡超 摄）

清光绪三年（1877 年），山西、河南、陕西发生特大旱灾，此时的阎敬铭已年过六旬，患有咳疾，形销骨立，需扶杖而走。虽自感病躯难膺重任，但目睹灾情不断加重、灾民愈来愈多，他深感自己不能置身事外，领旨前往山西稽办赈务，期间亦奉命查陕西赈事。

阎敬铭穿着朴素，只带简单的行李，辗转数千里到达灾区，并将朝廷拨发给他的一千两银子差旅费悉数捐出，用作赈灾。随着巡察的地方越多，阎敬铭看到的灾情也越严峻，他内心备受煎熬，却又束手无策。

阎敬铭派人赴南方采购米粮以应急需，直到第二年，虽费尽心力，也只购得少许。同时他四处求助，筹借钱粮，每日写下的求助信函不下八九封，效果却不理想。

然而更棘手的是，即使购买到粮食，也无法及时运抵灾区。因持续干旱，许多运河干涸，粮食无法通过水路运回，只能陆路绕行，路程远且道路崎岖，运费都是粮价的三倍，极大地增加了运粮难度和成本。

虽说到了清朝，防灾救灾机制已比较健全。但此时的清廷面临国外列强侵略和国内农民起义的双重压力，显得软弱无力。社会经济还未从凋敝中恢复，朝廷又遭边疆危机，左宗棠出兵新疆，作为后勤保障的粮草需求明显提高。阎敬铭反复请求朝廷拨款调粮救济，朝廷虽多次转调漕粮，但其数量与实际需求悬殊。

光绪三年年底，灾情继续蔓延，尤其是山西，饿殍遍野、触目惊心。阎敬铭万分痛心，向朝廷请求将江苏、湖北 6 万石漕粮调往山西应急，奏章中言"往来二三千里，目之所见，皆系鹄面鸠形；耳之所闻，无非男啼女哭""甚至枯骸塞途，绕车而过，残喘呼救，望地而僵。统计一省之内，每日饿毙者何止千人"。朝廷方意识到灾情的严重程度，紧急调运漕粮至山西。

这场自然灾害史称"丁戊奇荒"①，惨烈程度甚至达到人与人互食。光绪五年

---

① "丁戊奇荒"，又称"丁丑奇荒"，主要指发生在丁丑、戊寅（1877—1878）两年的特大灾荒，是中国历史上最大的灾荒之一，灾害极其严重，对中国晚清历史产生了深远的影响。

（1879年），灾荒才得以缓解。据统计，"丁戊奇荒"期间因饥饿、疾疫等原因死亡的人数达千万之多，更有 2000 万人流离失所、颠沛他乡。

回到阔别已久的故乡，满目尽是残垣断壁，阎敬铭辗转反侧，苦思冥想，决定修建义仓，以丰补歉。只有丰年储谷、荒年出谷，才能长远防旱备荒。他联合朝邑士绅详写奏章，并且五年间连续六次奏请，力谏朝廷批准。

光绪八年（1882年），义仓开建，选址于地势高、地表平坦的朝邑县城南寨子村的高坡上，此地向东扼黄河滩万顷良田，向西连八百里秦川，向南与华山相望。此外，这里还有丰富的黄土资源，可就地取材烧砖制瓦，最大限度地降低人力、物力的损耗。阎敬铭考察后，决定充分利用这些天然优势，筑窑建仓。

阎敬铭题名、朝邑县知县蔡文田书写的"丰图义仓"（田锡超 摄）

此地位于黄河西岸低处，遇旱大丰，遇涝大歉；丰则有余，歉则成荒。在此处修建义仓，可以作为一个调剂库，丰年储粮，歉年调出。当地住户根据自家实际情况，捐出粮食储存在仓中，遇饥荒之年，从仓借粮，丰收再悉数归还，如此反复，无须支付利息，又能解决粮食储存的问题。

义仓于光绪十一年（1885年）竣工，历时四年，耗费三万余两白银。温饱不忘饥寒、丰年不忘灾年、增产不忘节约，故取名"丰图义仓"，具有"丰收补歉，图报百姓"之意，后被慈禧太后御封为"天下第一仓"，从此驰名天下。

其实，这也不是阎敬铭第一次琢磨此事，早在同治十一年（1872年），他就劝人积谷，只不过那时，他的意见不被人理解，不过是南柯一梦。

据《大荔县志》记载，光绪二十六年（1900年），关中地区又发生大灾荒，夏秋不雨，麦歉产，秋无收。丰图义仓开赈放粮，按口散粮，并设粥厂，救民于水火。

《丰图义仓志》载："回忆辛丑赈济，全活无算，无不归功斯仓。"

此后一百多年来，丰图义仓一直起着为民囤粮、安定一方的作用。清末时期陕西大部分义仓逐渐消失，而丰图义仓依然完好地保存至今，基本上延续着其原有建筑布局，并一直用于粮食的储存。仓中可储藏大豆、玉米、花生、小麦、高粱、大米等粮食作物，尤以小麦和玉米为多。粮食虽大多为一年一储存，但丰图义仓的小麦最多可储存达 10 年之久。

新中国成立后，丰图义仓被陕西省政府命名为第三批省级重点文物保护单位，一直由该地粮站通过"以粮养仓"的方式保护着，每年可存储调运粮食两万余吨，是我国少数留存至今的古代大型粮仓之一，也是现今唯一仍在使用的古代粮仓，更是我国储粮品质最好的粮仓之一。

二、城中亦有城

丰图义仓建造在关中平原东部黄河西岸南寨子村的老崖上，地处黄河、渭河、洛河交汇处的关中盆地，有广袤的河滩和台塬，地质地貌和气候条件独特。义仓北倚临晋古道，南临黄河，无论陆路还是水路都十分便利，有效地保证了粮食的纳入和调出。

俯瞰丰图义仓（邵瑞 摄）

丰图义仓的主体建筑酷似一座壁垒森严的城池，集存储粮食和军事防御为一体，内仓城可存粮，也可屯兵，城北仓楼可作观察指挥之用，城内广场可操兵演练。纵观整个仓廪的设计，其建筑布局是城中有城，地势高燥，甚是威武雄壮。

丰图义仓充分体现了仓储的综合性功能，既满足了仓储囤粮之需，又兼顾了军事防御的需求，结构设计周密而科学。

内仓城坐北朝南，墙体为砖表土心结构，立东西二门，仓体均为单拱结构，不修大房而箍窑洞。这样设置，除了省时省料，还有一个重要原因，就是使窑洞恒温恒湿，冬暖夏凉，有利于保证存储粮食的质量，且封密严，便于防鼠防腐。存取食粮，互不打扰。

仓门与城内广场相对，节省了出入库时间，也方便调仓和晒粮。内仓城庭院设置为东西长，南北宽，增加了日晒面积，有利于保持粮食的干燥。同时，仓内还用坚实的墙体分隔成若干个小仓，以达到分储的目的，这样如遇火灾等意外情况，也只对其中一仓带来损失，规避了意外风险。仓内有宽敞大院，车马可自由通行。仓门中间为矩形院落，是仓吏办公和居住的地方。

光绪十七年（1891年），仓外又增修外围城墙，开辟护城河。外城与黄河西岸高出滩涂的河塬紧紧相贴，城北侧开辟出一条深壕，是关中盆地通往黄河古渡的驿道，形成东、南、北三面高显，西一面连塬的特殊地形。

作为一座高质量的古粮仓，丰图义仓有三个独特的设计：厚重的夯土仓墙、悬空仓体和分区排水法。这些设计让粮仓能够常年保持恒温状态，又利于通风，更隔绝了雨水侵蚀的隐患。

1.夯土仓墙

丰图义仓的58间仓房都依托厚重的内城墙而建，不另外单独设墙，既节约了建筑材料，又利用了厚重墙体的保温功能。而内仓城为了承载来自58间仓房的压力，将墙体设计成下宽上窄的梯形，底座更稳，地基的承载能力大大提高，也减少了粮食对墙体的侧压力。

每孔粮仓约能储存2000石粮食，如此大的存储量，非常考验粮仓的构造和设施。粮仓除了采用砖窑结构来增加温度和仓体的稳定性外，又增加了墙体的厚度。当地夯土厚重，热稳定性好，冬季辐射热量、夏季吸收热量。再加上夯土密度大，泥土中的空隙少，很好地隔绝了室外温度，起到绝热保温的作用。这样，粮仓的温度可以维持相对恒定，常年在18摄氏度左右，适宜粮食长久保存。这种粮仓存储的创新之举，既利用了墙体的厚实，便于恒定粮温，又节省了建筑材料，是综合功能利用较好的粮仓之一。

此外，黏土砖能承受 800~900 摄氏度高温，仓城导水隔墙实有防火墙的作用。仓房墙体为实体砖结构，同样能够达到防火的作用。一般防火墙（0.4~0.5 米）耐火极限为 4 小时，而此仓房墙体厚度达 0.8 米，耐火极限远远超过 4 小时，能达到较为理想的防火效果。

2. 悬空仓体

另外，为了防腐防潮，进一步改善储存条件，每间仓房表面及底部还做了灰土地基处理。采用的插板式仓门可根据粮仓粮食储存高度以及气候条件打开，释放仓内潮气，保持仓房干燥。

为了防止地下的潮气使仓内粮食受潮变质，仓洞内一仓一门，后墙有气窗，仓房木板离地基约 40 厘米，形成自然的通风道。粮仓墙体周围开凿了排气孔，这样设计能保持仓内仓外空气流通，潮气及时排出，达到粮食低温、低湿、低氧的"三低"仓储要求。

此外，仓面由松木板铺成，这种材料密度高，硬度强，耐磨性好，且耐虫性强，是理想的防腐木材，因而粮食不易霉变生虫，保障了储粮的食用安全。

3. 分区排水法

粮仓仓顶由抗氧化、抗水化和抗大气侵蚀的青砖铺成，大片面积亦可用于晒粮。仓顶分为 12 个排水区域，每个区域周边高中间低，形成东西南北四方的斜坡，巧妙地将雨水汇集于中间，再通过"U"形铁铸水槽向室外排出，可以避免雨水四散造成积水渗水。导水墙的设计一方面可以避免仓顶积水，使雨水快速向仓内广场流去，另一方面又可作为支撑墙、防火墙，大大提高了粮仓的防火能力。

这种分区排水的设计，水流通畅，直排檐下，雨停即干。由于仓内广场微微向南倾斜，雨水排入仓内广场后，会顺着广场南部的两处排水口，通过暗渠排出内仓城，再由明渠排至外仓城，流向城墙外的排水渠，最后排入东侧山崖下。

为了避免雨量过大对东侧山崖造成急剧冲刷，东门外建造了一处水池，既可以用来缓冲水势，又可以作为一个救火的蓄水池。

经历百年风霜，墙体院基虽留下了风化腐蚀的痕迹，但是几乎没有破损和裂缝，至今仍能使用，一切依赖于粮仓科学严密的建筑结构和有效的排水系统。事实上，历经一百多年，丰图义仓从未发生过渗漏。

丰图义仓 U 形铁铸水槽（田锡超　摄）

三、储粮与防御

粮仓在战乱或灾荒时期经常受到人为侵害，丰图义仓建造时就附加了军事防御和临时避难的功能。平时可用来储粮，如遇战争，则化身为朝邑军事重镇的守卫，守护着这一方的安全。

据《大荔县志》记载，丰图义仓建在朝邑城西塬阶之上，占据战略制高点，北临绝壁，东有断崖，有利于隐蔽、观测和射击。再加上丰图义仓"嵌套"式的设计，就为仓城穿上了层层防御"外衣"，给敌人的攻击带来重重困难。

朝邑是军事战略要地，是长安的门户。在此修建义仓，其意义也是显而易见的。一方面，可作为重要的粮食补给站，义仓的修建能够为军队囤积粮食，以备战时之需，另一方面，还可作为军事堡垒，既能守又能攻，视敌情而动，发动火力，也可拦截敌军过河。这样说来，丰图义仓可谓是清朝进行战争和维持统治的坚实后盾。

无论是在清朝晚期，还是在民国时期，历经炮火纷争、天灾人祸，丰图义仓在储存粮食和化解饥荒等方面创下了不可磨灭的功勋。就连抗日战争时期，丰图义仓也发挥了重要作用。1938年，日军来犯，炮击朝邑，形势异常严峻，当时，红军便充分发挥了丰图义仓的军事要塞作用，在此设指挥所，指挥全线作战，保障了军需。

《墨子》有"城者，所以自守也"。《孟子》也有"三里之城，七里之郭，环而攻之而不胜"。可见，"城"具有防御这一天然属性。所以，"筑城围仓"，几乎历史上每一个重要粮仓的建造都起到了这种作用。

华仓，山头而建，城墙筑立，可谓仓城；敖仓，山上临河，亦为山城。另外隋朝洛口仓、回洛仓等粮仓的选址原则，大抵类似，充分考虑储存效果、粮食安全、交通便利这些因素。

丰图义仓充分实现了平日储粮和战时防御的功能，与雅典卫城异曲同工。

丰图义仓建造之初，就充分考虑了储粮和防御的功能。无论是建筑选址，还是仓房通风、防潮、防火、防虫、抗震等设计，都较为科学合理，有利于粮仓日后的使用和管理。同时，还对仓储管理的发展有一定的借鉴和指导作用。丰图义仓并没有被发展的时代所淘汰，其构造及格局一直沿用至今，并发挥着重要作用。丰图义仓连续30多年被评为四无粮仓，成为近代仓廪建筑的一大代表。

丰图义仓从选址、布局、建筑设计及技术等各方面体现了中华民族的智慧与底蕴，承载了我国仓政、仓储历史、仓储文化的创新发展。

四、食为政首

我国古代以农立国，古人十分清楚粮草对于战争的重要性。正所谓"兵马未动，粮草先行"，所以历朝历代，在储粮之事上从未有过懈怠。储粮被视为国家的重要举措，勤劳作，勤储粮，成了代代相传的美好品德。

各类粮仓各司其职，正仓和军仓从农民或屯田兵那里征收税粮，主要用以供应军需；常平仓施行低价进高价出，调节市场价格；义仓通过赈济和贷借，在粮食不足时稳定民心；转运仓起转运储纳之用。两千多年来，这些粮仓的建造和运行，在赈济灾民，稳定社会和促进经济发展等方面都发挥了积极的作用。

民以食为天，粮食问题历来备受关注，"洪范八政，食为政首"的思想，体现了储粮的重要性；丰图义仓，也体现着古人丰富的粮食储备技术和管理经验。从摸索到熟稔，从土坑到智能，粮仓的千年变形记，不仅是技术的更迭，也体现了我国储粮事业的持续发展。

早在春秋战国时期，我国便有了仓廪制度，秦朝继承发展，西汉时盛行，隋朝时已形成一定的规模，到了唐朝，粮食仓储管理制度进一步发展，进入一个崭新阶段。清朝作为我国历史上最后一个封建王朝，其储粮制度集成了诸多传统因素，构筑了一套更为完善的体系。充实的粮食储备不但提升了国家的财政实力，更重要的是增强了国家对灾荒的抵御能力，为无数国民的生存提供了保障。

在社会建设和防灾救荒体系机制的构建、运行方面，官府和民间的协调及联动非常重要，特别是官府的统筹与主导、民间济贫扶困风尚的传承、粮食仓储制度的完善与维护、交通运输的畅达便利以及市场全局意识的建立都需要得到强化，而心系民生、廉洁勤勉的官员，更是社会建设和防灾救荒的关键。

镖局
——现代物流组织的雏形

　　2018年夏，山西祁县，民间武术家段天林正指导自己的外孙余志超练习家传的棍法。棍法不像影视剧里呈现得那样潇洒漂亮，它来来回回就是那么简单的几招。余志超马上要去太原参加全省武术大赛，这套一点也不令人眼花缭乱的棍法，很难让他脱颖而出。

　　直到一天，在与其他选手的交流互动中，余志超施展的棍法，处处直击要害，他这才发现这套棍法的精妙之处。他将自己的感受说与段天林听，段天林告诉他，这套棍法脱胎于戴氏心意拳，百余年前，由戴氏心意拳第四代传人戴魁传授给自己的先祖，由此沿袭了下来。

　　这套棍法狠辣至极，在祁县有"太极十年不出门，形意一年打死人"的俗语流传，由此可见其威力之大。由戴氏心意拳脱胎而来的棍法，自然藏着简单而凌厉的撒手锏。这是纪录片《十八般兵器》①中"棍"这个专题下的一个小故事。

---

① 2020年12月于央视科教频道首播，该片围绕中国古代兵器，解读古代政治礼制、军事制度、科技成就、战术，探讨古代武备中承载的中国传统文化的精神特质。

为何戴家会以如此刚猛的武术作为家传之术呢？原来，戴家祖上是开镖局的。

戴家所在的山西祁县，是中国古代主要商帮——晋商的大本营。晋商以对外贸易起家，而后涉及全国票号①事宜，从南方运往蒙古、俄罗斯的砖茶、瓷器、铁锅、丝绸、布匹大多会经过此地，货物以海量计算，而从大江南北的票号汇往山西的银子更是有百万两到千万两之多。

如此庞大的物资、钱财、人员流动，势必催生了第三方的物流加安保机构——镖局。交通问题和安全问题尤为重要，因此镖局在山西遍地开花，相当盛行。为了保证一路畅通，镖师们自然苦练内功，习得一门快捷、简单、能够震慑沿途觊觎金帛的宵小之徒的武术。以刚猛快捷现杀招的武术，也就成了镖局从业人主要修习的功夫了。

镖局，这个在历史上赫赫有名的机构，是怎样形成、完善乃至影响全国的？它涉及的范围广泛，运营有规矩而又灵活创新，堪称中国物流史的奇迹，它对现代物流的发展又有哪些镜鉴作用呢？

一、因需求而生

关于镖局的起源，众说纷纭。不管是哪种起源说，都认定镖局的"镖"是由"标"演变而来的。

那么，什么是"标"？

所谓标，最初就是标志、标识之意，后来因为饭店、酒家所用颇多，便有了"酒标"之意，酒标即酒家所挂的幌子。唐朝诗人杜牧的《江南春》中写道："千里莺啼绿映红，水村山郭酒旗风"，其中提到的"酒旗"，就是"标"。

在南唐，"标"的意思得到了进一步延伸。由于出现了"打标舟子"②之称，官府向竞渡胜者授以"彩帛银碗"，赋予端午竞渡争夺锦标之意，这便是"夺标"。北宋画家张择端除了创有中国十大传世名画之一的《清明上河图》之外，还有另外一幅名画《金明池争标图》流传后世，这里的"标"就是锦标之意。

到了明朝，"标"的含义继续扩展，在商界、军界都有了自己的解释，最终经过多重演变，汇集成了意义纯粹、指向明确的"镖"字的含义。

---

① 商业资本转化而来的旧式信用机构。
② 竞渡胜者的称号。

张择端《金明池争标图》页

于商界而言，在正德年间（1506—1521 年），松江府（今上海）产出一种新型棉布，因纱支匀细、布身紧密、结实耐穿，被视为上品的"标布"。此处"标"有标准、优胜之意。南来北往贩卖这些标布的客商小贩被称为"标客"，标客组成的机构也被称作"标行"。在明朝，标客们在北京、山东、江南地区之间往来，其中大多会集在山东临清、北直隶南宫县（今河北南宫）一带。史料中就记载有明朝松江府朱家角镇"商贾辏聚，贸易花布"的盛况。作为商贩的标客，因其携带物品价值较高，也会雇用一些会武术、善拳脚的人员来帮助运输以保证安全。被雇用的这些人员多为地方上"打行"的成员，打行即打手组织。久而久之，他们也被称为标客。标客的内涵开始向物流运输、安全押运方面演变。

于军界而言，军队里开始出现"标兵"一说。嘉靖年间（1522—1566 年），因南方有倭寇作乱，北方有鞑靼犯边，守卫当地的军队常常不堪重用，需由中央派人组织军队前往作战。通常，中央派员担任总督、巡抚时，须有一支护卫部队，称为中军。中军由各将领麾下最为精悍的军士组成，这些人武艺高强，力气惊人，被视为战士中的标杆，也被称作"标兵"。标兵除了护卫统帅之外，还有一个重要的职责，那就是押运、护卫军饷。

明朝末期，战乱频繁，从总督到巡抚再到总兵官，每人都有自己的中军，标兵也大大扩充。随着国力日颓，很多战败或者被打散的标兵，开始流落山野。为谋生计，有的变身响马，做起抢劫勾当；有的则从事护卫工作，成为南北客商物流的一支保卫力量。在护卫过程中，这些标兵出身的团队打出旗帜，也被称为"标旗"，以扩大影响力。

随着时间推移，打行出身的标客与军士出身的标兵，基本已经合流。清朝建立后，商品经济繁荣。"镖"的"金"字旁象征着传统的十八般兵器，部件"票"代表着货币，如此来看，"镖"表示用武力来捍卫财产。"镖局"是保护财产安全的武力组织。

镖师的兵刃（图片来源：华北第一镖局）

镖局自此登上了历史的舞台，成为当时民用长途货物运输的安全保护机构。不管镖局如何演变，但可以看出，镖局的出现，一定具备一个基本的条件：商品经济的高度繁荣。

明末江南地区经济发展迅速，南北货物运输急需安全保障。中国最早的镖局出现于清朝乾隆年间，这背后也是有康乾盛世、国内经济大发展的历史背景。

第一家被官方明确认可的镖局，是诞生于清朝乾隆年间的兴隆镖局。《山西票号史》记载："山西人神拳张黑五者……领圣旨，开设兴隆镖局于北京顺天府前门外大街。"

清朝是镖局空前繁盛的时期。在清朝中后期，镖局的业务范围逐渐扩大，它们不但接受民间托运人普通货物和贵重财产的运输业务，还会受地方官府委托押运饷银。继兴隆镖局之后，全国各地的镖局也陆续出现在文献中。据统计，当时全国镖局数量以北京为最，山西、河北、天津、江南地区等商品经济发达的地区也是镖局盛行之地，此间较为闻名的就不下 30 家。业务范围广阔、活动范围横跨南北东西的有十大镖局，它们按地域划分依次为北京兴隆、会友、源顺镖局，河北成兴、三合、万通镖局，山西同兴公镖局，河南广盛镖局，江苏玉永、昌隆镖局。

清末著名武术家王五

源顺镖局尤为出众。该镖局由清末著名武术家王五①，于 1877 年开设于北京半壁街。源顺镖局经营规范，定价合理，崇尚德义，客户源源不绝，招牌在短短几年内便闻名遐迩。镖局活动范围贯通南北，向北能至山海关，往南能达江苏淮安清江浦。

1898 年，王五接到了一个独特的"镖"，要为进京准备戊戌新政的变法派人士谭嗣同做安保工作。在交往中，王五与谭嗣同这位戊戌变法的重要推动者、满怀救国热情的忠义人士意气相投，成为莫逆之交。

慈禧太后发动政变后，戊戌变法失败，谭嗣同身陷囹圄，王五四处联络江湖人士，准备劫狱。但谭嗣同却以他希望用鲜血唤醒民众为由，劝退了王五②。

谭嗣同等"戊戌六君子"就义后，王五悲痛欲绝。1900 年，王五参加义和团运动，后被八国联军杀害，时年 56 岁。王五被杀后，头颅被惨无人道地悬于城门之上。一代武术名家霍元甲听闻此事，只身义愤赶往，趁夜将其首取下、安葬，此举成就了中华武术史上一段英雄相惜的千古美谈。

北京史专家方彪称，相比会友镖局，源顺镖局属于小型镖局，其人数有四五十。身为源顺镖局之主的大刀王五，一身正气，忠义爱国，他给整个镖界带来的震撼和影响是巨大的，将他称作"镖界楷模"可谓当之无愧。

---

① 王五，本名王正谊，河北沧州人，善使一口大刀，因师门中排行第五，江湖人称"大刀王五"。

② 谭嗣同说："各国变法，无不从流血而成，今日中国未闻有因变法而流血者，此国之所以不昌也。有之，请自嗣同始。"

二、因规则而兴

面对盗贼丛生、劫匪横行的环境，大家需要镖局来保证长途运输的安全。镖局从业人员面对黄白之物①，几百年来，很少出现监守自盗的情况，反而因为信守承诺，屡屡成为民间传说、武侠小说乃至影视作品中侠义之道、信义之道的典范。镖局是怎么做到这些的？这与镖局独特的内部管理机制有着莫大关系。或者说，镖局有着它十分独特的规矩来保障客户利益。

一个镖局一般由老板、总镖头、镖头、镖师、掌柜、账房先生、趟子手和杂役组成。大部分镖局的总镖头由老板兼任。当然，不是任何老板都能胜任总镖头，出色的总镖头大多为声名显赫的江湖"大佬"，有着一身拳脚功夫傍身，人脉遍布五湖四海。一般来说，镖局是凭武力来保护委托人的财产或人身安全的，因此，镖局的业务主要分为运输委托人钱财、商品的"走镖"和替委托人看护家门的"坐镖"两种形式。

根据运输对象分类，走镖分为六种，它们分别是信镖（捎送信函）、票镖（押送票号银两）、银镖（押送现银）、粮镖（押送粮食）、物镖（押送商品货物）、人身镖（保护雇主人身安全）。

根据保护目的不同，坐镖分为护院（守护私人住宅）、坐店（保护店铺正常经营不被打扰）、守夜（保障店铺的夜间财产安全）。前文所讲的大刀王五接下谭嗣同的镖，就是坐镖，主要履行护院的职责。

走镖按运输的方式可分为陆路镖和水路镖，陆路镖是镖师们骑马或乘轿在官驿大道上为护送的对象保驾护航；水路镖则是利用船舶进行水上护送。从事水路镖的镖师就得兼通水性，随船保护。走镖的路线取决于各镖局的镖头和镖师对沿路情况的熟悉程度。

镖局走镖，一般是依据运输的距离、货物的价值以及运输业务的难易程度计费，收取"镖利"。镖局与雇主签订"镖单"，在镖单上注明商号、货物名称、数量、起运地点、镖利等，双方确认无误后签字画押，留作凭证。镖师们将镖单上的货物完好地运送到指定的地点，交货完毕后获取镖利。

通常，总镖头或镖局分号的镖头率领几个镖师，带上接收货物的镖单和官府

---

① 即黄金和白银。

开具的通行证就可以上路了。

押镖路上，镖师们不但要经历漫长的行程，还会经常碰到劫匪，因此喊号子便成了镖队走镖时的必行之举。号子在镖界被称作"镖号"，镖师们喊起来前呼后应、抑扬顿挫，颇具威慑力，一来可以为镖队造势壮威，震慑一般的劫匪；二来又可起到自报家门与对方交谈对垒的作用。

当然，走镖的镖师与劫匪也有话不投机的时候。双方谈不拢，就会切磋过招，如果镖师赢了，劫匪自然让路放行；如果劫匪赢了，镖队就会被劫。于镖队而言，这便是"失镖"，除了要对委托人给予对应数额的赔偿外，镖局的名声还会受到一定的负面影响。这是为什么镖局多由武术名家开办，也是为什么镖局传下的武功都暗藏杀招。

镖局是一种特殊的物流组织机构，在运营管理上有着自身独树一帜的地方。

1. 权责明确，组织化程度高

在镖局的管理运行中形成了明确的行业准则。一个合格的镖师不仅要有基础技能傍身，还需要严格地遵守行业准则。例如，"三会一不"，即会搭炉灶做饭、会修补破鞋、会理发和不洗脸，因为走镖路途遥远且多途经荒无人烟的地带，做饭、修鞋、理发是必备技能，至于不洗脸，是因为风餐露宿，尘土覆盖后的脸，反而能抵挡风霜，保护面部。水路镖的"三规"，即押镖途中不能离船、夜晚不能入睡、忌讳与女性见面，这三种情况都有可能导致失镖。陆路镖的"三不住"，即娼店不能住、新开旅店不能住、易主之店不能住，这三种情况都有可能存在风险。睡觉时的"三不离"，即武器、衣服和车马不能离开可视范围。

同时，从人力资源管理角度来看，镖局分工明确，成员各司其职。镖局老板主要负责搭建镖局与黑白两道的关系网。掌柜精于盘算，主要管控镖局的日常事务，如看货、估价等。总镖头作为镖局的活字招牌，要以出类拔萃的功夫打响名声，还要担负重要程度高的货物护送任务。镖局的镖头与镖师则是货物运输的参与者和实施者，每一次走镖，都由一名镖头和若干镖师组成镖队护送货物。账房先生、杂役属于镖局的财务部门和后勤部门，从事镖局的记账和打杂事务。

2. 形成了自身的文化特色

镖局的发展产生了其特有的镖局文化，因其行业的特殊性，在内部形成了一种饱含凝聚力、创造力、传承力和支撑力的文化软实力，潜移默化地影响着镖界的每一个人。武术文化是镖局文化中贯通始终的核心支撑。传统武术的尚武精神和诚信价值观念与儒家倡导的仁、义、礼、智、信相交融，并在镖局文化中演变为诚信、尚武、果敢、谦和、正义、助人的核心价值追求和尊师重道、自省自律的行为准则。

3. 运输工具上的技术创新

镖局的发展过程中，人、马、驴、车始终是其运输的常用工具。随着镖局的发展，为了进一步追求运输货物的安全性，用于运镖的镖车和镖箱开始得到应用。镖车可划分为独轮推车、双轮车、马骡车、轿车、洋车等。镖箱是技艺高超的木匠用榆木打造的存储货物的货箱，其箱锁设计更为巧妙，是一种须将两把特有的钥匙拼合后才能开启的暗锁，而这两把钥匙分别由两位掌柜持有，也就是说只有二人都同意后箱子才能被打开，这极大地提高了箱内货物的安全性，同时又能防止运输途中监守自盗的情况发生。

镖车与镖箱（图片来源：华北第一镖局）

4. 运输的信息化管理

大镖局业务广阔，服务范围广，一次运距过长的业务结束后，如果镖师们空手而归，就如同现在货车的"空驶"[①]情况，会产生资源的浪费，造成镖局的无效费用支出。所以，镖局会利用其特有的信息网络，在上一单业务的终点处提前接收下一单业务，这样镖师们返程就不会空手而归了。为了不空手回归，镖师们

---

① 指（机动车辆等）没有载货或载客而空着行驶。

甚至会在上一单业务的终点处等上一段时间，以便回程时能够顺带接收到新的业务，减少不合理的运输。

5. 个性化定制

随着镖局的逐渐兴盛，许多平民百姓、商人巨贾乃至朝廷都会委托镖局押运商品货物。于是镖局送镖的种类也就越来越多，小到一封信件、一箱奇珍异宝，大到几车货物，甚至是朝廷的数百万两漕银。镖局会根据运输对象的不同，采用不同的运输方式，配备对应规模、能力的镖师，同时根据货物价值、运送路程以及运输难度制定不同的收费标准，获取镖利。

6. 资源整合

不同规模的镖局打通的镖路存在着很大差异，一些规模较小的镖局运送货物途经自己未打通的镖路时，需要向规模较大的镖局租借镖路，并向其缴纳"过路费"，在运输途中便可插上大镖局的镖旗，轻松抵达目的地。

三、没落与启示

繁盛了数百年的镖局进入没落时代，主要有以下几个原因。

一是达官贵人开始将大量金银财宝存入更有保障的英美列强所开设的银行之中，对镖局的依赖度降低。

二是火车、轮船等新兴运输工具的运用，使南北货运开始进入高效的大批量时代，进一步减少了对镖局的需求。

三是军阀混战，各地劫匪流寇横行，到处都是持有枪械的散兵游勇、黑白两道"城头变幻大王旗①"，镖局赖以沟通关系的江湖网络被破坏殆尽，在枪械盛行的时代下，走镖的危险性急剧增大。

四是同类型职业的崛起。进入民国以后，警察、保安等职业兴起，大大分流了镖局的固有业务范畴，替代了镖局存在的价值。

斗转星移，时间的指针拨到了20世纪末，以中国浙江桐庐办起的快递为发端，打破了固有的国有物流体系，形成了蓬勃发展的势头。随着中国经济的发展，物流行业成了影响国计民生的重要行业。

作为历史上特殊的物流组织机构，镖局的运营管理对现代物流有着新的

---

① 出自鲁迅的词，此句意为城头上还在变换着军阀们的各色旗号。指军阀混战时代，执政者换来换去，你方唱罢我登场，演出一场场闹剧。

启示。

对比镖局专业和规范化的管理体系，现代物流企业急需在人员分工界限不明、组织结构缺乏完整性、资源浪费严重等问题上进行对照改进。

镖局在数百年间建立起了独特的镖局文化，现代物流企业可以积极吸收借鉴镖局文化，结合行业现状，建设自身企业文化，以提升企业乃至行业的整体竞争力。

镖局十分注重创新，尤其是一线镖师对如何最省钱、最安全地运用车船等设备，都有一套独特的方法。现代物流企业应该充分利用技术创新，提高效率和竞争力，比如建立信息化平台，最大限度地利用资源，使利益最大化。

现代物流企业可以借鉴镖局针对不同顾客采用专业化、优质化和个性化的分镖模式，实行特殊定制化服务。

借鉴大小镖局资源重组，实行利益共享的举措，政府和现代物流企业应该联合起来，进行深入调研后，制定出相关的兼并重组政策，整合现有物流资源，提高效率，降低成本，扩大收益。

古代海关
——从军事重镇到贸易通道

"津海新关"匾额（现藏于中国海关博物馆）

唐贞观三年（公元 629 年）初冬的一天，西陲要塞玉门关外一阵喧哗，一张由大唐凉州都督李大亮亲手签署颁布的通缉令，张贴在玉门关城墙上。

围观民众与商旅对布告内容议论纷纷，原来一位名叫玄奘的和尚，不顾朝廷封锁边境的禁令，混入难民中，从长安一路西行，如今已穿越河西走廊，即将走出大唐的边境。为严肃法令，都督府颁布了对玄奘和尚的通缉令，沿途各关卡须仔细搜捕此人。

玉门关外的瓠庐河边，27岁的青年和尚玄奘正在芦苇丛中休息，陪伴他的是一个叫石

▲中国邮政发行的《玄奘》特种邮票之一（设计者：李云中、原艺珊）

磐陀的西域胡人，玄奘刚刚和他商量完怎么绕过玉门关，继续西行。玄奘和石磐陀没有想到，在九百多年后，会有一个叫吴承恩的人，以他们的西行经历为蓝本，结合民间传说，写出了不朽的中国古典名著《西游记》，玄奘是唐僧的原型，而石磐陀则是孙悟空的原型。

夜色降临，关城里传来了梆梆的打更声，巡察士兵的警觉性也随着夜色而降低起来。玄奘起身，整理好马匹上的行李，和石磐陀点头示意，两人开始沿着瓠庐河溯源而上。走了差不多十里地，他们才找到能够渡河的地方。水面宽一丈有余，石磐陀砍树作桥，铺草填沙，终于二人安然渡河。

骑在马背上的玄奘，还是禁不住回头望了望玉门关，这座代表汉族心理边界的雄关，正在广阔无垠的漆黑的夜里，熠熠生辉。离开了玉门关，玄奘从此就真正成为在异国飘零的旅僧了。过了玉门关，前面就是绵延百里的大漠了，玄奘紧紧缰绳，脸上写着的是四个大字——义无反顾。

时光荏苒，日月如梭。贞观十八年（公元 644 年）秋，西行学法多年后，已是得道高僧的玄奘在沿途西域各国的保护下，车载马驮着从天竺取得的佛教经书，浩浩荡荡行进在敦煌道外。玄奘的大名，在这些年已经传遍西域，唐朝也知晓了作为高僧的玄奘是何等地位，因此不再追究玄奘偷越国境的事情了，唐太宗李世民认为玄奘西行取经弘法中原是了不起的大事，敕令沿途关隘大开方便之门，迎接这位得道高僧。

回程的路，玄奘没有选择途经玉门关而是选择了阳关。或许玉门关外发生的事，令玄奘不忍心再回忆。当年，顺利渡过瓠庐河后，石磐陀反悔，不想再跟随玄奘西行，甚至一度动了谋害玄奘的心思。玄奘发觉后，立刻同意石磐陀回转的想法，放他归去。虽然安全得到了保证，但对玄奘的内心不能不说是一次打击。

距玉门关南面五十千米的地方是阳关。此时，几乎大半个西域已经被纳入唐朝的版图，玉门关和阳关已成为内陆。但它们依旧是扼守的关隘，与之前所不同的是，它们已经更倾向于成为收取商旅货物税钱的关市了。

望着熙熙攘攘的商队鱼贯出入阳关，玄奘不禁为祖国的强盛而自豪，也为东西交流的和平图景而欣慰。人说"西出阳关无故人"，关卡代表着离别，但此时，关卡已经成为财富聚集地的代名词之一，并最终演化为了今天人们熟悉的海关。

从雄关险隘到商贸海关，这中间到底经历了怎样的演变？又蕴藏着多少有趣的故事呢？

一、最早的"关"不收税

每个中国人，或多或少都能吟诵几句关于"关"的诗句，比如"秦时明月汉时关，万里长征人未还""劝君更尽一杯酒，西出阳关无故人"；或者能侃几句关于"关"的歇后语，比如"伍子胥过昭关，一夜白了头""过五关，斩六将"等。那么，什么是关？它又是怎么演变成今天的海关的呢？

"关"字的本义是门闩，后引申为关门。再后来，由关门的关引申为山川地势险要之地，即关卡。古代有很多关卡，如"一夫当关，万夫莫开"的剑门关，"天开函谷壮关中，万谷惊尘向此空"美誉的函谷关。曾经，战国大争之世，函谷关外，五国联军旌旗猎猎，却最终因各怀异心而被秦军的虎狼之师各个击破，最终流血漂橹，大败而归，成就了大秦帝国的赫赫威名。曾经，东汉末年，豪杰并起，虎牢关前，刘备、关羽、张飞大战董卓部将吕布，上演了"三英战吕布"的千古美谈。

但是，渐渐地，人们发现，除了军事用途之外，关卡还有另一项功能，那就是可以管理对外贸易，尤其是可以用来收税。

早在周朝时，周天子就设置了名为"司关"的官职，掌国境关卡稽查、给合法出入关境的货物发放通行证。据记载，关的重要目的是"执禁以讥"，也就是按照官方的规定，检查出入境的使节、官员、商人以及他们所携带的货物，"凡货不出于关者，举其货，罚其人。"而"节"则是官方允许货物出入境的一种凭证。

西周时，关卡不征税。到了东周时期，关卡增加了收税的功能。在春秋时期的古典书籍里面，出现了"关市之征"的文字记载。所谓的"关市之征"，是指国家规定货物通过边境的"关"和国内的"市"（此时的市，为其本意，就是货物交易的场所），都要进行检查和征收赋税。

春秋时期的鲁国大夫臧文仲，被认为是开创了关卡征税的典型人物。当时，臧文仲发觉国家财政不足，便有了充实国库的计划。他发现，鲁国有好多"关"，这些"关"是国家门户和门面担当，以及诸侯交往的必经之地，但它更多还是百姓往来的通道和货物流通的门户，如果在这些地方设立税卡，那么收税的利益一定是很可观的。说干就干，臧文仲一口气在鲁国设立了 16 个收税的"关"，一时间，税金如流水一般汇入国库。

不过，后来《左传》记述主张施行仁政的孔子，对臧文仲的举措持批评态度，他评价臧文仲是"不仁者三，不知者三"，原因就在于，臧文仲设关收税的做法与民争利，是不仁政的行为。

理想很丰满，现实很骨感。孔子所推行的不与民争利的观点，很多国家都没有采纳，反而由于关税有着明显的增加财政收入的功能，使得各级政府疯狂设立关卡要塞，并不断加强对关税征收的监管，特别是在战乱时期，老百姓的关税负担越来越沉重。就连一贯轻征关税的齐国、晋国，后来也走上了重征关税、暴敛无常的歧途。

在春秋战国时期，最富传奇色彩的"关"的故事，当属老子西出函谷关的典故。道家创始人老子（本名李耳），在道家思想大成之时，发觉中原时局比以往更加动荡，这与他所推崇的无为而治思想相悖，倍感失望之余，他骑着一头青牛，离开生活数十年的洛阳，准备向西去布施自己的思想。走到函谷关时，他碰到镇守函谷关的长官尹喜。尹喜负责稽查过往行人，颇爱老子的著述和思想。尹喜强烈请求老子归隐之前为后世留下其思想成就，于是老子著书上下篇，言道德之意五千余言而去，此为《道德经》。千百年来，众多海内外道家人士都到函谷关朝圣祭祖。

尹喜与老子的故事，见证了中国最早的"关"是如何运作的。结合司关制度和臧文仲的故事，我们也看到了"海关"的雏形正在慢慢形成。

西汉函谷关门楼所用"关"字瓦当（图片来源：中国海关博物馆）

二、丝路是条"关税"路

秦始皇雄才大略，一统六国。但秦朝政律严苛，对人民动辄加以罪名，加之繁重的徭役，最终不过短短十几年，便淹没在了秦末农民大起义的烽烟之中。

刘邦建立汉朝后，面对民生凋敝，废除严苛的秦法，采用黄老之道，实行"与民休息"的无为而治。西汉初年，为沟通各地财货、活跃市场和促进经济发展，并没有开征关税，汉文帝在位时把中原各地的关卡也撤了。汉景帝时，发生了"七国之乱"，汉朝中央政府复置了秦时的诸关，但仍没有开征关税。

不过，在元朔三年（公元前126年），出使西域多年的张骞归来后，汉朝与西域的双边贸易迅速兴盛起来。蓬勃的商贸活动、海量的物资互通，让财富迅速累积。汉武帝一改先前几代帝王的无为而治，开始大规模开疆拓土，这些伟业壮举都迫切需要大量的钱财来支撑。西汉王朝重要的财政来源之一就是利用关卡征税。

西汉王朝在内地和边疆地区增设了许多关卡，并开始征收关税。尤其，在长安通往西域的河西走廊，玉门关和阳关成为重要的征税关卡。

据《史记》记载，汉朝设立关都尉，对西域的商品贸易进行管理。关都尉在丝绸之路的主要关口稽查商旅和通关文牒，征收关税和市租（市场交易税）。而玉门关本身的名称来源，就是一次大型海关征税活动。玉门关始置于汉武帝开通西域道路、设置河西四郡之时，因西域输入玉石时取道于此而得名。后来，为了解决商客逃避过路关税，以及入侵者围攻玉门关的问题，汉朝又在玉门关南面新设置了一个关口，古人称山南水北为阳，此关因在玉门关以南，故而得名阳关。自此，玉门关与阳关既能相互照应，又能最大限度扼守隘口，防止商旅绕道逃税。同时，玉门关和阳关都作为都尉治所，屯有重兵，中原与西域的交通，都需要通过这两关。

汉朝既然设立了关税征集机构，那势必有相应的收税标准。汉朝设立负责关税收取的中央管理机构，它们对外贸实行官营垄断，进出关凭"符""传"放行，擅自与外商交易要受到其处罚，最重的可以处死刑。

汉朝确立了从量计征、从价计征这两种方式，来对关税进行计征。从量计征针对的是可分割、可储存的实物商品，比如丝绸、粮食、茶叶、金属等，以商品的数量或重量为计税依据，征收实物关税。假如有一个商人带了一车丝绸出关，那么他需缴纳关税的对象就是丝绸。而对于活体动物、皮革、药材等不能分割的商品，就以商品的市场价值为计税依据，以货币形式来征税，这就是从价计征。汉朝对出口商品除了征收关税之外，还收取市租，关税税率一般约为10%，市租以买卖成交额为计税依据，市租率约为2%。

不过，一些特殊商品的税率是很高的，要采用累进税率。比如粮食，国家严控粮食外流，如有人持大米出关，经汉朝的内关、中关和外关时，对大米征收的关税税率依次为七分之一、五分之一和三分之一，该大米出三关后的累进关税率为三关税率之和，关税税率达到约68%。而铁器、弓弩、马匹等都被列为违禁品，是不允许出关的。

从量计征和从价计征的方法，沿用至今，成为中国现代关税计征的基础。

三、市舶初露海关颜

东晋义熙七年（公元411年）的一天，狮子国（今斯里兰卡）境内的一座寺庙内，来自中国的高僧法显被知客僧告知，庙里刚刚供奉了一件宝贝，信众们正在围观。法显也忍不住出来瞻仰佛宝，当他看到宝贝的那一刻，潸然泪下，那哪里是什么佛宝，那是一把来自中原故土的白绢扇。很多当地人都没有见过这么精美的纺织品，于是将它奉为宝物。在那一刻，白绢扇突然唤醒了法显的思乡之情，他决定回国。

法显是中国历史上第一批到达天竺的僧人，而且是第一位从陆路去、海路归的僧人。比唐朝玄奘西行早了两百多年。后世玄奘西行的一个重要的原因，就是仰慕法显的壮举。法显将其游历期间的所见所闻，编撰成《佛国记》，为后世留下了研究西域、南亚的重要史料。

法显选择从陆地步行去天竺。他和几个僧人结伴从都城长安出发，穿过茫茫沙漠，历经千辛万苦，终于到达目的地。在天竺的几年间，他广泛研究佛法，后来，他来到狮子国继续弘法，直到两年后，他见到了那把白绢扇。

法显不想再穿越漫漫黄沙，因为这样不仅旅途危险，而且耗时颇多。归心似箭的他托人打听到有天竺商人的海船能够直达广州，耗时不过几个月。他大喜过望，赶紧联络商船，得到应允后，他激动得热泪盈眶。

法显在《佛国记》中记录了这条预计要走的航线：从印度恒河口出发，经斯里兰卡至印度洋，驶经马六甲海峡，随后由马六甲海峡进入爪哇海，由爪哇海进入南海，最后抵达广州。全部航程在两个月到三个月内完成。

不过，法显归国却困难重重，过马六甲海峡后，法显乘坐的商船受损，于是在耶婆提国足足修整了五个月，而后换了一艘船驶向广州，但突然遭遇大风天气，船只偏离航道，往东北方向开行几十天后，才看到陆地。等到法显上岸后，才发现自己已经到了青州长广郡牢山（今山东青岛崂山）。

历经九死一生，法显才最终回到中原地区。而他在《佛国记》中所记叙的这条海上通道，成为研究中国与印度、伊朗等国的海上贸易的最早记录。

随着海上贸易的渐渐发达，到了唐朝，这条航线被人们称为"广州通海夷道"。商船先在广州集结出发，向南行驶到珠江口的屯门港，经过海南岛东北方向的七洲洋，途经越南东南部海面，再通过新加坡海峡到达苏门答腊岛，向东南驶过爪哇海，然后驶出马六甲海峡，最终到达波斯湾的奥波拉港和巴斯拉港。这条航线全程长达 1.4 万公里，当之无愧是当时全球的最长航线，广州的繁荣也正由此而来。

公元 661 年，朝廷在广州设立"市舶使"这一官职，其职责是对往来贸易的船舶征收关税，代表宫廷采购一定数量的舶来品，管理商人向皇帝进贡的物品，对市舶贸易进行监督和管理。从某种程度上说，市舶使可以算作中国最早的"海关"关长。不过，有记载的真正有人担任市舶使的是开元二年（公元 714 年）右威卫中郎将周庆立被任命为安南市舶使。

唐朝政府向洋商征收的关税叫"舶脚"，又因为其征于洋船靠岸下碇之时，所以也称"下碇税"。唐朝规定外商缴纳舶脚之后，可以在境内自由贸易。当时，唐朝政府除了在广州征收舶脚之外，还在扬州等地设置征税处，税率由当地官员斟酌设置。当时的税率比较重，而唐朝名臣崔融要求在此基础上把"关"和"市"进行职能管理的划分，使其成为早期将海关税和其他税种进行区分的理论之一。"窃惟市纵繁巧，关通末游""关为御暴之所，市为聚人之地"。但同时，崔融又反对征收行人关税，认为关税阻碍商品流通，不利于社会稳定。"税关则暴兴……一关不安，则天下之关心动矣"。

唐朝在安史之乱以后，藩镇割据的局面更加严重，设置关卡、胡乱征税的现象增多。唐宪宗之时，外商乘船前来，除了缴纳舶脚，还要再缴纳一次"下碇之税"，所以外商常常对节度使以下各级官吏行贿宴请，以减少其通商的成本。唐朝政府也察觉到外商的负担有些重，遂下令不得多收银钱。据《全唐文》记载：

"南海蕃舶，本以慕化而来……其岭南、福建及扬州蕃客，宜委节度观察使常加存问，除舶脚、收市、进奉外，任其来往通流，自为交易，不得重加率税。"

四、开海，禁海，建海关

在今福建省泉州市，有一块刻着"宋泉州市舶司遗址"字样的石碑伫立在市区内，这也是现存仅有的一处古代海关遗址。

这里所说的海关，就是宋朝设立、繁盛三朝的外贸管理机构——市舶司。

唐朝的市舶使只是一个官职，宋朝则更进一步，设置了市舶司，是专门管理外贸的机构。宋朝在广州、杭州、明州、泉州、密州等海港开设了市舶司，几乎等同于如今的海关。市舶司的设定，也印证了宋、元时期水上贸易的兴盛。

宋朝编定了专业管理国外贸易的政策法规——《市舶条法》。市舶司的主要岗位职责包含依据生意人所申请的货物、船里工作人员数量及所去的地址，发给公凭，即出航许可证书；派人登船维护保养，避免带入武器、铜币、女性、逃跑士兵等；阅实回港船舶；对进出口的货物实行抽分制度，即将货物分成粗细两色，官府按一定比例抽取若干份，实为实物形式的市舶税，所抽货物要解赴国都（抽解），按照规定价钱收购船只运进来的一些货物（博买），历经抽解、博买后剩余的货物仍旧按市舶司的规范发给公凭，才允许运往别的地方销售。这已经是十分成熟的海关管理形式了，与今天海关的主要工作形式大体上相似。

市舶收入是宋朝国库收入的一项主要来源。北宋中期，市舶收入达42万缗（贯）上下。南宋早期，宋王朝执政危机深重，市舶收入对财政的影响更为关键。南宋年间，一年的财政收入只有1000万缗，而市舶收入就达到了150万缗，一定水平上支撑着国库。宋高宗赵构曾说，"市舶之利，颇助国用""市舶之利最厚，若措置合宜，所得动以

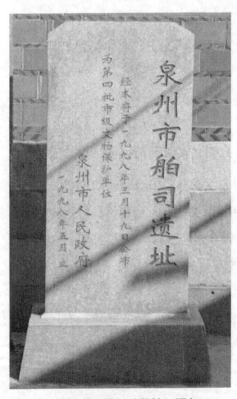

泉州市舶司遗址（林婕 摄）

百万计"。宋高宗赵构当政的绍兴元年、绍兴七年、绍兴十年，市舶收入都超过了 100 万缗，绍兴二十九年更是达到 200 万缗。

公凭是宋朝市舶司发给运营国外贸易的生意人的证明材料，也称公据、公验。中国海关博物馆展出有"李充公凭"的仿制品，其原物现存于日本，是现存最为完备的宋朝贸易凭证。崇宁元年（1102 年），李充一行人前往日本经商，两年后回国。1105 年，李充等人再次到日本，并向日本大宰府呈交本国公凭申请贸易。当年，因泉州没有设置市舶司，商船要北航到明州（今浙江宁波）办理出境手续，由两浙路市舶司发给公凭，然后航抵日本。这类公凭，实际上等同于如今的护照签证。

明朝建立后，北有蒙古袭扰，海上则倭寇猖獗，朱元璋就下令实行海禁政策，规定寸板不许下海。尽管明成祖朱棣时期，有过郑和下西洋的短暂辉煌，但海禁政策依旧是主流，全国只有一个对外通商口岸，那就是广州。海禁导致了民间物资贸易交流不畅，最终成为明朝中期沿海地区倭寇之乱的主因。一直到隆庆元年（1567 年），明穆宗消除海禁，调节国外贸易政策，容许民间开展国外贸易。沿海地区的民间对外贸易进入了一个新的态势，明朝出现了全方位的对外开放局势。

隆庆开关后，福建省漳州市的月港变成关键的通商口岸。明朝政府也在这里建立机构，完善税收制度。那时候，明朝政府部门要求进出海港的船只务必备案，详尽地汇报船舶尺寸、来源国家、所去国家及其货品的类型及总数，便于政府部门从中征收"引税""陆饷"和"水饷"。明朝还设定了专业的税收管理机构——"督饷馆"，政府部门在全国各省每年选派一名高官到海港轮流管理缴税，这类税制改革危害到了之后政府部门在广州和澳门的管理。

明朝灭亡后，后续的清王朝继续实行严厉的海禁政策，并废除了市舶司。清朝早期郑成功大家族在台湾海峡与清政府僵持，中后期沿海地区则遭遇西方国家殖民者势力的入侵，在这种背景下，清朝统治者选择了禁海、闭关的政策。明末清初颁布了"迁海令"，沿海居民都要向内陆地区回撤几十里，禁止开展对外贸易和打鱼捞虾，清朝中后期的政令明确提出：外出做生意的人两年不归即是大清国弃民，绝不准回籍。

但是，中西方庞大的贸易活动不能间断，清政府也需要通过中外贸易收取足额的税金供应国家的运转。因而，到康熙二十三年（1684 年），清廷施行谕旨，在广州市、漳州市、宁波市、江南地区开设海关，并宣布称之为粤海关、闽海关、浙海关、江海关。官府从内务府选派高官管理，称之为海关监管。那个时候的福建总督郝玉麟曾上奏："查闽省一年出洋商船约有三十只，或二十八九只，每船货物值或十余万、六七万不等，每年闽省洋船约得番银二三百万载回内地，以利息之盈利，佐耕耘之不足。"

"海关"之称，从此开始。但从制度上看，它是市舶制度的延续。1757 年，原设的沿海各关被乾隆皇帝宣布撤销，仅保留广东的粤海关对外开展商贸往来。广州十三行作为粤海关旗下的对外贸易机构，也是清朝唯一的合法外贸专区，中国与海外的商贸全都在这里聚集，直到鸦片战争的时候才结束，这个洋货行因此独占中国对外贸易达到八十多年之久。而广州十三行得以做独门生意的重大原因，在于皇帝将此视为私人小金库，时人称此为"天子南库"。

一部中国古代海关简史，背后折射的是中国人从陆地走向大海，又从大海回归陆地的历史趋势。开放包容的时代，海关制度不断创新，引领着国家持续向外开放；闭关锁国时代，海关被困一隅，成为满足统治者私欲的场所。

真正中国近现代意义上的海关制度，则是在鸦片战争爆发以后，西方列强借上海小刀会起义的契机，夺取海关管理权，由英国人赫德主政中国海关近半世纪的时候，才得以建立。

一饮一啄，皆是因由。历来海关多少事，尽附今人笑谈中。

漕运
——内河运输关系社稷安危

张择端《清明上河图》局部（现收藏于故宫博物院）

在漫长的中国封建时代，漕运是中央集权政体下的一项重要经济制度，漕运之制，为国之大政，历朝历代都十分重视。关于"漕"，《说文解字》的解释是"水转谷也"，即通过水道调运粮食，有河运、水陆递运和海运三种运输方式。在基础设施不发达的中国古代农业社会，征收赋税是国家运转的基础，需要将税粮等征收到的物资运往京师、边关等地，水运具有一定优势，于是漕运兴起。对于漕运，广义是指一切水路运输，狭义的解释如《辞海》所言，是历代对地方政府将所征粮食运往京师或其他指定地点的水路运输（有时包括部分陆路运输）的称呼。

漕运在中国有着数千年的历史，不仅起到平衡经济、保障供给的作用，也与政治稳定、国防安全、赈灾救济等紧密相连。漫长的漕运路程必然会耗费大量的人力、物力、财力，加之漕运又与各地安置的仓储设施密切相关，既有漕运、河道、仓储人员的管理，又有运丁、水手、沿途漕户的参与。

中国物流故事 STORY 古代辑 汉英对照

清乾隆时期的《漕运图》局部（作者不详，现收藏于天津博物馆）

漕运的兴盛，促进了贸易的发展，清朝"漕运四大都市"（扬州、苏州、杭州、淮安）应运而生。漕运一方面促进了经济的发展，水上交通和贸易也随之兴盛；另一方面，保障了粮食市场的供需平衡，缓解了市场粮食地域和季节不均衡的压力，对调节市场、平抑物价有积极意义。此外，漕运客观上改变了区域社会经济格局，运河经济带由此萌芽。

一、演进及变动

漕运的起源很早。春秋时期，晋国遭遇饥荒，晋惠公向秦国借粮。浩浩荡荡的运粮船从秦都到晋都，路途首尾相连，将粮食运至晋国，史称"泛舟之役"。

而到了先秦时期，大多数战争和土地、人口的控制有关，因此对军事后勤供应的要求也在增加。陆运不能满足日益增长的需要，此时水运规模化和经济效益高的优势日益凸显。秦汉时期，漕运制度和漕运体系逐渐形成，为之后的发展夯实了基础。秦朝建立的漕运制度核心是仓储管理，这一时期修建了很多大型粮仓，多建在都城或水路枢纽以满足转运和储粮之需，同时还积极挖凿漕渠，疏通漕运之道。

高效率的交通运输是军事战略实施的保证。如秦灭楚之战，大将王翦率 60

万大军出征，每日口粮总数约66667石，估须2600辆以上的车辆运送。陆运不足，必须借助江汉水运来补充。

古人称漕运负担国用军需，一是指借助漕运组织有效率的赋税征收和交通网络，来实现资源集中，维持国家财政运转服务；二是指满足国防军事需要。

春秋时期的吴国和越国最早修筑了运河开展军事活动，它们地处江南水乡，善于利用地理条件开展水运。关于邗沟的起源和路径，杜预考证为"于邗江筑城穿沟，东北通射阳湖，西北至末口入淮，通粮道也"。公元前486年，吴王夫差为北上伐齐，修建了邗沟。邗沟开通后，吴国又在"商鲁之间"开辟了连接沂水和古济水的菏水，一条新的运河通航。

秦朝统一六国后，因为形成了统一的中央集权，黄河、淮河、长江三大水系得以连通，贯通南北的漕运通道形成，漕运能力进一步提升，漕运系统也逐渐完善。

隋朝挖掘出的通济渠、永济渠，加修的邗沟、江南运河，将中原地区、河北平原和江淮地区紧密地联系到一起，形成贯通南北的交通大动脉。后修凿广通渠，大运河连接了长江、黄河、淮河、海河、钱塘江五大水系，构成了沟通全国水上交通的完整体系。唐朝逐渐把漕运重点放在南方，漕运线路也呈现出东南向、西北向的变动。唐朝中后期，常令宰臣兼转运使等职主管漕政。

到宋朝，南方经济崛起，成为朝廷物资供应的主要来源，尤其是江南地区，是供应漕粮的主要区域。北宋时期，中央三司使总领漕政，各处再设负责征集粮食的转运司（漕司）和负责运输粮食的发运司。各司其职，漕运更加专业化和高效率，加上运河条件的进一步改善，真宗、仁宗时期漕运年运量可达八百万石。到了南宋，漕运体系又做出重要调整，以临安（今浙江杭州）为中心，以长江及江南运河为运输主干，并形成以官运为主、商运为辅的漕运新模式。

元朝海运发达，漕运开启以海运为主、内河运输为辅的新阶段。元明清三朝，政治中心继续向东北迁移，而经济重心则越来越明确地确立在南方，尤其是长江中下游地区，漕运转变为南北方向，政治中心和经济重心呈北南分立的格局并长期延续，南粮大量北运。所以，从根本上说，政治和经济重心的转移决定了漕运线路的更新变化。国家制定各种措施，确保不遗余力地把漕粮从百姓手里征收过来，再顺利运往京城。

漕运随着时代的变迁而不断改革，直到明朝才基本完善。明初承元之漕运，以海运为主，河、陆兼运为辅。支运法、兑运法、改兑法等漕运方式相结合，组织与管理趋于成熟。漕粮，由南方供给为南粮、北方供给为北粮。

清朝开凿中运河，彻底结束了借黄河行运的时代，并建成黄、淮、运交汇枢纽，缓和水面比降，减轻浊流灌运，改善了漕运条件。清朝，由"漕标"负责漕粮的催缴和运输。据统计，雍正年间，每年漕运可供给 400 余万石粮食到京城。晚清，漕运受鸦片战争、太平天国、黄河改道等历史因素的影响，逐渐走向衰落，到 1901 年，运河漕运全线停摆。

二、制衡与调控

直达和转运，是古代漕运的两种基本形式。水路通畅则漕运顺行，如遇阻碍，则屯仓以待合适时机再作调配。

南漕北运之后，漕运线路趋长，漕粮运输成为一项巨大的工程，并在更大的运行空间中与途经的区域社会发生更紧密的联系。朝廷逐渐认识到漕粮运输对地方调控的意义和价值，并开始加以利用。贯通南北的漕运路线逐渐固定，漕粮征收、派转及运输的流程就相对稳定，为朝廷利用漕运解决政治问题提供了条件。

自宋朝开始，漕粮的社会功能逐渐被朝廷所认知。一个是籴粜[①]，另一个是赈济灾荒。籴粜，即通过买卖粮食平衡市场供需，从而稳定粮价。宋朝行和籴之法[②]，每年各地都有漕粮定额任务，如遇灾荒，有的地区无法完成缴粮任务，就可以以钱代之，缴纳价值相等的钱物，再由官府采购江南富裕地区的粮食代为上供，从而保证了漕运总额任务的完成。和籴之法逐渐发展，到宋仁宗时演变为代发制。负责收运粮食的发运司，有一定的采买资金，他们可以根据各地区丰收情况及时调整屯粮策略，丰收时籴米储备，如遇区域粮荒，就用储存的粮食上供，然后，再将漕粮和运费换算成钱，由被代地区上缴。"谷贱则官籴，不致伤农；饥歉则纳钱，民以为便。本钱岁增，兵食有余"，这个办法既保证了漕粮总体任务的完成，又维持了市场平衡，稳定了粮食价格，缓解了粮荒地区的粮食压力，还能有利于赈灾。

与宋朝相比，明清时期漕运的市场调节功能越发灵活。为了应对粮食市场出现的突发情况，官府可对运输中的漕粮随时进行截留和拨运。总的来说，明清时期改宋朝的"以籴为主"作"以粜为主"。

---

① 籴（dí）为买米，粜（tiào）为卖米，籴粜，组合在一起就是买卖粮食的意思。
② 对粮食供应进行国家管理的一种方法，官府与百姓议价出钱购买民粮。

截留和拨运，是指起运之前或者运输途中的漕粮，因为临时需要（仓储、兵饷或赈灾等）被转运司重新安排和调配，是官府平粜或赈济的主要方式。

清朝充分利用漕运的空间优势与便利条件，以及线路的流动性特点，在并不增加成本的情况下，实现其充实仓储、平抑粮价、赈灾备荒等社会作用，从而维持社会稳定。一旦区域性求助发生，可及时奏请转运，快捷、便利、高效地实现截漕赈济等社会功能。

随着漕运的发展，漕粮征运相关的制度也越来越先进和成熟。《户部漕运全书》① 于雍正年间开始编撰，并规定每十年更新一次。此书的内容涉及漕粮额征、征收事例、兑运事例、通漕运艘、督运职掌、选补官丁、官丁廪粮、计屯起运、漕运河道、京通粮储、截拨事例、采买搭运、奏销考成等，每一项制度还包括了多方面的子项，完全涵盖了漕运事务的各个方面，充分反映了清朝漕运制度的全面和严密。

三、运河经济带

北宋，建都开封，漕运主要走汴河再与江南运河贯通，运输的多为南方物资。元朝，定都大都，运河不能直达，漕运主要通过海运进行，但运河贯通南北的格局正式形成，这对货物运输的意义不言而喻。明清两朝，定都北京，大运河承载了南粮北运的重任，使其成为这一时期最富活力且最具辐射影响力的区域。南北物资互通、运河沿线经济的发展、沿线城镇的兴起与繁荣、商人的定向聚集以及贸易长距离开展等，这些经济现象开始引起人们的关注。随着历史的变迁，漕运与区域经济格局相互影响，形成了各具特色的区域经济发展模式，运河经济带也逐渐成形。

运河经济带是指运河水道承载漕粮运输的同时，促进了巨量的南北物资交流，不断促发更多的经济活动与联系，连接更多的区域、物资、行业与人群，所形成的一个相对成体系的、流动状态的、具有发散与辐射作用的经济带。

城市发展与交通息息相关，在古代，水路为主要的交通方式，便利的水道运输是当时经济发展的基本保障。每一座沿线城镇，都会随着漕运的行经而发展，形成坐落其中且经济发达的中心枢纽城市，这些城市又逐渐演变成漕运的交通转运枢纽和集散地，商人在这里会聚、商品在这里流动，促进了经济的发展。如此

---

① 清朝全面记载漕运制度的文册。

反复，运河经济带辐射形成的运河城市，经济水平高、发展迅速。

　　明清时期，苏州、扬州、淮安、济宁、聊城、临清、德州等运河城市和九江、芜湖、汉口等城镇构成了当时的运河经济带。漕船往来，多在这些站点停靠，无论是购买当地特产，还是商人们之间的物品交换，或是与运丁、水手及押运官吏的买卖，大多都在这里进行。商贾、客旅及市民百姓聚集在码头，形成了各具特色的贸易活动，码头文化逐渐形成，极大地促进了当地经济的发展。每年的漕运时节，漕船牵挽往来，帆樯如林，百货山积。

　　这些漕船停泊的码头、港口，成为全国货物的集散中心，也成为各地商人开展贸易活动的聚集地。据《歙志》记载："今之所谓都会者，则大之而为两京、江、浙、闽、广诸省，次之而苏、松、淮、扬诸府，临清、济宁诸州，仪真、芜湖诸县，瓜洲、景德诸镇。"

　　所谓因漕运而生、因漕运而兴，漕运的兴盛，不仅促进了南北商品流通和经济发展，还形成了具有辐射作用的经济带，带动一方繁荣。以"漕运之都"淮安为例，便利的交通条件、频繁的贸易活动和来往的商贾官员，都为淮安的发展提供了有利条件，无论是其城市面貌还是经济发展水平，都有显著改善和提升，使其与当时的扬州、苏州、杭州三大名城齐名。清朝还在此设置漕运总督①，盛极一时。

淮安总督漕运部院（蒋义　摄）

---

①　明清两朝专门管理漕运的高级官员。

以 1840 年为分界点，清朝的漕运开始衰落，其中最主要的原因是清朝国力衰退，内河和领海的航运权均被列强掠夺。加上太平天国运动的破坏，整个清朝的内河漕运，均受到摧毁。漕运经济渐渐退出历史舞台，沿岸城市也因此衰落。

四、靠水吃水

有船的地方就有江湖，千百年来依靠漕运"讨营生"的各色人物，无疑是漕运历史上浓墨重彩的一笔。

每年运粮期间，都会挑选运丁承担运输任务。各地运丁和漕船以帮[①]为单位运输漕粮。

漕粮运输工作十分艰苦，而水手待遇却非常差。在漫长的运河航行中，常常遇到逆行、搁浅、穿闸、过坝等情况，水手只得用纤绳拖着货船行进，如宋诗有云："百夫撑挽才得过，水浅舟大行无期。"他们大都无籍无贯，走食四方，无身家拖累，法纪观念淡薄，经常改帮换船，甚至临时出走，短工更是聚散无常。

▲张择端《清明上河图》水手拉纤部分（现收藏于故宫博物院）

---

① 每帮所辖船数不等，少则二十多艘，多则七八十艘。漕运队伍被称为漕帮、船帮。

历代以都城为中心的运河网，无不借助黄河、长江、淮河等大小河流和湖泊，在遇到洪水汛期、天气突变及河道淤堵的情况时，航行就有相当大的风险，如黄河三门峡险段，不知使多少水手葬身鱼腹。

漕运作为国家的经济命脉，在漕粮征收、船只运输和粮食入库等环节，牵扯数十万人员，无论是运粮的漕军和水手，河道上的闸官、监守和押运官员，还是沿途所经之地的地方官员、纳粮的漕户，都与漕运有着直接或间接的联系，都会影响漕运整体的局面。

为了确保漕运的正常进行，历代王朝采取了各种办法组织运输队伍。大体上，明朝及以前，封建政府主要通过强征民夫和组织职业运卒的办法，解决运输人员的问题，如汉、唐及宋初的服役民户，宋、明的运军等，在官府的严格控制下执行运送任务。但逃亡的现象相当普遍。

清初承袭明朝运军制度，在各地区组编了以帮为单位的旗丁①运输队伍。但不久就因缺乏运丁而难以维持。随着清王朝"摊丁入亩"制度的实行，传统的户籍控制政策也随之松动，人们有了较大的迁徙自由权，大批失业的农民、手工业者可以较以往更自由地改行或选择其他出路，他们有一部分转而投身到漕运中。

清朝雇募水手主导运输队伍，也给清政府的管理带来诸多问题。以往民户轮流充役，并不以承运为生，任务完成后可回家从事生产，运丁按月发放饷钱，有一定的生活保障。而清朝雇募的水手要考虑挣取工钱维持生计，每年停运期间便处于失业状态，其中大多数又是单身汉，随时可以改行换业，朝廷对他们难以实行有效的管理。另外，清朝船帮水手的成分极为复杂，不仅有大批失业农民，也有城镇无业游民、乞丐，甚至还有走投无路的地痞、流氓及罪犯等。当时的话本小说也不乏这方面的描写，如《葛仙翁全传》中就描写了一个无赖行骗失手后，流落到运河码头与人扯纤的故事。

大批流民转行成为水手后，虽常因竞争而发生口角、打斗，但也逐渐形成了互救、相助的意识和风气，久而久之，也就形成了一些帮派、秘密组织。那些资历老且争强好斗的老水手们便自然成为其中的首领。

漕运过程中，因力量的悬殊和利益分配的不均，运输者内部也会激发矛

---

① 指清朝时期运粮的军人。

盾。由于水手是应募而来，领运漕船的旗丁为其名义上的东家，水手会要求不断提高身价，清初每年每名水手原定雇银为一两，至嘉庆以后，渐增至数十两。另外，当船重难行时，水手要求增给钱文，谓之"窝子钱"；如遇水浅需要绕行时，水手会向旗丁要求增加脚费，谓之"性命钱"；漕船逆水过闸时，还需要增加"绞关"① 钱文。为应付入不敷出的境况，旗丁一方面在地方交兑漕粮时索取钱财，另一方面在运粮途中欺压民商船只，甚至劫掠财物，亦常常与其他船帮发生争斗。

针对不法行为，清廷一直很重视，采取了许多措施，数次整顿船帮秩序，加强各项限制措施，严惩滋事水手。但是因水手、运丁多达十几万人，延绵在运河南北数千里之地，所以很多制度虽成了具文，却不能得到彻底贯彻。这些惩罚只能流于形式，并不能从根本上解决问题，水手行帮间大规模械斗不断发生，造成社会动乱。清末运河断流，漕运停止后，大量水手加入太平天国、捻军、义和团等农民武装，从而加速了清朝的衰落。

五、余论

漕运成本高，然而，朝廷对这一事务的核算却没有成熟的体系。黄梦维在《停漕论》中对清朝漕粮运抵北京的成本作出过估算："通盘筹算，非四十金不能运米一石入京仓"。如此估算，朝廷每年漕运四百万石，耗费财力惊人。

晚清时期，漕运衰落，原因有很多。不仅因为漕运制度运转不灵，黄河改道和太平天国战乱也对其产生了消极影响，而新式交通工具和西方殖民势力的侵入都在改变原来的经济、地理格局，弱化了大运河的战略功能。

此外，漕运的各个环节充斥着官员贪腐与渎职的现象，钱权交易形成了不可逆变的积弊痼疾。清政府虽有策略性调整，但小修小补的办法仅能平息危机，不能革除弊病。在这种情况下，整个漕运机制呈现怠坏的趋势，漕运制度亦如其他制度一样出现僵腐的迹象。

再者，中国面临着前所未有的历史变革，地缘政治活动的表现形式也发生巨大改变，导致漕运的功能进一步被削弱。社会经济形态发生了重大变化，自给自足的以农业为主的经济结构被打破。漕运衰落首先表现为漕运的功能性降低，即

① 水文测量的时候要跨河布设绳子之类的东西，绞关是用来把绳子拉直的设备。

漕粮转运的物质成本和时间成本提高，运输效率降低。河道淤浅、通航条件逐渐变差，这也是导致漕运衰落的重要原因。漕运被历史淘汰成为必然。

往事越千年，历经军事要道、运输航路、文化纽带等多重身份的转换，伴随着河道枯竭与现代交通方式的冲击，曾盛极一时的漕运在清朝逐渐衰落，漕运作为沟通南北交通要道的时代走向终结。

紫禁城

——世界宫廷建筑群的物流奇迹

紫禁城全景（图片来源：故宫博物院）

　　明朝建文四年（1402 年）六月，从北平起兵的燕王朱棣，率领大军攻入都城南京。皇城内燃起熊熊大火，建文帝朱允炆不知所终，自此成为一桩历史悬案。

　　朱棣发布了建文帝自焚而死的消息，在一片非议声中即位，改次年年号为永乐，是历史上赫赫有名的永乐大帝。

　　朱棣虽然以血腥的杀戮应对所有的质疑声，然而这样并不能使他心安。加之当时北元对北方地区的侵扰加剧，朱棣提出"天子守国门"的主张，并决定将都城迁到他的起兵之地——北平。

明成祖朱棣像轴（杨令莼摹，现收藏于故宫博物院）

这次迁都不仅创造了一座雄伟的城市，也给后世留下了一个世界上伟大的宫殿建筑群——紫禁城。伟大不仅因为它是世界上现存规模最大的宫殿，而且因为，这座庄严的宫殿的一草一木、一砖一瓦，皆是匠心凝聚，它带着历史的记忆，折射出历史的梦幻想象和中华民族无穷无尽的智慧。

建造这座雄伟的都城，耗时近十五年，但是历史的记载出现了不同的版本，这是为何呢？

据《明典汇》载："永乐四年（1406 年）闰七月，淇国公邱福等请建北京宫殿备巡幸。"《明成祖实录》载，永乐十四年（1416 年）十一月，"复诏群臣议营建北京……自永乐十五年（1417 年）六月兴工，至十八年冬（1420 年）告成。"我们从这些史料可以看出，紫禁城从 1406 年开始修建到 1420 年建成一共用了十五年，而这十五年里实际建造时间只有大约三年半（1417 年 6 月至 1420 年）。那前面的十多年，紫禁城难道停止建设了吗？

事实上，前面长达十几年（1406 年至 1417 年）的时间，建造紫禁城最主要的工作，是在劳动力和材料的准备上。换而言之，在这十几年里，为了建造这个世界建筑史上的奇迹，整个中原王朝开始了前所未有的物流总动员。

一、前奏：迁徙人员

在这座城市改名叫北平之前，它曾经是辽国的燕京、金国的中都、元朝的大都。尤其作为元大都的时期，这座城市的规模已达五十平方公里，是当时世界上最繁荣的世界都市。意大利传奇旅行家马可·波罗曾描述元大都，"外国巨价异物及百物之输入此城者，世界诸城无能与比"。

明洪武元年（1368 年），明朝大将军徐达率北伐大军包围大都，元朝的皇亲贵胄携带金银珠宝逃遁，守军兵力不足，大都城很快被明军攻破。接着，一把烈火摧毁了这座繁荣的城市。为了纪念平定北方地区，明太祖朱元璋将元大都更名为北平。

后来，当朱元璋第四子、获封燕王的朱棣来到他的封地北平时，这个他日后的龙兴之地已经沦为北方一个荒凉偏远的城市了。这里不但人口稀少，而且资源匮乏、基础建筑极其薄弱。所以，很多年后，坐上皇位的朱棣准备迁都北平时，面临的最重要的问题，就是宫殿的修建和城市的发展，这些都需要大量的劳动力。

永乐元年（1403 年），朱棣将北平改名为"北京"，并将其地位升级为"行在"①。这年，他还下旨迁山西九个府的两万户、直隶和江浙富户四千户至北京，以增加京畿的人口。这些人普遍比较富有，很快便在北京做起了他们以往经营的生意。另外在北京的近郊区，也多了许多农户开垦土地，规模性的移民工程逐渐开展起来。

永乐三年（1405 年），朱棣派皇三子、赵王朱高燧负责北京的军事，并下令顺天府及邻近两个府免缴田赋两年，以此吸引人员内迁北京。

永乐五年（1407 年），明成祖从中国各省征选了一支由匠人、士兵和一般劳动力构成的精兵去往北京，其中包含 7000 多名被虏获并押运到北京的安南匠人。同时，朱棣下令从河南、山东、山西、陕西、中都（今安徽凤阳）等地选民丁和军丁，第二年到达北京动工。劳动大军人数应该高达几十万。

到此，浩浩荡荡的北京紫禁城建造打开了序幕。这时候，一个难题摆在了这群建造者的眼前，工程建筑急需的砖、石、木材究竟从哪里来呢？

这个难题抛给了负责全国建筑事宜的总负责人——工部尚书宋礼，宋礼将从哪个方面打开局面呢？

二、开局：疏通运河

以紫禁城的建造规模和规格，需要大量的顶级建筑材料。在确定建造北京宫殿的诏书里，永乐皇帝指派工部尚书宋礼、吏部右侍郎师逵、户部左侍郎古朴等奔赴各地，采办各种材料。最终，他们精挑细选，敲定了建设紫禁城的建筑材料的产地：石料来自北京房山、河北曲阳，金砖来自苏州，石灰来自河北易州，五色虎皮石来自河北盘山，殿基所用的精砖石来自山东临清，松木多来自东北，而楠木多来自四川、云贵、江浙等地。

北京、河北的材料产地距离紫禁城建筑工地还不算远，可以通过人拉马驮的方式勉强保证进度，但是距离数百里乃至上千里的江浙、四川、云贵等地的建筑材料，势必要通过层层转运才能到达北京，水运成了最方便快捷的物流方式。而从南方地区到北方地区，货运能力较大的，就数京杭大运河了。那时候的京杭大运河是什么情况呢？

大运河最早是春秋战国时期开凿的，隋朝时期进行了大幅扩修。自隋炀帝杨

---

① 天子行銮驻跸的所在，即天子所在之地。

广开通连接西起洛阳，北至涿郡，南起余杭的大运河后，南北物资运输驶上了快车道。大运河沿岸经济在唐宋时期极其兴盛。但是，随着朝代更迭、战火损毁以及黄河泛滥等因素，到元朝，大运河已经只剩下部分河段在运行了。元世祖忽必烈统一全国后，为了更便捷地将南粮北调，决心对隋朝大运河裁弯取直，即把原先以洛阳为中心的横向的大运河，修建成以大都为中心、直通杭州的竖向大运河。一声令下，开凿了济州河、会通河、通惠河等，大运河此后无须绕河南省，只需要由淮安经宿迁、徐州直上山东到达北京。至此，诞生了现今的京杭大运河。新的京杭大运河比绕道洛阳的大运河缩短了九百多公里。

元朝末年，黄河再次改道，京杭大运河山东段被黄河泥沙侵袭，开始淤塞。朱元璋建立明朝后，政治中心南京一直处在富庶的江南地区，对南北连接的要求没有元朝迫切，大运河的作用有所降低。洪武末年，黄河再次泛滥，运河的某些河段再次被淤塞。到朱棣决定迁都北京，建造紫禁城时，重构南北交通成了朝廷重要的施政方向。朝廷发现，京杭大运河山东段，尤其是会通河段，淤积了大量黄河泥沙，丧失了快捷运输的价值。要解决这个问题，就需要快速清淤，重新使会通河发挥作用。

大运河南旺枢纽考古现场发掘的分水龙王庙建筑群古遗址（徐速绘 摄）

永乐九年（1411年），明成祖下令工部尚书宋礼、漕运总督陈瑄疏通淤积多年的运河。宋礼将目光集中到了从山东临清到须城（今山东东平）安山的会通河段。这一地段属丘陵地带，地势高，水源不足，因此多数河段岸狭水浅，不能通行重载船只。而元朝在修建闸坝时，将分水点选在了并非地势最高点的任城，导致南水多北水少。宋礼此次名为疏浚河道，实则需要重新对该河道进行梳理，更科学地安排水源高度，促使南北运河都能行驶大船。

宋礼深谙智慧在民间的古训，他常常微服下乡，实地深入勘察沿运水系、地形，遇到不懂的问题，虚心向当地百姓请教。在汶上县城白家店村探访时，村里有人向他举荐了乡老白英，乡亲们对宋礼说，白英是藏在民间的水利专家。

白英曾是运河民夫的一个小领班，年轻时，他带领十多人的团队，往来于运河之上，十分熟悉山东境内大运河及其附近地势、水源状况，积累了丰富的行船、治河经验。白英为人正直，不慕名利，视官宦锦衣、肉食者为蠹材，老百姓亲切地称他为隐逸君子。

起初，白英对宋礼的印象不好，以为他也是高高在上什么都不懂的官老爷。但他听说宋礼秉性刚直，又见到宋礼与老百姓相处的坦诚姿态后，他终于明白宋礼和其他官员不一样。因此，当宋礼找上门来的时候，白英立刻将自己思考了十多年的治河方略同宋礼进行了讨论。

白英的运河疏浚方案是这样的：通过筑坝拦住大汶河和大清河抬高水位，开挖小汶河，将大汶河河水通过小汶河引入大运河，高出南旺（会通河地势最高点），从而保证"运河之脊"南旺水源充足。

白英依据会通河的地势和雨情，明确提出了治河方式。以汶水作水源，筑堤引水渠，西注地势最高的南旺，随后向南北分离。分离的其中六份北流到临清，接入卫河，正中间设水闸 17 座；四份南流至济宁，下发泗、淮，正中间设定水闸 21 座，从源头上应对会通河水源不够的难点。

宋礼听取了白英的提议，依照白英设计方案的工程图纸安排工程施工。宋礼征调民工上万人，开始了这个艰巨浩大的工程。经过 9 年的艰苦奋战，终于疏浚河道，并开掘了汶上至济宁段运河，使河河相通，渠渠相连，湖湖相依，汇成一派巨大水系。

会通河的疏浚工程，让大运河再次容光焕发，产生了新的活力。南方物资可以安全快速地向首都调运，而且可以解决正在修建的紫禁城的材料运输问题。

二百年后，明朝万历年间来华的传教士利玛窦在《利玛窦中国札记》中写道，经由运河进入皇城，他们为皇宫建筑运来了大量木材、梁柱和平板……供皇宫所用的砖可能是由大船从约 2414 千米之外运来的。仅是为此就使用了很多船只，日夜不断运行。沿途可以看到大量建筑材料，不仅足以建筑一座皇宫，而且还能建成整个的村镇。

老北京人爱念叨一句话，"咱北京城是漂来的"，可见这条南北通畅的水路作用何等巨大。

三、高潮：材料运输

就在大运河艰苦疏浚的同时，紫禁城的建筑材料也在准备中。

皇城用砖颇多讲究，城墙用砖、地面用砖各有不同，有的地面还得铺三层砖。据统计，整座皇城建筑用砖达 8000 万块之多。

古城墙和宫殿用砖，绝大多数为临清砖。临清砖因产自山东临清而闻名。临清砖的官窑是明永乐年间专门为建造紫禁城而设立的。明清两朝在临清共建有砖窑约 384 个。

临清砖的制作工艺流程繁杂而严苛。工匠们在当地取土后，先用大小筛子各筛一遍，然后用水过滤，储入水池中。等土壤沉淀后，加水踩土，不断踩匀，才可以脱坯。脱坯时，要先在砖模里铺一层布，再取一块重约 30000 克的泥头，在地上来回滚动成团，然后用力举起，精准地摔入砖模中。摔出的泥头的大小要掌握得恰到好处，一个摔砖工匠每天只能摔 300 块砖坯，即使是年轻力壮的快手，每天最多也只能摔 400 块。

砖坯入窑后，需要用棉柴、麦秸 40 多吨，烧旺火半个月，洇半个月，方成砖，因此一个砖窑一年最多生产 12 窑砖。如按每窑每年产砖 30000 块计算，384 个砖窑一年可出砖 1152 万块。

修建紫禁城所用的临清砖要求极高，每块砖必须长一尺五寸，厚三寸六分，外观棱角分明，六面光滑平整，敲之声音清脆，否则不得用黄表纸包裹托运上船。解送通州后，工部官员还要再进行一次严格的敲验检查，方可运进京城使用。由于临清砖制作工序烦琐，检验严格，所以每块砖的造价较为昂贵。

铺设在几个主要宫殿地面上的砖，一般以金砖居多。这种砖约两尺见方，因其质地坚硬，表面有光泽，敲之有金属声，并且据称每块造价高达一两黄金，故称为金砖，是明清时期皇宫的专用砖。金砖的制作要经过取土、制坯、烧制、出窑、打磨、泡油六个步骤，制作时间长达两年。建造紫禁城时，经苏州香山帮工匠的推荐，陆慕砖窑被工部看中，决定"始砖于苏州，责其役于长洲窑户六十三家"。

金砖（图片来源：《太和殿》，周乾　著）

因为苏州的金砖、临清的贡砖都邻近大运河，所以在运输上，其得以快速利用运河的便利，大规模地向北京供应。但是，石料的采集运输，则是另一番情景。

石料在宫殿建造过程中用量也非常大。建筑下面的台基、台基四周的栏杆、石头桥、皇城中主要的路面都用石料建造。

为了减少运输困难，对于石料，尤其那些体量很大的石雕，例如天安门前面的石狮子和华表石柱，都尽量在附近的房山、曲阳取材。这里面最大的石料要数故宫保和殿北侧的一块丹陛石，它长达16米，宽3.17米，重200余吨，这是其加工完成后的重量，如果按原来的毛料计算，分量还要重得多。

不管是从房山，还是曲阳，向紫禁城运输石料，只能采用陆运。路运又分四种方法：人力、畜力、旱船、冰船。其中人力和畜力只能运输重量较小的物料或者制品，吨级别的物料就要用另外两种方式了。

旱船运输是在大型货物下垫圆滚木，以人力或畜力拉拽前行，要求道路十分平坦。冰船则是使用泼水成冰的方式，通过减少道路的摩擦力方便运输的一种方法。这里最富有创造性的就是那块丹陛石的运输了。这块丹陛石采自距北京市中心70公里的房山，为了将石头运到紫禁城，数万名劳工在运输的道路两旁修路填坑，每隔一里左右掘一口井，在隆冬严寒中，从井里汲水泼洒在地面上冻成冰道，约两万名民工和一千头骡子用了整整 28 天，才将石料送到宫里。这块费尽心力运往北京紫禁城的大石头被放置在故宫中轴线的御道上。

不过，论起材料采伐难度最大、运输最复杂、耗时最久的，当属紫禁城木料的采集与运输工作了。甚至很多时候，紫禁城的修建速度都依赖于木料运输的速度。

紫禁城宫殿的柱子、梁枋、四周门窗全部由木料做成，对木料不仅需求量大，而且质量要求也高。其中最珍贵的是产自四川的金丝楠木，这是一种极其高档的木材，美丽淡雅的色泽、坚硬细密的材质、优美匀整的纹理、温润柔和的质地以及收缩性小、遇火难燃、不挠不裂、耐湿不腐、有幽香等特点使其成为古代木建筑的上乘选料。这些生长在原始森林中的庞然大物被运到北京，贴金沥粉缠龙为饰，摇身一变成为支撑太和殿的七十二根大柱，直径最大的达一米。

开采木料十分不易，金丝楠木多生长在南方的崇山峻岭，那里常常有虎豹蛇蟒出没，砍伐艰辛异常。由于地形条件的复杂多变，天时阴晴、水枯水荣的把握不定，伐运常伴随着危险和不确定因素，加上有些产木之所在瘴疠毒雾之乡，更增加了采运的难度。后代描述是"入山一千，出山五百"。永乐十三年（1415 年），因采伐进度不如预期，朱棣特命宋礼亲自前往四川督办皇木采伐事宜。宋礼和当地官吏、工匠一起研究问题，探寻解决方法，最终完成了此项任务。在伐木工九死一生的操持之下，木料终于出山，并最终运送到了北京。

水路联运是木材运送的关键方法。楠木被砍倒之后，从高山上扔下，滚入溪谷中，在那里被捆扎成木筏。这一过程危险重重。明人王士性说，木非难而采难，伐非难而出难……上下山阪，大涧深坑，根株既长，转动不易，遇坑坎处，必假他木抓搭鹰架，使与山平，然后可出。一木下山，常损数命。这些木筏在溪谷中一直等到山洪暴发将它们带入河流。于是木筏沿着纵横的水道到达长江，而长江与大运河相连，木材进入运河后，再由纤夫一路协助拉上京城，这一路每个站点都有官员沿岸值守，木材被运至京城后集中码放等待使用。这也催生了很多与之有关的地名，比如台基厂、皇木厂等。这些珍稀的木材砍伐下来漂流 1000 多公里，耗时短则 2 年，长则 4 年，才能漂到北京。

这个过程虽没有山中拽运那么危险，但由于路途遥远，水势不统一，也会导致木材不能全部顺利到达京城。明朝天启年间，在天津入海口两岸附近的芦苇荡里，发现了历代王朝漂下来的一千多根大楠木。

四、尾声：后世荣光

会通河疏浚工程完工后，南北物资大动脉彻底打通，源源不断的砖石木料通过这个水道被运送到紫禁城的建设工地上，紫禁城建设速度明显加快，并最终于永乐十八年（1420 年）完工。

紫禁城完工在即，宋礼放下督造事宜，风尘仆仆地来到大运河边，接他的伙伴白英一同进京复命受赏。因多年在工地操劳，白英早已劳累过度，当队伍行至德州桑园时，他不幸呕血去世，时年 56 岁。宋礼只能独自失落地回到北京。

永乐十九年（1421 年），紫禁城刚建成不到四个月，奉天、华盖、谨身三座大殿因雷击起火，火势汹涌，大殿被烧为灰烬，十几年的建造心血付之一炬。

后来，新一轮的施工启动。此时，宋礼已经疾病缠身，常常卧病在床，不能亲临工地现场。但他已经在多年的紫禁城建造中，选出了一位出色的副手，那就是工部侍郎蒯祥。蒯祥是一代建筑设计大师，被后世誉为故宫的总设计师，当然，这是另一个传奇故事了。

永乐二十年（1422 年），因紫禁城建设木料缺口依旧很大，宋礼再次挂帅出征，前往四川寻找巨木。同年七月，宋礼病逝在任上，享年 62 岁。

疏浚运河、改兴漕运、采伐皇木、领建故宫，都是花钱如流水的工程，但是，宋礼财不妄费，役不妄兴，"锱镠亿兆经其用，棉帛毫丝不曾吞"，《明史》定论其"卒之日，家无余财"。

宋礼病逝的消息传到山东，运河两岸百姓哀痛不已，他们自发为宋礼建造祠堂供奉祭祀，亲切地尊他为"河神"。

明正统五年（1440 年），奉天、华盖、谨身三大殿以及乾清宫得以重建。自此，经历永乐、洪熙、宣德、正统四代，紫禁城终于修缮如新，以其巍峨壮丽之观展现在世人面前。

紫禁城凝结了多少劳动人民的智慧结晶，多少匠人的辛勤劳作，又有多少人为其殚精竭虑，甚至牺牲性命，才成就了如此举世无双的豪华宫殿！而为了营建紫禁城，整个古代中国的物流水平也借此得到了前所未有的提升，实现了质的飞跃。紫禁城营建背后的物流事业，为中国物流史写下了光辉的一页，堪称人类物流史上的奇迹，值得永志流传。

中国物流**故事**古代辑 汉英对照

《万国来朝图》轴（现收藏于故宫博物院）

Beijing-Hangzhou Grand Canal

—The Pinnacle of Interactive Civilization between People and Water

Gongchen Bridge(Photo by Wang Ping)

During the Spring and Autumn Period, Chinese people started to dig Beijing—Hangzhou Grand Canal. Beijing-Hangzhou Grand Canal has the longest span and the oldest history in the world. It serves not only as a grain transport artery, but also as the source of irrigation. All the places where the Grand Canal flows are people's livelihoods. The Beijing—Hangzhou Grand Canal, which was excavated in the Spring and Autumn Period, constructed in the Sui Dynasty, flourished in the Tang and Song Dynasties, straightened in the Yuan Dynasty, dredged in the Ming and Qing Dynasties, ran about 1797 kilometers from north to south, playing an important role as a golden waterway for north—south grain transport. The Beijing—Hangzhou Grand

Canal promotes the cross-regional flow of resources, catalyzes the further development of the commodity economy, breeds the bud of the market economy, and nourishes the rich tangible and intangible culture.

1. Leaving the Merit to the Present Generation

In ancient times, land transportation mainly relied on manpower and animal power, with small carrying capacity, slow running speed, much time, and high cost. Therefore, water transportation was the first choice for bulk cargo transportation. Most of China's natural rivers flow horizontally from west to east. In addition, the economic and cultural environment around the Yellow River Basin has been destroyed by war, and the Yangtze River Basin has developed, thus China has gradually formed a situation in which the economic and cultural center was in the south and the political and military center was in the north. The canal played an important role in strengthening the connection between the north and south centers and ensuring the materials from the south can be continuously transported to the north, thus, opening up and maintaining a canal running through the north and south was particularly significant for the dynasties.

The history of Chinese people digging canals has spanned more than two thousand years. In 486 B. C., in order to crusade against Qi in the north, Fu Chai, the king of the state of Wu, built the "Han Ditch", which ran from Yangzhou to the northeast through Sheyang Lake to Huai River in Huai'an. "Han Ditch", with a total length of about 170 kilometers, connects the Huai River and the Yangtze River. It is the earliest section of the Beijing-Hangzhou Grand Canal. In addition, during the Warring State Period, the chasm built by the state of Wei and the Zhengguo Canal built by the state of Qin are all famous canal projects in history.

The Grand Canal of the Sui Dynasty is the peak of canal excavation. "Feel happy in the southeast", Emperor Yang Guang excavated the canal for the convenience of visiting Yangzhou to see the beautiful scenery of guelder rose, which is a common opening remark of ancient storytellers. However, this is not the case. "Although people say that the Sui Dynasty was destroyed because of the opening of the Grand Canal, it has played a great role." People are more willing to believe that this is the courage and foresight of an emperor. Therefrom the grand project that spanned thousands of years and benefited thousands of years got started.

In the first year of kaihuang (581 A.D.), Yang Guang was conferred as the king of the state of Jin. During the period of defending the northern Turkic, thanks to the land transportation network opened up by the Qin Dynasty, Yang Guang made many achievements in defending the frontier.

Yang Guang succeeded to the throne and moved the capital to Luoyang. He began to build a canal with Luoyang as the center. On the one hand, opening up a canal running through the north and south was contributed to using waterway transportation to transport rice from the south to the north; on the other hand, Yang Guang paid attention to the expansion of territory and the stability of jurisdiction, dredging the canal was conducive to centralizing imperial power, strengthening the control, connecting the political center of the north with the economic center of the south, and forming the unity of the north and the south.

In the first year of Daye (605 A. D.), Emperor Yang of the Sui Dynasty organized millions of people to excavate the Tongji Canal, which started the construction of the Grand Canal of the Sui Dynasty. With the support of today's advanced technology and concept, it will take a lot of time to dredge waterway. However, more than 1000 years ago, relying on manpower and the most primitive tools, Emperor Yang excavated a complete canal network with a total length of more than 2000 kilometers in only six years. Among them, Tongji Canal, Yongji Canal, Han Ditch, and Jiangnan Canal connected Central Plains and Hebei Plain with Jianghuai Region closely, forming a traffic artery centered on Luoyang. Together with the Guangtong Canal, which ran toward the west to Daxing City and was built during the Sui Emperor's period, the Grand Canal connects five major water systems, that is the Yangtze River, the Yellow River, the Huai River, the Hai River and the Qiantang River, and constitutes a complete system that communicating the national water transportation.

The Grand Canal in Tang Dynasty developed on the basis of the Grand

Canal in Sui Dynasty. In historical circles, the canals in the Tang Dynasty which were built in the Sui Dynasty are collectively referred to as the Grand Canal of the Sui and Tang Dynasties. The Grand Canal of Sui and Tang Dynasties is divided into two branches, one is Yongji Canal, which connects to the northeast; the other is Tongji Canal, Han Ditch (also known as Shanyangdu) and Jiangnan Canal, which connects to the southeast.

The Grand Canal of Sui and Tang Dynasties connected the two economic circles of the Yellow River and the Yangtze River. It was an important economic lifeline for Sui and Tang Dynasties. It was mainly used for grain transport, which not only saved huge logistics costs, solved the problem of bulk transportation between the north and the south in ancient times, but also promoted the economic development of areas along the canal. At the same time, the north had the material support from the south, and the logistics pattern of "feeding the soldiers of the northwest with the food of the southeast" gradually took shape.

2. A Matter of National Importance

The Grand Canal of the Sui and Tang Dynasties played an important role in connecting the north and the south. However, with the collapse of the Tang Dynasty, China entered the era of the Five Dynasties and Ten Kingdoms, which was chaotic and fragmented. When Bianliang (now Kaifeng) was the capital of the northern Song Dynasty, the grain supply was transferred to the south of the Yangtze River. During the Song and Jin Dynasties, the Yellow River suffered from frequent floods, which broke its mouth repeatedly and destroyed the river course, resulting in the navigation suspension of part of the Yongji Canal.

After the capital of the Yuan Dynasty was established in Dadu (now Beijing), the national center moved to Beijing, and the old Grand Canal of the Sui and Tang Dynasties was still used for grain transport. At that time, affected by the long-term war and the flood of the Yellow River, the canal was mostly blocked, and the transshipment between water and land was quite inconvenient.

Guo Shoujing, an irrigationist, proposed to Kublai Khan, the emperor of the Yuan

Dynasty, the canal management plan that had been planned for many years: first, taking Wenshui and Sishui as water sources, excavating Jizhou River, then Huitong River, building gates and dams to facilitate water transportation; second, building the canal with greater transportation capacity, excavating the Ba River and Tonghui River to solve the problem of weak navigation ability of the old rivers. In this way, transforming the canal into an inland waterway that directly connected Beijing and the south of the Yangtze River.

Kublai Khan ordered the partial repair of the Grand Canal of Sui and Tang Dynasties, from which the Beijing-Hangzhou Grand Canal came to the stage of history. Although the starting and ending points are the same, the total length of the Beijing-Hangzhou Grand Canal is about 1797 kilometers, about 903 kilometers shorter than that of the Grand Canal of Sui and Tang Dynasties. The Beijing-Hangzhou Grand Canal passes through six provinces and cities, including Beijing, Tianjin, Hebei, Shandong, Jiangsu, and Zhejiang. Its main water source is the "Four South Lakes" composed of Weishan Lake, Zhaoyang Lake, Dushan Lake, and Nanyang Lake. Up to now, it is still an important shipping waterway, which is called "the three great projects in ancient China" together with the Great Wall and Karez.

Ships on the Beijing-Hangzhou Grand Canal (Photo by Zhu Jipeng)

中国物流故事
古代辑
汉英对照

The Grand Canal in Sui and Tang Dynasties ran south-north and east-west in a "herringbone" shape, while the Beijing-Hangzhou Grand Canal ran south-north in a straight line. In order to avoid bypassing Luoyang and keep it straight, it was necessary to build a new artificial river channel, abandon the previous route via Luoyang and Kaifeng, and divert to Shandong. Built the original horizontal canal into a vertical canal, which was generally in a straight line from north to south. "Load rice at the dock in Hangzhou and transport it directly to Beijing", the saying of the Beijing-Hangzhou Grand Canal tells the historical origin of the two cities taking the river as the medium.

The Beijing-Hangzhou Grand Canal not only solved the problem of grain transport but also promoted the economic and cultural exchanges between the north and the south. Through merchant shipping, silk, tea, bamboo, sugar, and other goods from the south, and pine, fur, coal, and other materials from the north are exchanged and shared, so that the regional commerce is prosperous.

In addition, the Beijing-Hangzhou Grand Canal is also an important hub connecting the ancient maritime Silk Road and the land Silk Road, which promotes the development of industry and commerce in coastal areas. The Beijing-Hangzhou Grand Canal is connected to the land Silk Road in the north and the maritime Silk Road in the south, forming a complete channel. Starting from Beijing Tongzhou at the northern end of the Beijing-Hangzhou Grand Canal to the north, there are mature post roads or commercial roads, which are connected with the land Silk Road, stretching to the northern grasslands and then extending to Europe; from Hangzhou at the southern end of the Beijing-Hangzhou Grand Canal, there is a part extending from the East Zhejiang Canal to Ningbo, which is connected with the maritime Silk Road and leads to South Asian countries. China's excellent culture has spread to all parts of the world and has had a wide and far-reaching impact on the world.

The connection of the Beijing-Hangzhou Grand Canal further strengthened the connection between the south of the Yangtze River and the northern grassland area in the Yuan Dynasty, and further promoted the connection between the land Silk Road and the maritime Silk Road. According to *Travels of Marco Polo*, Macro Polo came to Shangdu of the Yuan Dynasty along with the land Silk Road. On the return journey, he went to Zhenjiang via the Beijing–Hangzhou Grand Canal, then to Quanzhou, Fujian, and returned to his hometown via the maritime Silk Road. Another traveler, Odorik, came to China from Italy through the maritime Silk Road, reached Dadu along the Beijing–Hangzhou Grand Canal, turned southwest along the Yellow River, entered Hexi Corridor, and returned to Italy through Central Asia, which happened to be the land Silk Road.

3. Canal of Gold

The Beijing–Hangzhou Grand Canal is not only an artificial river but also a logistics and transportation system that can connect east and west horizontally and north and south vertically. The driving and radiating effects of economy and culture should not be underestimated.

From Beijing in the north to Hangzhou in the south, the Beijing–Hangzhou Grand Canal runs from the North China Plain to the Yangtze River Delta. With the construction of the Beijing–Hangzhou Grand Canal, the political center and the economic center were more stable, which provided the north with material support and guarantee from the south. A magnificent transportation network was formed, and China's political and economic structure was basically fixed.

The flow of the canal not only determined the pattern of urban development but also affected the functionality of urban development. The Beijing–Hangzhou Grand Canal played a huge role in promoting the economic development of the coastal cities, and the south–north trade flourished for a time. The flow of goods and materials catalyzed the accumulation of wealth, and cities along the coast gradually became rich. With the development of commerce, large blocks rose and prospered, and the patterns of cities changed. The brands of cities gradually became prominent and began to form national business centers represented by Yangzhou, Suzhou, Jining, etc.

These canal cities with developed industry and commerce, built on the canal, inherited the spirit of the canal with the characteristics of logistics, and gradually attracted the attention of the world.

Piaohai Lu, written by Cui Pu, recorded the traders who were always on the move, as well as the coastal features and traffic conditions of the canal at that time.

Ming and Qing Dynasties maintained the basic pattern of the Beijing-Hangzhou Grand Canal, adapted to local conditions, and after many large-scale repairs, the Beijing-Hangzhou Grand Canal played an important role in transporting grain and maintaining the coordinated development of the country in long term.

Entering modern times, with the development of sea transportation and the opening of the Jin-Pu Railway, Beijing-Hangzhou Grand Canal fell into depression, but it still has extraordinary transportation value. After the founding of New China, the Beijing-Hangzhou Grand Canal became the main channel for transporting coal from north to south, and also became an important part of the East Route of the South-to-North Water Transfer Project. Living by water, there are still about 300 million Chinese people living by the canal.

Although modern transportation is very developed, in modern cities like Suzhou, more than 6000 ships pass through the Beijing-Hangzhou Grand Canal every day, and the canal water network bears roughly half of the freight volume.

The sparkling Grand Canal bears a heavy history. The United Nations Educational, Scientific, and Cultural Organization (UNESCO) summed it up that the Beijing-Hangzhou Grand Canal represents the migration and flow of human beings, the reciprocal and continuous exchange of multi-dimensional goods, ideas, knowledge, and values, and the exchange and mutual nourishment of the resulting culture in time and space, which has been continuously reflected through tangible and intangible heritage for a long time.

The Beijing-Hangzhou Grand Canal passes through lots of lakes and canals. Why did the emperors of all dynasties prefer to use a lot of manpower and material resources to excavate and maintain the Grand Canal, rather than use the

existing lakes?

This is because the Beijing-Hangzhou Grand Canal has shouldered the responsibility of material transportation in the north and south regions of China for generations. Transportation must be efficient. Every place on the route is an excellent material transfer place. The distance setting of the whole line should be efficient. In addition, "force majeure" is the most feared thing for transportation on lakes. Although there is plenty of water in the lake on this route, as long as the season and the climate are wrong, even if there is only one dry place, the whole route will be paralyzed. The vast lakes are the favorite of the "water bandits" . Moreover, due to the limited shipbuilding technology in ancient times, the tragedies of ship destruction and people' s deaths occurred from time to time. Therefore, "by the lake" seems to be an "unflattering way" , it is an extremely wise choice of the ancient people, which also gave birth to the earliest design of land and water inter modal logistics system.

4. Benefit Future Generations

4.1 Logistics Thought from Living by Grain to Segmented Transportation

In the early Tang Dynasty, the Stationary-Troop Service System was implemented. Soldiers farmed in peacetime and fought in wartime, and their food was basically self-sufficient. Even if the transportation is difficult and the navigation is slow, the food supply can still be maintained, and the disadvantages of canal transportation do not appear. With the aggravation of the central government, during the reign of Li Longji, Tang Xuanzong, the Stationary-Troop Service System gradually changed to the Mercenary System, and the separation of soldiers and farmers made the government' s demand for food further increase. However, the land in Guanzhong was narrow, and the grain output could not meet the needs of the capital. When transporting grain from the south of the Yangtze River with high grain yield, the cargo ship was blocked in the area of the Mainstay of Sanmenxia, and it could not be transported directly by water, the problem of transportation of grain gradually became prominent. The supply of grain was short of demand, the central government was blocked, and the emperor began the life of "living by grain" . Luoyang is located in the Central Plains, with developed agriculture, convenient transportation, and abundant grain reserves. Whenever the materials were insufficient, the emperor would lead the officials of civil and military to move to Luoyang together, and "eating at the east capital" effectively eased the pressure on the court.

In the 18th year of Kaiyuan (730 A.D.) in the Tang Dynasty, Pei Yaoqing suggested changing the previous way of direct transportation of grain by water, and put forward the idea of segmented transportation. He suggested that a warehouse should be built at the entrance of the Yellow River. The grain, rice, cloth, and silk from the south of the Yangtze River will be transported here and unloaded into the warehouse, and ships will return immediately. When the Yellow River is suitable for navigation, the goods will be delivered to the destination.

The segmented transportation reduced the loss of grain transport and saved the expenses. Segmented transportation can keep ships in the south of the Yangtze River from entering the Yellow River, which saved the waiting time due to the difference in water level, and avoided the Sanmen barrier. The transportation cost was greatly reduced, and the transportation efficiency was greatly improved.

The "transshipment method" of setting up warehouses and transshipment also reflected the logistics concept of segmented transportation, which has a positive and far-reaching impact on the development of grain transport and even Chinese logistics.

4.2 Logistics Thought from Segmented Transportation to Direct Transportation by Waterway

The Sanmen barrier is located in the throat of the Yellow River grain transport, which is the key to the whole Yellow River grain transport. The special geographical environment of the Sanmen barrier poses a great threat to the passing ships, which will lead to the tragedy of ship destruction and human death.

The grain transport management of the Yellow River in the past dynasties was carried out around the Sanmen barrier, but the results were not ideal. After that, most of them adopted circuitous tactics, abandoned the ship and landed at the Sanmen barrier, and had to change between boats and vehicles many times, resulting in huge transportation costs. Because of the insurmountable natural barrier, the grain transport of the Yellow River was intermittent.

In order to overcome this barrier, in 741 A. D., Li Qiwu, followed the example of the predecessors to carve the mountain as the plank road, and the trackers helped pull the fiber on the plank road to help the ships pass the Sanmen barrier. Although the construction of the plank road was helpful for the passage of ships, it did not completely solve the navigation difficulties, even caused frequent death accidents of boatmen falling into the river, thus aggravated the suffering of the people.

After that, the transportation plan of direct access by waterway was proposed. Digging the New Kaiyuan River near Sanmenxia, avoiding the Sanmen barrier by manually digging the river, and making the ship reach Chang'an directly.

In only about three months, the New Kaiyuan River, paralleling to the Yellow River was navigable. When sailing on New Kaiyuan River, ships can avoid torrents, and the navigation was relatively safe. Direct transportation by waterway was similar to segmented transportation, and it was more advanced. It was too troublesome to load and unload by segmented transportation. After the opening of the New Kaiyuan River, the passing ships no longer transferred from Jijin warehouse to land transportation, but directly passed through the Yin River warehouse to Yongfeng warehouse in Weikou, which greatly improved transportation efficiency.

4.3 Logistics Thought from Direct Transportation by Waterway to Segmented Transportation

After the An-Shi Rebellion, the northern economy was severely damaged, agricultural production was abandoned, people' s livelihoods were depressed, and people were starved all year round. Since Emperor Suzong of Tang Dynasty, emperors of all dynasties have racked their brains to think about how to transfer materials from the south of the Yangtze River to Chang' an. At that time, the grain transport was interrupted because of the war, and the canals were in disrepair for a long time, especially the Bian Canal, which had been blocked by the soil and could not pass at all. It was not until 764 A.D. that Liu Yan was ordered to rectify the grain transport in the face of danger.

Liu Yan extended Pei Yaoqing' s segmented transportation to all sections of the canal, which made "ships from river don' t enter Bian River, ships from Bian River don' t enter stream, ships from stream don' t enter Wei River" . He adopted the method of segmented transportation, the problem that each section of river is difficult to pass continuously due to different water flow was solved.

In order to cooperate with this plan, the method of building a warehouse and transferring nearby was implemented, namely, a shipping terminal was set up in Yangzhou, the south of the canal, and a transshipment granary was set up along the river. The grain from the south of the Yangtze River was transported to Yangzhou and segmentally sent to the government for storage. The ships returned immediately, and then the grain was transported by the government ships. Each waterway has its own ships for transportation. Ships went back and forth in specific river sections. The boatmen were more familiar with the situation of sailing in their river sections and knew how to avoid dangerous beaches during navigation, which reduced the loss on the way, saved the shipping time and alleviated the worry of capsizing.

After Liu Yan' s reform and dredging of the river, the Grand Canal regained its former prosperity, which met the food needs of Chang' an.

4.4 Logistics Thought of the Standardized Management

Liu Yan built 10 large-scale shipyards in Yangzhou. According to the different water level characteristics of the Huai River, Bian River, Yellow River, and Wei River, he built standard ships, each of which was a big ship with a grain weight of 1000 Dan, and each ship had 35 boatmen.

When passing through the Mainstay of Sanmenxia, it is stipulated that ten ships should be taken as one class, and ten ships should be tied together. Each class is equipped with 50 boatmen who are responsible for stabilizing the hull, and the shore is equipped with 300 trackers who are responsible for towing the ship. In addition, the rope position, team formation, and spacing were all standardized management, under the unified bugle, all the people worked together, thus the fleet was unstoppable to break through the natural danger.

After Liu Yan's reform, compared with the period of Emperor Xuanzong of the Tang Dynasty, the transportation time was shorter, and the transportation cost of grain per Dan was reduced. More importantly, it no longer consumed huge manpower and material resources.

4.5 The logistics Thought of Inventing Sluice to Improve Equipment

With the rapid development of the canal, the construction of the canal project in the Song Dynasty has also been greatly improved. On the basis of using single sluice to control water in the Tang Dynasty, double-sluice and cove sluice were created.

In the first year of Yongxi (984 A.D.), when Qiao Weiyue was appointed as Huainan transshipment ambassador, he began to build the first standard ship lock in China, which replaced the weir by the ship lock to overcome the limitation of the canal topography. The work of ship lock is to use the principle of "When the river rises, the boat floats high". Although it has advantages over the weir, the water loss is still unavoidable when crossing the ship, which requires certain measures to reduce the water loss.

The cove sluice, which appeared in the middle of the Northern Song Dynasty, was used to solve the problem of storing water and sailing. The water released from the sluice chamber is stored in the cove, and when the water is insufficient, the water in the cove is used to return to the sluice chamber. Cove sluice can effectively save water and solve the problem of the water sources. In addition, it is easy to build cove sluice, which has been widely popularized in Huainan Canal and Jiangnan Canal.

Song Dynasty is the peak period of the development of canal sluice technology. This technology, which relies on the lake to store water and uses sluice to control the flow of the canal, ends the history of "relying on heaven" . It is a major breakthrough in the history of human canal engineering.

4.6 Logistics Thought of Digging Tonghui River to Form an Intermodal Transportation between Inland River and Sea

Yuan Dynasty had a large population, and its food supply mainly depended on the south. When Kublai Khan was the emperor of the Yuan Dynasty, he dug Huitong River from Dongping to Linqing in Shandong Province, and Tonghui River from Tongzhou to Dadu. In addition, he opened up sea transportation, sea transportation is cheaper than river transportation, and it can also avoid the trouble of land transportation and stranding.

Yuan Shizu not only opened the inland river to the capital, but also collected goods from ocean-going ships and inland river ships in Zhigu, and reached the capital directly through Tonghui River, which increased the grain transported to Beijing by more than 3 million Dan every year and became the key to the prosperity of Yuan, Ming, and Qing Dynasties. This great feat has made the rivers, seas, and lakes connect with each other, realizing the situation of combined transport between inland river and sea, and playing a vital role in realizing the combined transport between the maritime Silk Road and the inland river and promoting the initiative of "the Belt and Road" .

5. Rejuvenation

Since ancient times, ship transportation has been the most advantageous form of transportation in terms of volume and cost and has always been known for its low energy consumption[1]. Looking at the world regional economy, from the role of the Mississippi River in promoting the development of industry and agriculture along the coast of the United States to the driving force of the Rhine River in promoting the sustainable economic development of Germany and even

---

[1] The average transportation cost of ship transportation is only 1 / 2 of railway and 1 / 8 of highway, and the unit energy consumption is only 1 / 4 of railway and 1 / 9 of highway.

the whole European Union, to the catalytic function of the Beijing—Hangzhou Grand Canal in the canal economic belt, almost all of them indicate that great rivers are important economic growth axes.

The Beijing—Hangzhou Grand Canal, which flows thousands of miles from north to south, has been artificially excavated, but it has changed the geographical pattern of China. It is a historical witness of the achievements of ancient transportation civilization and modern inland navigation. In June 2017, President Xi Jinping said, "The Grand Canal is a precious heritage left by our ancestors and it is a flowing culture, which should be well protected, inherited, and utilized."

Time has not made the Beijing—Hangzhou Grand Canal a cold relic. Today, the Beijing—Hangzhou Grand Canal still plays a huge role in supporting the country's economic, social, and cultural development. It is a history worthy of awe in the hearts of Chinese people, and it is also a national sentiment that inspires us to be the first and pursue excellence.

Story 2

The Silk Road

—The Millennium Agreement of the Intersection of Eastern and Western Civilizations

One day in the spring of 1871, in the yellow sand of the Gobi Desert in the Western China, a foreigner with blond hair and blue eyes was riding on a camel, led by a guide, trudging step by step. The camel team was very long, and the luggage boxes were filled with geological exploration tools, mineral drawings, and paper records describing local traditions and customs.

Sculpture of Richthofen—Namer of the Silk Road (By Xiang Jinguo)

This foreigner is Richthofen, a German geographer and geologist. He persuaded Li Hongzhang, the Minister of Beiyang, to allow him to visit China. From 1868 to 1872, he conducted seven inspections along different routes, from coast to inland, from northeast to southwest, and left his footprints in China.

Richthofen had a habit that not only recording the local products but also paying special attention to the roads for transporting them in each research. Wherever he visited, it was necessary for him to describe the land and water traffic conditions in the research report and record the urban transit and commercial routes constructed on the basis of the traffic, thus forming the main line of the report. Gradually, he found that there was a close relationship between the ancient Chinese trade roads and the Western records of "the Silk Country" , and he had already grasped the historical context.

After Richthofen returned to his country in 1872, he served as the President of Berlin University. He spent most of his later years writing *China: The Results of My Travels and the Studies Based Thereon* (hereinafter referred to as *China*). In the first volume of *China*, Richthofen clearly put forward the concept of "Silk Road" for the first time.

In 1936, Richthofen's student, Sven Hedin, published a book in the name of *The Silk Road*. Since then, the word "Silk Road" has been slowly accepted by the public and spread rapidly.

Since then, a shining term has entered the minds of the Chinese people and even people all over the world. The road of economy, trade, and culture, which is covered by the yellow sand, has also come alive again, telling people legendary historical stories.

1. Opening Trade Routes

At the beginning of the 2nd century B.C., the Western Han Dynasty became more and more powerful after the Enlightened Administration of the Reign of Emperor Wen and Emperor Jing. The aspiring young emperor, Emperor Wu of the Han Dynasty, Liu Che, decided to declare war on the Xiongnu, who had threatened the border security of the Western Han Dynasty for more than 80 years. He hoped to wipe out the humiliation for many years.

In the second year of Jianyuan (139 B.C.), Liu Che decided to unite with the kingdoms in Western Regions to fight against the Xiongnu, and he sent envoy Zhang Qian to contact the people of Greater Yuezhi[①] who were expelled from the Hexi Corridor by the Xiongnu.

Zhang Qian, opening trade routes to the west (Stamps) (Designed by Gao Yun)

At that time, the Greater Yuezhi had migrated to the Amu Darya Valley in Central Asia to escape from the invasion of the Xiongnu. To get in touch with them, Zhang Qian had to cross the Hexi region controlled by the Xiongnu. However, it was no easy task to cross the desert and quicksand, which covered more than 7000 kilometers in the Western Regions. Moreover, he had to pass through the territory controlled by the Xiongnu to seek a military alliance with the Greater Yuezhi, who was the enemy of the Xiongnu. This was an area that Han people never set foot in before. It was covered with deserts and snow-capped mountains all the way. Sometimes it was full of strong winds, flying sand, and stones, sometimes it was silent and deserted.

However, Zhang Qian resolutely embarked on the journey. Guided by Tangyi Fu, Zhang Qian led a delegation of more than 100 people. He set out from Longxi to the kingdom of the Greater Yuezhi, igniting wildfires and marching along water and grass, keeping away from all suspicious traces of hooves. However, unfortunately, they met the Xiongnu cavalry in Hexi Corridor, and all the others were killed except Zhang Qian and Tangyi Fu.

The Xiongnu did not want to kill Zhang Qian, so they tried to persuade him, but failed, they enslaved Zhang Qian and Tangyi Fu. Later, Shan Yu, the chief of the Xiongnu, betrothed a wife to Zhang Qian, Zhang Qian married the wife. It took 11 years for Zhang Qian and his guide Tangyi Fu to escape from the

① The Greater Yuezhi was a nomadic tribe in Central Asia in the 2nd century B.C.

Xiongnu. After experiencing this shock, Zhang Qian did not return to the Han Dynasty, but continued going westward without changing his original intention, vowing to complete the mission of visiting the Western Regions.

Zhang Qian crossed the Pamir Mountains to the west and arrived in Dayuan after dozens of days of trekking, that is, Fergana Valley of Uzbekistan in Central Asia today. Then the king of Dayuan dispatched troops to escort Zhang Qian to Kangju (between the Amu Darya and the Syr Darya in Central Asia), and then from Kangju to Greater Yuezhi. However, the people of Greater Yuezhi had elected a new king and annexed large tracts of land of the local tribes. The people of Greater Yuezhi had already lived up and worked in peace and contentment, and they were too far away from the dynasty of Central Plains in ancient China at that time, so they did not want to unite with the Han Dynasty to take revenge on the Xiongnu.

Zhang Qian lived with the people of Greater Yuezhi for more than one year, but he still had no way to persuade them to attack the Xiongnu, so he had to return to the east. On the way back, Zhang Qian chose to enter the Qaidam Basin along the southern foot of the Tarim Basin and returned home by detouring the Qinghai area, mainly in order to avoid the blockage of the Xiongnu, but he was captured again with bad luck. Fortunately, one year later, the Xiongnu leader Shan Yu died and civil strife broke out. In the midst of chaos, Zhang Qian escaped and finally returned to Chang' an, in the third year of Yuanshuo (126 B.C.) of Emperor Wu of the Han Dynasty.

Zhang Qian' s first mission to the Western Regions lasted for 13 years. Although he did not achieve the political goal of forming an alliance with the people of Greater Yuezhi, he learned about the politics, economy, geography, culture and customs of the Western Regions, which laid a foundation for strengthening the ties between the Central Plains and the Western Regions. Soon, Zhang Qian took advantage of his knowledge of the Western Regions when he participated in Wei Qing' s attack on the Xiongnu. Thanks to his knowledge of the location of water and grass, he made great contributions to this military operation and he was granted the title of Marquis of Bowang by Emperor Wu of the Han Dynasty.

When Zhang Qian was visiting the Western Regions, the Western Han Dynasty also launched a series of attacks against the Xiongnu, which eliminated the Xiongnu's military power in Monan and Hexi corridor.

However, the Western Regions were still controlled by the Xiongnu, which still threatened the security of the northwest border of the Western Han Dynasty. Therefore, Emperor Wu of the Han Dynasty sent Zhang Qian on a diplomatic mission to the Western Regions again, he tried to develop ties with people in the Wusun and other countries in the Western Regions to establish an alliance against the Xiongnu. This time, there were 300 attendants, and the diplomatic corps was well prepared, carrying plenty of money and silk. When Zhang Qian arrived in the Wusun (Ili River and Chu River Basin), what happened was that the Wusun was politically unstable because of the dispute over the throne, and the Wusun had no intention of forming an alliance with the Han Dynasty to fight against the Xiongnu. During this period, Zhang Qian sent deputy envoys on diplomatic missions to the Dayuan, Kangju, Greater Yuezhi, Anxi, and Shendu (now India) in Central Asia, West Asia, and South Asia respectively. In 115 B.C., Zhang Qian returned to the Han Dynasty, and the Wusun dispatched an interpreter and an envoy to accompany him on a journey to Chang'an. The envoy saw that the people of the Han Dynasty were rich and generous, and after returning to the Wusun, he widely publicized it, which greatly enhanced the prestige of the Han Dynasty in the Western Regions. Soon, the deputy envoys sent by Zhang Qian also returned home one after another and brought back many envoys from the countries they visited. Since then, the communication between the east and the west officially started, and the friendly exchanges between the government of the Western Han Dynasty and the Western Regions, Central Asia, West Asia, and South Asia developed rapidly, and envoys from the west met each other on the road.

It is said that from the Western Han Dynasty, from five to six to over ten diplomatic corps would be sent out to the west in the course of one year, the places they visited were far away, and it took at most eight or nine years to visit at a time. The largest of these diplomatic corps numbered hundreds of people, while even the smaller parties included over 100 members. "Being entertained at frontier fortress every day", what complements the diplomatic corps are groups of businessmen. After that, the land transportation between China and the west continued to extend westward.

The travel of Zhang Qian opened up the land transportation between the east and the west which had been blocked by the Xiongnu for a long time, promoted the economic and cultural exchanges, established the friendly ties between the Central Plains and the northwest frontier, and opened a new era of direct exchanges between China and western countries. The pioneering significance of Zhang Qian's mission to the Western Regions is great. Sima Qian praised it highly in *Records of the Historian*, which named his achievement as "opening trade routes".

2. Shocking the West

Zhang Qian's visit connected China with Europe and Africa with a safe road transport channel. Starting from Chang'an, the capital of the Han Dynasty, this route traversed the Hetao Plain and then divided into two branches. One road starts from Yangguan, passes through Shanshan, goes west along the northern edge of Kunlun Mountain, passes through Shache and the Pamir Mountains in the west, through Greater Yuezhi to Anxi, goes west to Li Qian, or enters Shendu along the south of Greater Yuezhi. The other road starts from Yumen Pass, passes through Jushi Qian Country, goes west along the foot of Tianshan Mountain, through Shule, passes the Pamir Mountains in the west, then passes Dayuan, and arrives at Kangju and Yancai.

The emissaries of the Han Dynasty went westward, and the emissaries of Western Regions also came eastward. Chinese silk and other textile products were transported from Luoyang and Chang'an to Alawa via Hetao Plain and

Xinjiang Uygur Autonomous Region today, and then shipped to Europe, and brought rare treasures of the countries in the Western Regions to China.

In about 50 B.C., the consul led 40000 people to attack the Anxi (located in Northeastern Iranian Plateau) in the east and was surrounded by Anxi people. The two sides fought a fierce battle, which lasted for a long time. The Anxi people suddenly waved a colorful flag, and the Romans were in a mess since they thought it was the Anxi people who got God's help, thus immediately losing their fighting spirit and countless people died in the chaos.

This was the worst badly defeated one in Roman history. The pity is that they were scared to lose, not defeated. And the bright and eye-catching military flags that suddenly appeared were made of Chinese silk.

At that time, the Romans dominated the Mediterranean, and the upper class regarded silk clothes as a symbol of wealth. Caesar loved this kind of silk very much and always wore it into the Senate. Silk became the Roman's crazy pursuit.

Even if the Romans were not in shortage of money, it was not easy for them to buy silk. Because silk transportation was a difficult and long process, it had to pass through Lop Nur, Taklimakan Desert, Pamirs, then Samarkand in Central Asia, and reach Persia before it was transported to Rome. Because Persia imposed transit tariffs, some merchants were discouraged, and the Romans had to buy silk from Persia at a higher price. To meet the demand for silk, the Romans had to tear down silk and add wool and other cheap materials into it.

Silk was always in short supply, although the Romans had traded with Anxi, Kushan, and Axumite empires. The desire for silk stimulated the traders to actively explore trade routes. According to many new archaeological discoveries, there is a prairie economic belt connected by many intermittent small business roads around the 50-degree north latitude line and in the vast grassland north of the Nile River Basin, the Two River Basin, the Indus River Basin, and the Wei River Basin. It is the prototype of the Silk Road.

At the end of the Western Han Dynasty, the Xiongnu banned the Silk Road. In 73 A.D., Ban Chao of the Eastern Han Dynasty once again connected with the Western Regions which had been blocked for about 58 years, and extended this road to Europe for the first time. The envoys of the Roman Empire also arrived at Luoyang, the capital of the Eastern Han Dynasty, along the Silk Road for the first time. It is the first recorded connection between Europe and China.

Following this road connecting Asia and Europe, Chinese products like brocade and satin were continuously transported to East Asia and Europe. Therefore, in ancient Greece and Rome, China was called Seres country, and the Chinese were called Seres people[①].

This Silk Road became the longest and most important international business road in the world at that time. Old Pliny, a writer in Rome, once said, the distant Eastern Silk country obtained raw materials for silk products in the mountains, which went through the processing of soaking and so on, then exported them to Rome, this promoted Rome to gradually respect silk clothes. He also said, "It is conservatively estimated that Indonesia, Seres, and the Arabian Peninsula can make a profit of 100 million silver coins from the Roman Empire every year by trade, which is what the women in the Roman Empire spend on luxury goods every year."

The Silk Road is like silk. Sometimes, it is a silk thread, some intermittent and some clear; sometimes, it is like a vast net, and gorgeous colors emerge from time to time.

3. The Rise and Fall of Silk Road

A large number of officials, businessmen, scholars, and travelers from all over the world came and went along the Silk Road all year round, some of them stopped in towns along the way to live and get married locally. Their lifestyles interacted with the local's, which promoted national integration and brought prosperity to countries along the way.

The Silk Road started in Chang'an and Luoyang respectively in the Western and

---

① In ancient Greek, "Seres" means "silk".

Eastern Han Dynasties, which were the economic and cultural centers of China at that time. However, no matter where the Silk Road starts, it usually meets in Zhangye and Wuwei, and then goes straight along Hexi Corridor to Dunhuang.

The Silk Road began to be divided into several branches at Dunhuang. Because after arriving here, further ahead is the Taklimakan Desert. It is unrealistic for the caravan to cross the desert and move westward. So the caravan could only walk along the edge of the desert.

Walk along the southern line of the desert, pass through ancient Yangguan, bypass the Taklimakan Desert, and pass through Shanshan, Hotan, Shache, and finally arrive at the Pamir Mountains. When people of the Han Dynasty arrived here, they saw that the Pamir Mountains were more than 7000 meters high, and the top of the ridge was straight into the sky, so they thought they had arrived at the legendary Buzhou Mountain.

Walk along the northern line of the desert, pass through Loulan, Jushi, Gaochang, Yuli, Qiuci, Gumo, and Shule, and finally arrive at Dayuan. In addition, there is another route further north, which starts from Anxi and passes through Yiwu, Tingzhou, Yili, and so on.

The Pamir Mountains is a transfer station of the ancient Silk Road, from which people can reach Europe through the Middle East. Similarly, there are three routes from the Pamir Mountains to the west, which correspond to the three routes to the east of the Pamir Mountains.

The first route is along the north coast of the Aral Sea, the Caspian Sea and the Black Sea, passing through Suyab, Taraz, and Etiel to Constantinople. The second route starts from Kashgar, crosses Fergana Valley, passes through Samarkand and Bukhara, and reaches Mashhad, where it meets the third route. The third route starts from the Pamir Mountains, passes through Kashmir to some countries like Pakistan, and can also go to Europe through Peshawar, Kabul, Mashhad, Baghdad, and Damascus.

To sum up, the countries through which the Silk Road passes mainly depend on the nature and destination of the caravan, and different routes pass through different countries. But the Silk Road, like a radiation line, extended to countries in the Middle East and Europe at that time.

The Silk Road is a "living" passage. Therefore, in different historical periods, because of the role of politics, nature, and religious beliefs, the Silk Road will choose different directions. For example, during the Northern and Southern Dynasties, the Xianbei rulers who occupied the northern part of China were not only hostile to the Southern Dynasties but also often fought against the Rouran in the north. The record of Kan's Gaochang Kingdom escorting envoys from various countries to leave the country from 474 A.D. to 475 A.D. was unearthed in Turpan, Xinjiang. A few short lines of words show that the envoys from Zihe, Yanqi in Tarim Basin, Wuqi in Northwest India, and Brahmin country in the Central India all had to go through Gaochang before going to Rouran in Mongolia Plateau. This document outlines the route of north-south and east-west exchanges in the second half of the 5th century A.D., which means that the Silk Road connecting the East Asia, North Asia, Central Asia, and South Asia was still unobstructed, despite the turbulent war times.

From Han Dynasty to Sui Dynasty, the Silk Road developed rapidly. In the Tang Dynasty, the imperial court defeated the East and West Turks, and the territory in the middle and west stretched to the periphery of Amu Darya. The prosperity of the economy and culture, coupled with the extensive and convenient connection with the Western Regions, made the trade of the ancient Silk Road reach a peak. China exported exquisite silk, porcelain, and tea to the west, while Persian silk, gold, silver wares of western countries and other products entered China.

In addition, Chinese and Western religious and culture and art also spread thanks to the Silk Road. In 627 A.D., master Xuanzang set out from Chang'an, went west along the traditional north road of the Silk Road, and finally arrived in India. Eighteen years later, with his carefully collected Buddhist scriptures, master Xuanzang once again set foot on the Silk Road and returned to his hometown. The precious historical material of the Silk Road, *The Great Tang Dynasty Record of the Western Regions*, was written by him according to what he saw and heard along the way.

4. Rejuvenate

After the Ming Dynasty, the Silk Road gradually declined. After the 15th century, the Ottoman Empire[①] developed and established a huge empire spanning Asia, Africa, and Europe. This empire controlled the important sections of the Silk Road, imposed high tariffs and monopolized silk trade, which made it very difficult for western countries to trade through the Silk Road.

European businessmen were not willing to go through this road again, but instead, carried out technological innovation to improve the level of the shipbuilding industry and maritime navigation ability. Eventually, Europe developed a navigation route that bypassed the Ottoman Empire and reached the southeast coast of China from the sea. From then on, the era of great navigation came, and the trade between the east and the west ushered in a new era. It can be said that the decline of the Silk Road is not because the Silk Road is difficult to pass through, but because there are better ways of logistics.

After the 16th century, the main passage between China and the west, which was formed in the Han Dynasty, was gradually sparsely populated, and business travel was cut off. The prosperous time was gradually submerged in the long river of time with the dancing yellow sand. The world is gradually entering a period of economic development dominated by marine trade.

After entering the 19th century, the Industrial Revolution finished in the west, the great powers rose, and western countries began to expand wildly. Countries and regions along the Silk Road were plundered and oppressed one after another. The Middle East was controlled by British and French forces, Central Asia was swallowed by Czarist Russia, and China was bullied by great powers and entered a semi-colonial and semi-feudal society. The Silk Road countries and regions were basically in a situation of poverty and backwardness.

---

① Ottoman Empire is a military feudal empire established by Ottoman Turks.

With the passage of time, the pointer of time points to the 21st century.

Because of the disputes over geopolitics, oil and gas resources, nationalities and religions, great powers were frequently caught in "tug-of-war" in Central Asia and the Middle East in the western section of the Silk Road, which made the situation complicated. Some western experts and scholars have indicated that it is a place where expectation and loss coexist, and also a place where elegance and exclusion coexist and intersect.

However, in the east of the Eurasian continent, the starting point of the Silk Road, there is dawn to change the situation in the region. China has entered the road of becoming a powerful country in the east.

In 2001, China advocated the establishment of the Shanghai Cooperation Organization. Initially, with the aim of cracking down on terrorism, separatism, and extremism, the countries made joint efforts to manage the anti-terrorism affairs in Central Asia. After that, the organization expanded its content and cooperation scope to foreign economic and trade, environmental protection, high and new technology, culture and art, culture and education, financial industry, transportation, and electricity and energy, which aimed to promote the creation of a fair, democratic and effective new international political and economic direction.

In 2013, Chinese President Xi Jinping delivered a speech in Astana, the capital of Kazakhstan, which clearly put forward the proposal that China and Central Asian countries create the Silk Road Economic Belt together. Central Asian countries actively responded to "the Belt and Road" Initiative and committed themselves to jointly establishing friendly and cooperative relations of equality, pragmatism and mutual benefit. During the implementation of "the Belt and Road" Initiative, China not only invested in oil development in Central Asia, but also brought many development funds for infrastructure and opportunities for economic and trade development. Alfred McCaughey, an American historian said, with the accelerated process of Asia-Europe-Africa economic integration, a unified "world island" centered on China began to take shape.

The past is irretrievable. Zhang Qian, who opened the trade routes to the west, Ban Chao, who gave up civilian pursuits to join the army, Xuan Zang, who learned from the west, and the Sogdian merchants who accompanied the camel bell from west to east have all become our historical memories. However, the glory of the Silk Road will not dissipate with the passage of time, on the contrary, it will increasingly show its endless charm.

China-Europe Railway Express（Photo by Zou Jingyi）

The Silk Road is not only a trade channel connecting the east and the west but also a great road to promote the development of human civilization and world history. Through this ancient path, the long history of Chinese culture, Indian culture, Arab culture, ancient Greek culture, and Roman Empire culture are interconnected, which promotes the communication between Chinese and western civilizations. The Silk Road shows the diversity and innovation of China.

In the 21st century, win-win cooperation has become the main theme of international multilateral cooperation. China's clear proposal to build the Silk Road Economic Belt has received rapid response from many countries and regions along the Silk Road. It shows China's complex of opening up to the outside world for in-depth exchanges and cooperation in Eurasian continent, and shows China's sense

148

of mission and responsibility for the cooperation and development of Asian and European countries and regions.

Oil wells, power stations, China—Europe Railway Express—a new Silk Road is unfolding in Eurasian continent. The Silk Road in the new era is glowing with its endless charm of the times.

Hanjia Granary
— The World's Number One Granary

The gate of the Hanjia Granary site protection area (Photo by Shi Yunpu)

As a populous country, food security is an important work related to the national economy and people's livelihoods in China, which has been highly valued by the government. In today's society, China still need to use huge grain reserves to meet people's production and living needs, support various state expenditures, and deal with problems such as war supply, famine relief, and sudden changes in the international market that may occur at any time. How to solve the problem of storage and circulation of grain, so as to make the storage and circulation safer and more efficient to store and circulate grain, the world's number one granary— Hanjia Granary, may give us some enlightenment.

中国物流故事 古代辑 汉英对照 STORY

1. Widely Building of Granary

"Granary" is the general name of grain warehouses in ancient China. According to *Shuowen*, "Granary is used to store grain, take the grain and put it into the granary in a hurry, so it is called granary."

Chinese granaries have different names because of their different architectural forms and various storage forms. The granaries on the ground are called Lin, Qun, and Yu, ancient Chinese People first stored grain in the form of open-air accumulation and simple houses, and later evolved into simple granaries, square granaries, and granary houses with various forms and complete functions. The granary above ground is easy to build, easy to access, and has good ventilation and moisture-proof performance, but it is limited by grain storage time. It also has to deal with the problems of fire, insects, and rat plague.

The granary below the ground is called pit and sinus. From the initial bag shape, rectangle shape, and ellipse shape, it has gradually developed into a large granary with a larger capacity, more perfect storage technology, and a more reasonable mechanical structure. Although the underground granary has higher requirements for the construction area and is not easy to access, it has a large storage capacity, which can reduce the natural damage to grain, and has lower construction cost, so it meets the demand for long-term storage of grain, therefore it became an important form of national granary in the Sui and Tang Dynasties.

In the era of Emperor Yang of the Sui Dynasty, due to the lack of materials and poor grain transport in Guanzhong, in order to meet the food needs, the capital city was moved to Luoyang, the Beijing-Hangzhou Grand Canal was built with Luoyang as the center, and large granaries including Hanjia Granary, Luokou Granary and Huiluo Granary were established along the Luo River which served as the destination and transfer station for grain transport.

Hanjia Granary was built in 605 A.D., the first year of Daye in Sui Dynasty. It was officially put into use at the end of Sui Dynasty. Its main purpose is to store grain from the states and counties in the east of the capital city. This construction was a huge project, which took tens of thousands of people at its peak of constructing time and took more than ten years to complete. Until the Zhenguan period, the granary built in Sui Dynasty was still used by the central government of Tang Dynasty.

In Sui and Tang Dynasties, granaries were widely built and formed. Two granary centers in Daxing (now Xi' an) and Luoyang were formed. At that time, there were Tai Granary and state-level transshipment granaries directly managed by the court, including Tai Granary in the Western Capital and Hanjia Granary in Luoyang. There were Zheng Granary managed by the local government and supervised by the court, Charity Granary set up by the people, Ziluo Granary to store grain, salt, and ancient coins, Ever-normal Granary[①] to stabilize food prices, as well as military granaries to store ordnance supplies.

With the development of granaries, there produced independent areas—the granary city, with walls as the boundary of outfield and granary as the unit of storage. The advent of the granary city not only meant that the granary in ancient China was moving towards maturity but also improved the safe storage of grain and formed a systematic plan for grain storage and management.

With the construction of the Grand Canal, the grain transport in Sui Dynasty developed rapidly, and the artificially built canal efficiently transported grain from the south area to the northern capital. A large number of transshipment granaries were built in Yongji Canal and Tongji Canal in Sui Dynasty, which effectively improved transportation efficiency.

Continuing the trend of Sui Dynasty, the economy of Tang Dynasty flourished and the grain production was enormous. The Hanjia Granary replaced Huiluo Granary and became the largest granary in China, which was called "the world' s number one granary" in Tang Dynasty.

In every historical period of our country, because of the cold and dry

① The granary that when the grain price is low, the state will buy grain from people at a higher price, when the grain price is high, the state will sell grain to people at a lower price thus benefiting people.

weather in north area, grain storage time was generally relatively long, so a lot of cellars had been built. In south area, due to the humid and warm climate, high groundwater level, humid soil, large grain production, and short storage time, granaries were often used to store grain.

After a long period of experience, the ancient granary has formed a complete set of construction systems and management methods, among which the technology of grain preservation is still very practical till now. In the Song and Yuan Dynasties, the granary continued to coexist on the ground and underground; in Ming and Qing Dynasties, the basic construction of granary cities entered a new period, and granaries on the ground occupied the vast majority of the proportion.

Inscribed brick unearthed from the No. 19 cellar (Photo by Zhang Bin)

2. Carry on

Hanjia Granary is not a granary, but a granary city with huge grain storage. The city not only used the terrain to reasonably arrange more than 400 cellars but also realized the transfer and storage of water and land transportation combined with the waterway. The whole granary city is divided into a living management area and a granary area. The living management area is located in the northwest of the granary city, separated from the granary area by walls in the south and east, where the management personnel and the soldiers guarding the granary city were placed.

Prior to this, Hanjia Granary was the Hanjia City in Luoyang, the eastern capital built by Emperor Yang of Sui Dynasty. With the turbulent situation in the late Sui Dynasty, Luoyang city fell into a state of chaos. The granaries outside the city were occupied by different forces. The famous Luokou Granary and Huiluo Granary became the goods of Wagang army, Liyang Granary became Dou Jiande's family property, Yongfeng Granary was the key cornerstone for Li yuan, Emperor Gao of Tang Dynasty to win the world. Great changes had taken place in the pattern of grain storage in Luoyang. Granaries outside the city were easy to be looted, and food security was at stake. Instead of helping the Sui Dynasty, these granaries filled with grain were used as powder kegs for national subjugation.

While enjoying the fruits of the Sui Dynasty, Li Shimin, Emperor Taizong of the Tang Dynasty, was keenly aware of the disadvantages of granaries outside the city. It was the safest way to accumulate a large amount of grain in the city. He decided to build granaries in Luoyang City to ensure the food supply in Luoyang City at any time and avoid repeating the mistakes of Sui Dynasty. This grain hoarding location, which was carefully planned by Li Shimin, was Hanjia Granary in the northeast corner of Luoyang.

The name "Hanjia Granary" is meaningful, which completely presents the phenomenon of prosperous Tang dynasty and the wealth of the Royal Granary.

The location of Hanjia Granary is very scientific. It is located in Hanjia City in Luoyang, close to Gonghuang City in the central city and the eastern city. From the geographical conditions, it belongs to the highest terrain area in the northeast of Luoyang, and the Valley Water, one of the four major water systems in Luoyang, runs northeast. The groundwater level in the north of Luoyang city

中国物流故事 STORY 古代辑 汉英对照

is relatively low, which is a key factor for the construction of large and medium—sized granaries. At the same time, due to the vertical characteristics of the loess in the north of Luoyang, the stability of cellar is enhanced, which is very suitable for digging cellar.

As an important node of the transportation network, Hanjia Granary not only supplied grain to Luoyang City, but also transported grain to Chang' an to the west, and also had the duty of storage and transfer, which played the role of the transshipment station between Guandong and Guanzhong. The grain was transported to the city by ships through artificial channels and then transported to Luoyang by land transportation. Moreover, in the southeast of granary city, there was a relic of the grain transport wharf, and the Valley Water was connected with the Chan River and the Cao Canal to the east, so the water transport was also convenient and smooth, which was very convenient for ships.

The distribution of cellars of Hanjia Granary (Image source: CCTV's "Exploration and Discovery" program)

Based on archaeological excavation and literature records, it could be inferred that there were four gates in Hanjia City: to the north is Deyou Gate, to the south is Hanjia Gate, to the west is Cangzhong Gate, and to the east is Cangdong Gate. Hanjia City was built with stocky and tall city walls, with a bottom width of about 17 meters, an upper width of 11.3 meters. The city was divided upward, and the section of the city wall was trapezoidal, which was made of rammed earth and had very high safety performance.

3. Standard Configuration

After the Mid Tang Dynasty, the increasing population in Chang' an formed a great population pressure. During this period, the frequent floods and droughts in the vicinity of Chang' an posed a serious threat to the food problem of millions of people in Chang' an, and the grain supply was increasingly tense.

At this time, Chang' an still mainly relied on land transportation, by carriage transportation, the transportation capacity was extremely limited, and each carriage could only transport about 600 Jin of grain. The explosion of population and the deterioration of the environment caused the eastward movement of the Tang Dynasty regime, which promoted Luoyang to become a new political and economic center.

Luoyang is not far from Chang' an, but the threat of drought to Luoyang is lower than to Chang' an. Luoyang has a good waterland transportation network, the Grand Canal, which is a bridge connecting the land Silk Road and the maritime Silk Road, and also the fate line of ancient China to transport materials. Luoyang was the only intersection of the land Silk Road and the Grand Canal. It brought the north and south together. The grain produced in the south of the Yangtze River can reach Luoyang by water. The shipbuilding technology of the Tang Dynasty could meet the requirement that each ship could transport more than 500000 Dan of grain, which was beyond the carriage' s reach.

Therefore, from the period of Empress Wu Zetian in Tang Dynasty, Hanjia Granary became the "Tai Granary" in the true sense, and the grain from all over the country continuously gathered here through the Grand Canal.

The main types of grain stored in Hanjia Granary were millet and rice. According to historical records, in the eighth year of Tianbao of Emperor Xuanzong of Tang Dynasty (749 A.D.), the total amount of grain stored in the main large granaries in China was 12656620 Dan, and Hanjia Granary accounted for 5833400 Dan, accounting for nearly 1/2 of the total, so it was known as "the world's number one granary".

The situation of Hanjia Granary is very neat, similar to a rectangular frame, with four walls. It is about 615 meters from east to west, 725 meters from north to south, the wall is 15~17 meters wide and 1~6.5 meters high, with a total area of 430000 square meters. There are more than 400 cellars in the city, which are arranged in rows from east to west and from north to south. There is a certain distance between the cellars, which are arranged in rows and regularly, accounting for more than half of the area of the city. The paths are crisscrossed. On the about two-meter-wide road, the ruts left by the two wheelers and mono-cycles are still vivid. The minimum diameter of the cellar of the cellar is about 8 meters and the depth is 6 meters, and the maximum diameter of the cellar is about 18 meters and the depth is 12 meters. The plane of the cellar is circular, and the profile structure is also large at the top and small at the bottom. There are different sizes of cellars, the smallest one can store thousands of Dan of grain, and the largest one can store from thousands to ten thousand Dan of grain.

The first step in building the cellar is to dig a pit, that is, firstly, dig an annular foundation groove from the ground, then tamp the foundation groove to form a solid pit mouth, and then dig a round cylinder-shaped pit with a big mouth and a small bottom. The sectional shape with the big top and the small bottom is not only easy to dig, but also makes the cellar firmer. When carrying out waterproof and moisture-proof work in the middle and later periods, the operation is also more convenient.

The bottom of the cellar is mostly flat, and there is an arc-shaped ditch close to the cellar wall. One end of the ditch is high and the other end is low. The high end is flat with the cellar bottom, which can make the small amount of rainwater seeping from the cellar top flow into the ditch after reaching the cellar bottom, so as to ensure the dryness of the cellar.

After the cellar is excavated, lay a layer of dry soil on the bottom of the cellar[①], and then tamp it. This can not only increase the firmness, but also increase the density of the soil, so that the moisture is not easy to rise. In addition, it is necessary to burn the bottom of the cellar hard, and then spread a mixture of braised soil fragments, black ash, and other stuff as a moisture-proof layer, then cover wooden boards or overlapped boards mixed with wooden boards and straw rolls on it. In addition, the mixture of Hanjia Granary is also smeared with a layer of compounds consisting of broken slag soil, broken coal cinders, embers, and blenders.

It can be observed from the wooden remains left at the bottom of the cellar of Hanjia Granary that it was a common practice to lay wooden boards to prevent moisture, but the arrangement and combination of wooden boards didn't follow the same form, and the laying methods and sizes of wooden boards were different.

According to *Tian Sheng Ling*, at the bottom of the cellar, straws were laid with a thickness of five feet(about 167 centimeters). On the straws, two layers of bundled straws were laid and straws were also laid on the walls of the cellar. Where large bundles of straw were used, several bundles of straw were also used to block the gap. After laying double straw, there were covered with one layer of straw mats, this was the way to store grain.

When the grain was put in, the information such as the total amount of grain, the date of storage, and the name of the operator must be recorded on the inscribed brick, and then covered with straw mats. Spread five feet of soil above the straw mat, and then spread double-layer straw on it. After that, dig and fill seven feet (about 233 centimeters) of soil to close it, and erect wooden signs to

① According to archaeological records, the thickness of the soil in each cellar of Hanjia Granary is different, normally 2~4 centimeters.

describe the corresponding information, so that granary officials can search and evaluate the situation anytime and anywhere.

4. Optimization

During the excavation of Hanjia Granary, Bafang inscribed bricks were unearthed from three cellars No. 19, No. 50, and No. 182. The bricks were square and polished on the front. The contents of the bricks included the name of the granary, the location of the cellar, the source of the grain, the variety of the grain, the quantity of the grain, the date of entering the cellar, the mode of transportation, and the names of the officials who handle the grain. The discovered inscribed brick, combined with the literature records, reveals that the grain storage in Hanjia Granary has reached the degree of institutionalization and scientization.

Inscribed brick played a role similar to an account book. When taking grain from the cellar, the inscribed bricks would be taken out together and reviewed. If there was a big difference between the grain stored in the cellar and the figures on the inscribed brick, the management personnel would be held accountable.

The excavated inscribed bricks were all discovered in the backfill soil at or near the bottom of the cellar. These inscribed bricks were put into the cellar together with grain and discarded after the grain was taken out of the cellar. This system of laying inscribed bricks and monuments is the product of the great development of underground grain storage in the Sui and Tang Dynasties. It is also a new and effective management system invented by people constantly summing up the advantages and disadvantages of the past underground grain storage management. It also has a great reference role in modern storage.

It can be seen from the inscribed bricks unearthed from Hanjia Granary that Hanjia Granary is managed by districts. This regionalization management is convenient for the number identification and location check of cellars, so as to facilitate the management of grain.

On the basis of doing a good job in cellar storage, the storage period of different kinds of grain in different storage environments was clearly defined in Hanjia Granary, for example, according to *The New Book of Tang*: "The storage period is five years for millet and three years for rice in the wet environment" ; even considering the difference of actual storage time caused by different transportation distance, "with the same time, far first and then near" , that is to optimize the storage time of granary by considering the storage period of grain.

In addition, Hanjia Granary also considered replacing the old with the new to preserve the grain for a long time. According to *Tang Liu Dian*, "Millet can be stored for nine years, and rice and hybrids can be stored for three years" .

The structure of the cellar of Hanjia Granary (Wang Xu)

5. Baptism

With the fully enclosed storage method, after being stored once the grain was taken out, all storage steps would be destroyed. It can be seen that the grain in the cellar was not often used, but as a long-term reserve. Once all the grain was stored, it would basically maintain this state for a short period of time.

This method has been confirmed in *Tang Liu Dian*, when taking grain out of the cellar, only after the grain in one cellar is completely exhausted can another cellar be opened. When putting grain into the cellar, it also needs to fill one cellar and close it before opening and installing the next cellar.

In order to prolong the storage time of grain, the top of the cellar must be sealed by tamping and compacting after being filled with grain, so as to reduce the air residue between grain particles. Cover the grain with a mat, then pad the mat with chaff with a thickness of 40~60 centimeters, and then add another mat to the chaff. The method of sandwiching chaff in mats can isolate moisture and keep warm, and prevent grain from heating, sprouting, and rotting. Then seal the cellar with loess into a conical roof, which totally looks like a hill.

In ancient times without advanced pesticides and preservatives, it was these effective measures that, on the one hand, made bacteria and insects unable to survive and reproduce in the cellar, made the seeds basically dormant without metabolism; on the other hand, without the heat of seed metabolism, the cellar could keep low temperature continuously, which ensured a dry, low-temperature and anoxic storage environment in the cellar, thus forming a stable environment benign circle.

The walls and top of the cellar were made of incombustible materials, which would not cause fire under normal conditions. The top of the cellar completely depends on the grain to make self-close. Its fully closed state is conducive to the prevention and control of insects. In the construction, Hanjia Granary follows the principles of low cost, high efficiency, and practicality. All kinds of dismantled materials can be reused.

The No. 160 cellar of Hanjia Granary was still sealed when it was excavated, and there was about 500000 Jin of grain in it. After more than 1400 years of baptism, about half of the millet in the cellar had become moldy and carbonized, but the degree of carbonization was different. Millet was divided into three colors according to the depth of accumulation layer, the upper layer was light brown, the middle layer was brown, and the bottom layer was black.

In 1969, by chance, fifteen "tomb-shaped buildings" were discovered on the north side of Luoyang Old Town during the construction of Jiaozhi Railway.

Archaeologists unanimously thought that they were octagonal tombs in the Western Zhou Dynasty. It was not until the inscribed bricks were found near the bottom that people suddenly realized that this is the famous Hanjia Granary.

When archaeologists carefully dug the surface soil, these carbonized grains were detected by instruments, and it was found that there was still much organic matter in rice. What is more surprising is that some particles found in the wall of the cellar sprouted on the third day after being taken out, and were sent to the Luoyang Academy of Agricultural Sciences for cultivation. In the second year, they even grew to knee height and produced fruit.

Storage of grain in cellar and digging ground for pits were the methods that Chinese ancient laborers created in the long-term social practice of production and manufacturing. As far back as the Yangshao culture period, people used bag-shaped cellars with small mouths and large bottoms to store grain, and they knew to dry the bottom with fire.

The No.160 cellar of Hanjia Granary site (Photo by Zhang Bin)

In Sui and Tang Dynasties, the ancestors' working experience was continuously summed up, the structure of cellars was improved, and the way of storing grain in large and medium-sized cellars was created. The grain cellar at this time was not a bag cellar with a small mouth and a big bottom, nor a vertical cellar with a slightly equal size, but a cylinder cellar with a big mouth and a small bottom. This kind of cellar can disperse the weight pressure of grain around the cellar according to the distribution of wood boards, thus relieving the load of wood boards of the next layer.

6. Closing

People regard food as their prime want, and grain is a top priority for food. Grain, as a special commodity, is the foundation of the country in both ancient China society and modern society.

As an important place to reserve war materials and national strength, Hanjia Granary played a very important role in the prosperity and stability of the Tang Dynasty. However, the Tang Dynasty was in great danger at its peak. After the An-Shi Rebellion, with the gradual decrease of the flow of the Grand Canal and the poor management of grain transport, Hanjia Granary also ushered in a huge turning point. Luoyang City, which lost its important political status, gradually declined in the late Tang Dynasty, and Hanjia Granary, which witnessed the prosperity of the Tang Dynasty, gradually lost its important position, making it difficult to reproduce the prosperity of the past.

After the capital of Song Dynasty was established in Bianjing (Now Kaifeng in Henan Province), grain from Jiang, Huai, Hu, and Zhe was transported to Kaifeng every year through Bian river. As a result, the influence of Luoyang's grain transport gradually decreased, and Hanjia Granary was gradually ignored, and finally withdrew from the stage of history. Many ancient people's construction experience and management skills on Hanjia Granary have been used till today, and the civilization and wisdom are worthy of further study and thinking.

Today, Hanjia Granary, as a key site of the Grand Canal, has entered the global historical and cultural heritage list. Looking back on the past, Hanjia Granary has a miraculous scale and storage. It writes about the glory of a nation and reveals the details of the ancient dynasty. What it stores is not only the grain that is full of people's hard work but also the ambition of a country.

Grain is the material condition of economic development, social stability, and national security. The management mode and rules and regulations of its logistics and storage have been highly valued by China, a large agricultural country with a large population.

Today, in the era of globalization, all countries can obtain their own resources in short supply from other countries through international trade. However, with Various uncertain factors, China's grain imports have also been affected to a certain extent, and the emergency characteristics of grain storage management are more obvious. This requires managers to pay more attention, think deeply about the problems existing in the original model, and optimize and innovate in combination with practical work, so as to improve the efficiency of grain storage management.

"Uniform wheelbase"

—Logistics Standardization that Has Been Practiced for Thousands of Years

The Portrait of Qin Shi Huang in *Sancai Tuhui*

There is an endless stream of vehicles on the street, roads and viaducts crisscross, buses, taxis, private cars and school buses shuttle, bicycles, tricycles and electric vehicles drive slowly, vehicles go their own ways, and the traffic is busy and orderly, all of this is thanks to scientific traffic rules and modern traffic indicating equipments. In ancient times, without modern traffic command systems and intelligent navigation, how could roads play an effective role?

1. Introduction

According to *Records of the Historian*, more than 4000 years ago, there have been records of ancient people riding a carriage in China, that is, the roads for vehicles in Xia Dynasty have taken shape. In the Zhou Dynasty, roads were built for people to use. *The Book of Songs* mentioned that "The roads in the Zhou Dynasty are smooth and unimpeded" and "Service cars with large trunks are running on the road", which described the flat and straight roads in Zhou Dynasty. And China's radial transportation network has begun to show its scale. The Zhou Dynasty built wide and flat "Zhou Road" to connect Haojing, the capital, and the states. At the same time, the official "Yelushi" was set up to manage the roads from the capital to various places, organize the maintenance of vehicles, and level off the roads to ensure they are smooth and safe. During the Zhou Dynasty, strict grade standards were set for transportation: the emperor took a carriage with six horses, while the princes could only take a carriage with five horses. The lower the grade, the fewer horses. This is the earliest perfect road system in world road history.

In this ancient road system, not only perfect national roads to major states were built to ensure the road infrastructure, but also special traffic management agencies were set up with professional management personnel and management systems. Each department and personnel of the traffic management organization performed their respective duties, and managed and implemented the procurement of means of transport (horses and vehicles), vehicle manufacturing, vehicle transportation and overall transportation. However, the unified standard of transportation, character and moral standards in Zhou Dynasty became an ideal state after the split and scuffle in the Spring and Autumn Period and the Warring States Period, and the development of all regions deviated.

Driving obstacles caused by nonuniform tracks

During the Spring and Autumn Period and the Warring States Period, the sizes of vehicles in each state were different, and the wheelbases were also different. And one state's vehicles were only suitable for riding in that country. When cross-border long-distance riding occurred, it was difficult to ride on the track that had been formed for a long time because the specifications of foreign vehicles were different from those of local vehicles. For example, when a person from the state of Qin drives to the state of Zhao, he has to change to the carriage of the state of Zhao as soon as he arrives at the boundary of the state of Zhao, because the wheels of the carriage of the state of Qin can't fit into the track of the state of Zhao.

There are two reasons for this situation. First, the technical exchanges between states were not intensive. Second, during the period of seven states striving for supremacy, chariots were the most common armament in the army. When manufacturing vehicles, all states had a set of unique standards for the wheelbase, thus forming a fixed track in their own territory, which was convenient for local vehicles to drive and prevented foreign chariots from entering. "Different track for vehicles" , when enemy vehicles entered the state, traffic obstacles would occur because the wheelbase didn't adapt to the track. This is also a way for states to use track defense intentionally to stop other states from invading.

All this changed after Qin Shi Huang unified the six states. After Qin Shi Huang unified China, he wanted to build a unified empire. However, different states had different standards for the track, which seriously affected the development of transportation and hindered the country's economic development.

At that time, Qin Shi Huang had just conquered the other six states, the world had just been unified, and the 515 yearlong split situation had just ended. He abandoned the original fortifications of the six states, confiscated all the military weapons and began to unify the different wheelbases, which was called "the uniform wheelbase" . According to *Records of the Historian*, the number of six is the standard, Fu and berretta are six Cun, the wheelbase should be six Chi, with six Chi as one step, and a carriage should be driven by six horses.

Qin Shi Huang abolished the Feudalism and promoted the system of prefectures and counties[1]. The riding grade system implemented in Zhou Dynasty was also abolished, and the carriage in the world was unified and standardized— "The wheelbase is six Chi, with six Chi as one step", that is to say, the wheelbase of the vehicle was changed to six Chi, so that the distance between the two wheels was the same.

The sizes and specifications of vehicles were the same all over the country. Whether they were pulled by six horses or four horses, the widths of the vehicles were the same, and the standards of axles and wheels were the same, so it was convenient and fast to replace any damaged parts. The use of "uniform wheelbase" greatly improved the transportation efficiency of the army and commercial forces. "Uniform wheelbase" enabled Qin to have an efficient army, which ensured the security and operation of the unified empire economically and militarily.

Qin Shi Huang promoted the standardization of carriage in the world with "uniform wheelbase", which ensured the most effective operation of the national economy and military, thus laying a solid foundation for long-term stability. The function of traffic had changed from defense to trade and cultural exchange, and the nationwide "uniform wheelbase" promoted the development of national logistics.

2. Promotion

As early as the Zhou Dynasty, there was the cognition of "uniform wheelbase", but it was not until the Qin Dynasty that it was promoted and implemented as a standard. According to *Records of the Historian*, "Uniform measuring tools should be used when weighing goods, the wheelbase of the carriage should be uniform, and the same characters should be used when writing". The decree of "uniform wheelbase", which was implemented by Qin Shi Huang throughout the country, is of great

① A local administrative system (similar to the present administrative division) of counties led by prefectures almost prevailed throughout the whole feudal era.

significance to guarantee political stability, and promote economic development and cultural prosperity.

Ancient wheels were all made of wood, which was very hard and heavy. The friction between the wheels and the ground caused the wooden wheels to wear rapidly so that their service life was short. In order to reduce the friction between the wheels and the ground, and make the wheels more durable, the makers made the wheels narrower and put a layer of iron around the wooden wheels, which was called an iron cage in historical records. In this way, the wheels were not only durable, but also ran briskly.

The wheels had been rolling on the mud road and the flagstone road over the years, due to the effect of gravity and friction, two deep wheel grooves had formed on the road, which was called the track.

When the vehicle is driving on the rugged road, if the wheels are pressed into two tracks, the carriage and ox cart will be more labor-saving, faster, and more stable in long-distance transportation. During long-distance transportation, when the wheels are running on the hard tracks, the vehicle can move more stably, which can significantly reduce the consumption of animal power and axle wear, so as to reduce the transportation cost. On the contrary, if the wheel does not press into the track, it will be bumpy, laborious, and slow.

Front of the Copper Carriage (Image source : Emperor Qin Shi Huang's Mausoleum Site Museum)

Wheels wrapped in iron sheets

If the vehicle ran out of track, it would face great risks. Once "get off the track", it would "get into the track" again. The light ones were just bumping, and the heavy ones might have accidents such as tilting or even overturning the vehicle. When there was a track matching the wheelbase standard on the road, the vehicle ran along the track, and the wheels were confined in the track, so the vehicle could run smoothly and efficiently. When the groove marks on the road were deep to a certain extent, a track gully was formed, which had a certain fixing effect on the running wheels, which was the "track" in "uniform wheelbase". The significance of "uniform wheelbase" for ancient transportation lies in: the tracks of the whole country were unified, which means that the tracks rolled out by vehicles across the country were all six Chi wide, and the vehicles, horses, and related resources can be mobilized at will. Its influence didn't fade out people's vision until the appearance of rubber tires in the 20th century.

In order to protect the pavement and improve the use efficiency of the road, Qin Shi Huang not only promulgated the decree of "uniform wheelbase", but also limited the specifications of the carriage. He required the car to be six Chi wide (about 1.4 meters) and the number of spokes of the wheels to be 30. At the same time, he made a unified specification for the size of the carriage and the standard of using the vehicle in the whole country.

The tracks of ancient post road (Photo by Shan Xin)

The width of the track is equal when the wheelbase of vehicle is the same, and "uniform wheelbase" was actually a measure of road standardization. With this standardization, the Qin Dynasty took ten years to form a national traffic trunk line with Xianyang as the center, a highway for the emperor as the main route and radiating to all directions, which met the needs of army mobilization, intelligence transmission, and transportation of civil engineering materials in the whole country.

The unification of wheelbase not only realized the convenient passage of vehicles on the transportation network extending in all directions, but also realized the standardization of vehicles. The body of the chariot and its parts unearthed from the tomb of Qin Shi Huang in China showed a high degree of normalization, standardization and systematization. There were more than 3000 parts of bronze chariots and horses unearthed from the pit. Similar parts had the same structure and size, and are commonly used. The number of spokes of the wheels was 30, which was the same as the number of wooden spokes unearthed from the Terracotta Warriors Pit, which conformed to the "30 spokes to symbolize the sun and the moon" in *Kao Gong Ji*. The specifications of vehicles manufactured in strict accordance with the production process standards were highly consistent, the machining dimensions of parts were accurate, and the values were close to the modern series of preferred numbers. The efficiency of transportation of vehicles and horses and allocation of parts in the whole country was improved, which realized the mass production of vehicles, and was conducive to the maintenance and replacement of vehicle parts, and formed the "standard system" in Qin Dynasty.

The strategic power can reach wherever the road for traffic is made ready. Whether for war or trade, it should begin with the transport. Qin Shi Huang understood this truth more than 2000 years ago.

"Uniform wheelbase" was an important strategic measure after the unification of Qin state, which made unified and standardized planning for the national infrastructure, especially the road construction. In fact, the reason why Qin Shi Huang required "uniform wheelbase" was closely related to another large-scale construction project of the Qin Dynasty, that is, highway for the emperor[1].

The realization of unimpeded and efficient transportation requires not only standardized means of transportation, but also developed road networks. On the premise of vehicle standardization, Qin Shi Huang built a road network extending to all directions on the basis of renovating the existing complicated traffic routes, which greatly promoted the development of land transportation and the political, economic, and cultural exchanges in various regions.

In the second year of the unification of the Qin Dynasty, Qin Shi Huang ordered the construction of highway for the emperor with Xianyang as the center and radiating to all directions. Highway for the emperor means high-speed road. On the basis of the existing old roads, Qin Shi Huang took Xianyang as the center, " dredge the river and build the highway for the emperor" , built the trunk line connecting major cities, formed the transportation network at the central level, radiated to the surrounding areas with the central cities as the origin, and built and completed the nationwide transportation network. All parts of the country were connected by highway for the emperor and its branch road

---

① Highway for the emperor is the earliest "national road" in Chinese history, which began in Qin Dynasty.

network, which made the exchanges between different regions more convenient and promoted economic exchanges and development.

Greening was carried out on both sides of highway for the emperor, with trees planted in a unified way. The road formed three lanes for people to walk on both sides and the emperor to use in the middle. This transportation network became the foundation of logistics roads and nodes in Han Dynasty, Sui and Tang Dynasties, and some road lines are still in use today.

Highway for the emperor could not only run horses, but also had a large number of tracks for vehicles, which was the "railway network" of Qin State. The unification of wheelbase is the foundation of "railway network" construction. The "uniform wheelbase" initiative of the Qin Empire formed the main national traffic trunk line with Xianyang as the center, highway for the emperor as the main route and radiating to all directions. In addition, the Direct Road leading to Jiuyuan in the north was also a remarkable national defense project at that time.

3. About Modern Logistics

3.1 Road System

The development of China's ancient road system was driven by political, military, economic, and cultural needs. The road traffic network began to sprout in the Spring and Autumn Period, and a convenient and efficient traffic network was built in Qin and Han Dynasties, and a system of post communication system and overall management of transportation affairs was formed. The Han Dynasty followed the road administration system of chariots and horses in the Qin Dynasty, and expanded the site to a wider area. Since then, the prosperity and development of economy and trade have given birth to various modes of logistics transportation and laid a foundation for the development of private transportation. In Chinese history, different dynasties were influenced by their political background, transportation systems and economic development levels, and the scale of transportation network was different. But on the whole, China's highway transportation capacity was constantly improving, the transportation scale was increasing, and the road system was gradually mature and systematic. At the end of the 12^{ed} Five Year Plan, the total mileage of China's comprehensive transportation network reached about 5 million kilometers, and the operating mileage of high-speed railways, expressways, urban rail transit and the number of port berths ranked first in the world.

3.2 "Uniform Wheelbase" in Railway

In the 19th century, due to the different railway technology and topography in different regions, and in order to prevent the inflow of agricultural and industrial products from other regions, there were at least 9 kinds of tracks in North America, which made it difficult for trains to travel on different tracks.

In 1937, the International Railway Union stipulated 1435 millimeters as the standard gauge, which promoted the overall development of the railway, made the existing railway realize its maximum application, and gave full play to the advantages of continuity of railway transportation. At present, China and most European countries adopt the standard gauge, Japan and African countries adopt the narrow gauge, and Russia and some Central Asian regions adopt the wide gauge. China mainly uses a standard gauge, but Yunnan still has meter gauge[1] in operation. China's mining enterprises have their own railways, and most of them use gauges other than standard gauge; the width of the railway built by Japan in Taiwan, China is 1067 millimeters, while the width of the sugar industry railway in Taiwan and the forest railway in Ali Mountain is 762 millimeters.

International railway freight transportation is a kind of transportation mode second only to ocean transportation. Most of the import and export goods of ocean transportation rely on railway transportation for distribution. In recent years, China has also opened the international railway inter modal transport business of the New Eurasian Continental Bridge from Lianyungang to Rotterdam, Netherlands. In international rail transport, goods must be reset

---

[1] The meter gauge with a gauge of 1 meter (1000 millimeters), which is still used in France, Vietnam, Myanmar, Malaysia, and so on.

at the border between the two countries before cross-border, transport can be realized since the track gauges are different. For example, for trains from China to Russia, every time they leave the country, they need to replace the bogies in the wheelhouse of Erenhot station in China.

In the 1920s to 1930s, Yan Xishan[1] built Tongpu railway with self-raised funds in Shanxi Province. This railway starts from Datong in the north and ends at Fenglingdu in the south of Puzhou town in Yongji City in the south, with a total length of more than 800 kilometers. It can be called a north-south railway trunk line running through the middle of Shanxi Province. At that time, the economy of Shanxi was backward, and the construction of railway was naturally beneficial to people's livelihoods. However, due to the narrow-gauge design of Tongpu railway, trains from other provinces could not enter Shanxi. Later generations have different opinions about the narrow-gauge railway. Some think that this practice closed the province to the outside world, while others think that it is economical. However, the narrow-gauge railway limits the railway freight transport capacity and economic exchanges with other provinces. From this story, we can see that the unified "standard" has great contributions to promoting the development of culture, economy, and even the whole society.

3.3 Standardization of Logistics

The Qin Dynasty enacted the decree of "uniform wheelbase" , which made vehicles all over the country unified and standardized, and standardized road traffic provided a guarantee for transportation. Roads are suitable for vehicles, which reduced the transportation costs of goods and military supplies, and at the same time greatly improved the material transportation efficiency of the army and caravan and the transmission speed of government decrees. "Uniform wheelbase" is the first national technical standard for means of transportation in ancient China, which is similar to the modern logistics standard in China. It stipulated the basic standards such as the

---

① Yan Xishan (1883-1960), born in Wutai, Shanxi Province, was an important political and military figure in the Republic of China.

size and specification of the carriage; specified technical standards for the dimensions and materials of parts "the wheelbase is six Chi" "make the vehicle individually, and when it is used, it can match the track on the road" ; stipulated the operation standards of "taking six Chi as one step a car is driven by six horses" , as well as the road use and road management standards. The standardizations of roads and tracks are of great significance to the development of transportation in Qin Dynasty and the formation and development of the national common economy.

"Uniform wheelbase" is of great significance to the development of modern logistics standardization in China. Logistics standardization is to formulate unified standards in all aspects of the logistics industry for reference, so as to improve the current situation of "different tracks and different characters" in the logistics industry. Modern logistics standards also stipulate roads, vehicles and equipment. In addition, the basic general logistics standards stipulate equipment such as containers and pallets; the public logistics standard specifies several categories, including logistics facilities and equipment, logistics technology, operation and management and logistics information and so on; there are professional logistics standards such as agricultural and sideline products, food cold chain logistics and automobile logistics.

It can be said that the development of the modern logistics industry is based on logistics standardization, and the mature logistics standardization system guarantees the high-quality development of logistics industry. On the one hand, the logistics standardization improves the working efficiency of the industry and saves resources. On the other hand, the logistics standardization in our country integrates with international standards which can enhance the competitiveness of Chinese logistics enterprises in the international logistics market. Frequent international trade and exchanges accelerate the development of logistics industry. The realization of efficient international logistics depends on the internationalization of logistics standards. The consistency of domestic logistics standards and international logistics standards is conducive to the convergence of goods transportation, promoting international economic and technological exchanges and cooperation, and improving the quality and efficiency of logistics services. Especially in the background of "the Belt and Road", logistics standardization will be an important link and basic guarantee.

Modern logistics standards are more comprehensive, scientific and standardized. It takes logistics as a large system, and formulates work and technical standards in different fields and systems, such as transportation, warehousing, distribution, circulation, processing, packaging, loading and unloading and information management, and forms a national and international standardization system to realize the cooperation between logistics system and other related systems.

4. Ending

In 2016, the opening ceremony of the 39th International Organization for Standardization was held. President Xi Jinping sent a congratulatory letter: "Standards are the fruits of human civilization progress. From ancient China's 'uniform wheelbase, unified character' to modern industrial scale production, they are all vivid practices of standardization. With the in-depth development of economic globalization, standardization plays an increasingly prominent role in facilitating economic and trade exchanges, supporting industrial development, promoting scientific and technological progress and standardizing social governance. Standards have become the 'universal language' in the world. The world needs the coordinated development of standards, and standards promote the interconnection of the world".

The quotation "uniform wheelbase, unified character" by President Xi Jinping is aimed to explain the important role of standardization, which is reflected in promoting economic and trade exchanges, supporting industrial development, promoting scientific and technological progress, and standardizing social governance. This "standardization" is particularly important for the sustainable and efficient development of modern logistics industry.

Since the reform and opening up, China's standardization has developed rapidly with the progress of the times. In recent years, China has significantly enhanced its comprehensive national strength and has developed rapidly in the cause of standardization. China has constantly contributed to China's wisdom and offered Chinese plans for the construction of global economic system, and has made every effort to "community of human destiny".

中国物流故事 STORY 古代辑 汉英对照

Zheng He's Voyages to the West

— Milestone of Human Civilization in the Era of Great Navigation

Commemorative stamp for *The 600th Anniversary of Zheng He's Voyage to the West* (Small sheet) (Designed by Cui Yanwei, edge decorated by Wang Huming)

The sea, mysterious and moody, makes people fear and yearn for it. Since ancient times, Chinese people have never stopped exploring the ocean. Generation after generation, our ancestors sailed to the sea again and again. And the yearning for the sea cannot be blocked by danger. More than 600 years ago in China, a fleet was sailing, and it was about to create a miracle in the history of world navigation. The leader of this huge fleet is Zheng He.

1. Origin

In 1398, Zhu Yuanzhang, the Ming Emperor, died, and the throne was passed to his eldest grandson Zhu Yunwen, whose era name of the reign was

Jianwen, and was called Emperor Jianwen and Huizong of Ming Dynasty. Before his death, Zhu Yuanzhang had enfeoffed the princes to various places for the reasons of "strengthening the border defense and defending the royal family" , and the power of the princes became increasingly huge. In order to weaken the power of the princes and consolidate the imperial power, Emperor Jianwen began to plot with Qi Tai, Huang Zicheng, and other trusted ministers to weaken the vassals. In the first year of Jianwen (1399), the king of Zhou, the king of Dai and the king of Qi were demoted to common people, and the king of Xiang was killed.

The king of Yan (Zhu Di, the fourth son of Zhu Yuanzhang) guarded Peiping and had the strongest power. Emperor Jianwen transferred the elite troops of the king of Yan to weaken his power in the name of border defense. The king of Yan knew that he was doomed, so he dispatched troops in the name of "Clear the disloyal people around the king, and pacify the war within the country" . Since then, the battle for imperial power broke out, which was called Jingnan Campaign. Zhu Di led the Yan army to occupy the capital, and the country changed hands. Zhu Di succeeded to the throne and was called Chengzu of the Ming Dynasty. His era name of the reign was Yongle. Emperor Jianwen disappeared in the palace fire and his whereabouts became a mystery.

According to historical records, Zheng He's ancestor was a nobleman in Bukhara, Central Asia, who served as Pingzhang of Yunnan Province in the early Ming Dynasty and was later named Xianyang King. His great-grandfather used to be Zhongshu Pingzhang, and his father was named Yanghou in Yunnan.

Zheng He's yearning for the ocean and long journey originated from his grandfather and father' s experience, who believed in Islam and had visited many countries and cities, such as Mecca (Holy Land of Islam). They were very familiar with foreign cities and countries and told Zheng He what they saw, heard and felt. Therefore, Zheng He planted a seed of longing for a long journey in his heart.

In the 15th year of Hongwu (1382), the army of the Ming Dynasty launched a unified war against the forces of the king of Liang in Yunnan. The army of the Ming was overwhelming and the king of Liang was defeated. Eleven-year-old Zheng He was taken to Nanjing as a prisoner and was castrated as a eunuch. In the 17th year of Hongwu, Zheng He was assigned to serve in the palace of the king of Yan. During this period, he was deeply liked by the king because of his excellent qualities, such as intelligence, diligence, studiousness and caution, and stayed as a personal bodyguard. After that, with his talent and leadership gradually revealed, Zheng He began to show up prominently and became the trusted person of the prince. During the Campaign of Jingnan, Zheng He fought with Zhu Di, and made many achievements. Especially in the battle of Zhengcunba, Zheng He and Zhu Di successfully broke the seven battalions of soldiers and horses under the command of General Li Jinglong, which made this battle a key to the winning of the Campaign of Jingnan.

In 1402, Zhu Di ascended the throne, and Zheng He was promoted to be an official and eunuch. It is said that Zhu Di gave Zheng He the surname "Zheng" in order to commemorate his credit in the battle of Zhengcunba. Zheng He became one of the most trusted eunuchs of Zhu Di.

In the last years of Hongwu, after decades of hard work, the Ming Dynasty became rich and peaceful. After Zhu Di ascended the throne, the emperor with great talents set a bright tone for the Ming Dynasty. The economy continued to grow and the culture continued to prosper. Under the rule of Zhu Di, who was born to like grand plans, *The Yongle Canon*, an ancient encyclopedia, was compiled. The Grand Canal connecting the north and the south was dredged. The Forbidden City, the largest palace group in the world, was built, and his political and military achievements reached the peak. According to *The History of Ming Dynasty*: "His military achievements are comparable to those of Zhu Yuanzhang. He sent troops to pacify the northern desert area. In his later years, his fame spread far and wide, and neighboring countries surrendered to the Ming Dynasty, with more than 30 countries paying tribute to the Ming Dynasty. The territory is vast, far exceeding the Han and Tang Dynasties. His political and military achievements are unprecedented."

Zheng He's voyages to the west were an important part of Zhu Di's grand plan.

As for the reasons for the voyages to the west, it is recorded in *The History of Ming Dynasty* that "Chengzu suspected that Emperor Hui had died overseas, and he wanted to find him, and show off his troops in the foreign land to show that China was rich and strong". In the view of historians, it is an important reason why Emperor Yongle sent Zheng He many times to the west to search for the suspected missing Jianwen Emperor. However, Zhu Di, the emperor of the Ming Dynasty, who prides himself on Yongle Emperor, probably cared more about "showing China's prosperity and strength by showing off his troops in the foreign land".

At that time, a royal edict to Zheng He by the Ming Emperor Chengzu said, You should make my (Ming Chengzu) intention clear to the whole world, what's my intention? It is people of all ages who could live their lives. In other words, Ming Chengzu wanted all people to live a good life. From this point of view, carrying out overseas trade, showing prosperity, spreading the civilization of the Ming Dynasty, and showing the majesty of the emperor through Zheng He's fleet may be Zhu Di's real purpose.

2. Climax

On June 15, 1405, the Liujia Port in Taicang, Suzhou was very busy. At the confluence of Liu river and Yangtze River, colorful flags were flying and gongs and drums were noisy. People flocked here from all directions to witness Zheng He's fleets maiden voyage to the west.

Zheng He's fleet chose to start from Liujia Port after careful consideration. In the 26th year of Hongwu (1393), Zhu Yuanzhang began to build granaries for grain transport, and 919 granaries were built at the south wharf of Taicang to hoard the grain. According to *Taicang Fuzhi*, it stored millions of tons of rice during the Yongle period, and the autumn grain in Zhejiang and other places was transported here, so this was the most prosperous warehouse at that time. In the early Ming Dynasty, Suzhou contributed 12% of the national tax, of which 12% was borne by Taicang. With surplus money and sufficient materials ready, Zheng He's voyages to the west were imperative. After worshipping Mazu in Tianfei Palace, Zheng He led his team to board the big ship. This fleet, which consisted of more than 200 ships and more than 27800 people, was loaded with silk, cotton, porcelain, grain, fresh water, fuel, fruits, and vegetables, medicinal materials, tea and other goods. The fleet left Liujia Port and went southward along the coast to the mouth of Minjiang River. After winter, it followed the northeast monsoon and headed for the vast sea. Because these ships were full of valuable treasures, they were called "treasure ships".

The coastal residents who were lucky to see this huge fleet passing by were amazed. Because in the vast waters of southern China, they have never seen such a spectacular sea scene. Hundreds of ships lined up on the sea, and sails blocked the sky. During the day, the flags and banners flutter and drums riffle. Looking around, the blue sea is like a field with flowers blooming in spring. When it comes to night, bugles are heard one after another. There are lights on the sea. The lights reflected in the sea and the stars in the night sky complement each other, just like the markets in the sky. Only a powerful empire can support such a grand voyage and direct such beautiful scenery.

After leaving the territory of the Ming Empire, Zheng He's fleet first arrived in Zhancheng (now the south-central part of Vietnam), then visited Java, Old Port, Manraja, and Sumatra, then crossed the Straits of Malacca today, entered the Indian Ocean, and reached the regions and countries such as Cuilan Island, Ceylon, and Kezhi, and then continued northward along the Indian coast. After visiting Gambari and other countries, the fleet began to return.

After more than two years of sailing, Zheng He led his team to return triumphantly and brought back the treasures presented by envoys from various countries to the Ming Dynasty, which inspired the whole empire.

Then the Ming Emperor sent Zheng He to the western countries again. From 1407 to 1421, Zheng He's fleet went to the west five times.

At that time, China was in the heyday of the Yongle, but the Asian and African countries through which Zheng He's fleet passed were relatively backward. Most of them were in primitive tribal states or slavery society, and some of them were even uncivilized. For instance, in Guli state, there obviously carries the remnants of matriarchal clan society. Most of these countries did not have a complete political system and legal system, and still had primitive tribal customs. In terms of customs, these countries basically did not have the concept of "propriety" , and it was very common for men and women to enter the pool naked together.

When Zheng He went to Asian and African countries, whenever they went to a place, they always "opened the casket and reward" for trade, and exchanged with Chinese specialties such as gold, silver, jewelry, silk and porcelain. These things were exquisitely crafted, fully demonstrating the Chinese people's adept manual skills and superb craftsmanship. They were the fruits of labor that condensed the wisdom and sweat of the Chinese people, which were full of Chinese culture. For these things that had never been heard and seen before, the people of Asian and African countries were astonished, warmly welcomed, and had an extremely strong desire for appreciation and possession.

These countries began to understand China's artifact culture, and then hungrily pursued and absorbed the system culture, resulting in a strong desire to "change its habits" . Wherever Zheng He's mission went, they fully demonstrated the etiquette and demeanor of diplomacy of a powerful country, which was in sharp contrast with the vulgar folk customs and rude manners of the places visited, thus bringing great shock to the local people. They found that Zheng He's mission brought not only beautiful things, but also beautiful style, words and deeds. In the process of Zheng He's voyages to the west, they often appointed kings, chieftains or leaders of various countries on behalf of the emperor, and gave them crowns and clothes. This kind of material reward and spiritual honor not only met their demand for respect, but also made them feel the beauty of China's rites and music. So they came to China one after another to take the initiative to ask for the crown clothes, so as to realize their requirement of "being willing to follow the Chinese style in their state". At present, "China's ritual and music civilization are famous in foreign countries, which made everyone influenced by its moral uprightness." In the sixth year of Yongle (1408), the king of Yini (now near Brunei) visited China, but unfortunately died of illness, his last words were "buried in China". It can be seen that Zheng He's voyages to the west are of great significance to the spread of Chinese culture, and also have a far-reaching impact on the economic, political and cultural development of countries he visited.

3. Ending

In the 20th year of Yongle (1422), Zheng He, who returned from his sixth trip to the west, was criticized by civil servants. At that time, Zhu Di was obsessed with fighting everywhere, and the national treasury could not make ends meet. The scholar-bureaucrats, who were dissatisfied with the emperor's policy of going to the west, took advantage of the reason that it cost a lot to persuade the emperor. Zhu Di began to hesitate. At this point, Zheng He's voyages to the west temporarily withdrew from the stage of history.

Two years later, Zhu Di died on his way to the northern expedition of the Mongolian grassland. Prince Zhu Gaochi ascended the throne and changed his reign title to Hongxi, and was known as Emperor Renzong of Ming Dynasty. When Zhu Gaochi came to power, he wanted to get rid of his father's maladministration. As an important part of maladministration, the voyages to the west were abandoned and all western treasure ships were suspended. In 1425, Renzong of Ming dynasty died of illness, and Prince Zhu Zhanji acceded to the throne, who was called Xuanzong of Ming Dynasty. Zheng He was demoted to Nanjing as a guard eunuch, repairing Dabao'en Temple.

In the 6th year of Xuande (1431), Xuanzong of Ming Dynasty found that there were fewer countries that came to pay tribute, and he was deeply moved by the grand occasion when all nations came during his grandfather's time. So, despite the minister's opposition, he decided to restart voyages to the west.

The 60-year-old Zheng He was rehired, and boarded his familiar treasure ships again, and started his seventh and last voyage to the west in his life. In the 8th year of Xuande (1433), the fleet returned and passed through Guli (now India's southwest). Zheng He died of illness at the age of 62. Wang Jinghong, the vice envoy and eunuch of the fleet, took over the command of the fleet and took the coffin home. At that time, more than ten western countries sent envoys to Beijing to pay tribute with the fleet.

In the 10th year of Xuande (1435), the Emperor Xuanzong of Ming Dynasty Zhu Zhanji died of illness, and 8-year-old Prince Zhu Qizhen ascended to the throne, and was named Yingzong of Ming Dynasty. In the first year of Zhengtong (1436), Zhu Qizhen, the Emperor Yingzong of the Ming Dynasty, issued an imperial edict that "all activities should be stopped", officially declaring the end of "the voyage to the west" activities since Yongle years.

Forty years after Zheng He's death, Zhu Jianshen, a young Chenghua Emperor, took the helm of the Ming Empire. On this day, an old eunuch who had witnessed Zheng He's voyages to the west told the emperor about the magnificent scenery of that year. Emperor Chenghua was so excited that he ordered people to the Ministry of War to get the chart drawn by Zheng He. When the news reached the Ministry of War, Liu Daxia, an official of the Ministry of War, immediately hid the chart, and denounced that Zheng He went to the west, wasting hundreds of thousands of money and food, killing thousands of soldiers and civilians, although many rare treasures were brought back, these things are of no benefit to the country and the people. The minister should earnestly advise the emperor to abandon this malpractice. If there are old cases, they should be destroyed. Later, it was said that Liu Daxia burned up the chart in order to destroy the emperor's mind of going to the west.

Since then, the vigorous voyage to the west completely withdrew from the historical stage.

4. Influence

Looking back at Zheng He's voyages to the west, although the magnificent epic picture is far away, it has left lasting significance for all walks of life. For example, the shipbuilding industry can deepen their understanding of Chinese ships history by studying Zheng He's treasure ships, historical researchers continue to explore the relationship between Southeast Asia countries and China after the voyages to the west.

For the logistics industry, one of the purposes of Zheng He's voyages is to carry out trade activities with overseas countries, which cannot be separated from the support of the logistics system. It provides a reference for us to analyze the significance of logistics.

From the perspective of logistics, the historical contribution of Zheng He's voyages to the west lies in that it not only opened up new ocean routes, further promoted the international trade activities of the Ming Dynasty, but also established logistics nodes along the routes, established the foundation of an international logistics system. The specific influences of Zheng He' s voyages can be defined in three ways.

4.1 Opened up a New Navigation Route

Zheng He's fleet opened up a new route in the history of world navigation, and realized direct navigation between the western Pacific Ocean and the Indian Ocean. There are 42 major routes opened, with the westernmost route reaching the south of the equator, and the west end of the route extending to Bila and Sunla. This is probably the farthest African country that Zheng He' s fleet had reached, reaching Java, Indonesia in the southernmost, and reaching Tianfang (Mecca in Saudi Arabia) of the Red Sea in the north, with a total voyage of 160000 nautical miles, which is equivalent to more than three circles around the earth. This route crosses the Indian Ocean from Sumatra to East Africa via Maldives and Mogadishu. The opening of this new route is the greatest significance of Zheng He's voyages to the west.

4.2 Established Logistics Nodes

According to *The History of Ming Dynasty* that Zheng He traveled to 36 countries and regions during his seven voyages to the west. Each voyage can be as short as a few months, and as long as a few years. If there is no transit station for supply and rest, how can they continue the long voyage. Thus, on the long and vast maritime Silk Road, Zheng He's fleet established four major maritime transportation centers, two major maritime trade bases and two east—west trade bases.

These nodes selected by Zheng He not only considered the geographical location and economic conditions, but also considered the human environment. Such as Zhancheng, Sumatra, Malacca and Guli, these transportation center stations are not only the main traffic routes, but also the places where businessmen gather. Since the 11th century, Quanzhou merchant ships have chosen these places as trade centers and berthing ports when they sailed to the Indian Ocean, and many Quanzhou people sailed here every year. It is conceivable that when Zheng He's fleet landed, they were greeted by their compatriots and indigenous people who were very familiar with China, and the communication was smooth.

When Zheng He's fleet went overseas for trade, although they were "giving more and getting less" , they still paid great attention to economic benefits. In order to carry out the trade and economic plans for overseas countries, in addition to the use of transportation centers and maritime trade bases, the ancient Guli as a center for east—west trade was also used as a base camp. According to *Ying Yai Sheng-lan*, which was written by Ma Huan, there were two leaders who were promoted by the court in Guli, under the appointment of the Ming government, they were responsible for assisting Zheng He' s fleet in handling foreign trade affairs in Guli. Taking Guli as the trade link between East and West, on the one hand, Zheng He' s fleet can trade with South Asian countries here, on the other hand, it is convenient for Zheng He' s fleet to trade along Southeast Asia, West Asia, and East Africa, which is beneficial to promote the trade connection between East and West.

Zheng He led the fleet to achieve continuous development in marine transportation, which not only made great contributions to the economic exchanges between China and Asian and African countries, but also greatly promoted the development of the marine economy in the early Ming Dynasty, making China the most powerful maritime power in the world at that time. Therefore, Zheng He's voyages to the west was undoubtedly a great achievement of human civilization in the 15th–16th century.

4.3 Applied and Developed the Most Advanced Marine Navigation Technology

Zheng He's route to the west is still known as the golden waterway, which connects the Pacific Ocean and the Indian Ocean. Every year, about 100000 ships sail on the waterway. The fleet relied on advanced communication tools and navigation technology to ensure the safety of shipping. For example, the Global Positioning System (GPS) equipment is used, the fleet will be guided to the destination port after inputting the starting point and terminal point, and each ship will sail independently along the established route at sea. Without advanced information technology and communication technology at that time, how did Zheng He ensure the fleet reached its destination safely?

In *Zheng He's Nautical Charts*, which records the navigation technology of Zheng He's fleet, a great deal of information about navigation route and course, ocean current, water depth, reef distribution, berthing location, compass, and astronomical navigation are preserved, which has become a precious cultural heritage left to us by predecessors. According to *Zheng He's Nautical Charts*, they used the most advanced navigation technology at that time, namely, Star–guided Ocean Crossing Technique and Zhenjing of the Sea Routes.

According to historical records, the ancient people's astronomical navigation mainly relied on Star–guided Ocean Crossing Technique, which was used to determine the navigation direction and orientation of ships. During the Yuan and Ming Dynasties, Star–guided Ocean Crossing Technique began to be used to measure the geographical latitude of ships. The working principle Star–guided

中国物流故事 古代辑
STORY
汉英对照

Ocean Crossing Technique is to determine the geographical latitude of the ship by measuring the angle between the stars and the horizontal plane of the ship with the Star-guided Fixing. Although this tool and measuring principle are simple, it embodies the wisdom of the ancients for thousands of years and represents the world's most advanced astronomical navigation level at that time. According to the records, the ancients took black wood as the material of the Star-guided Fixing, and a pair of the Star-guided Fixing consisted of twelve regular quadrilateral boards of different sizes and an ivory square with a length of about 6 centimeters and gaps left at four corners, and the templates were arranged according to their sizes. The lengths of the four sides of the ivory square gap are also different. The user holds the center of one end of the the Star-guided Fixing with his left hand, adjusts his arm posture to make the line of sight and the lower edge of the the Star-guided Fixing on a horizontal line, and makes sure that the upper edge of the the Star-guided Fixing is aligned with the measured star. At this time, the included angle between the horizontal plane where the ship is located and the stars can be measured, and the geographical latitude where the ship is located can be calculated by putting the included angle into the existing formula.

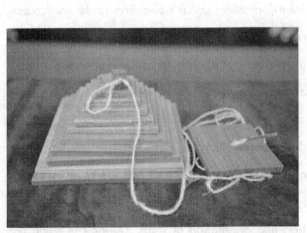

The restoration of the Star-guided Fixing (Photo by Chen Biao)

The measuring principle of the Star-guided Fixing (Image source: Wu Chunming)

It can be seen that navigation technology was very advanced at that time. *Wu Bei Zhi*[1], written by Mao Yuanyi, a scholar at the end of Ming Dynasty, has 20 pages of Zheng He's charts, among which there are 4 charts about Star-guided Ocean Crossing Technique. As early as in *Huai Nan Zi*, it is recorded that Arab navigators are good at a kind of technology, which determines the latitude position of ships by observing the stars. Arab navigators had landed in Quanzhou in the Tang Dynasty. In the middle ages, Quanzhou people learned this technique from the Arabs in their frequent contact with the Arabs. They became the direct applicators of the technique and were familiar with it.

The navigation compass in Yuan, Ming, and Qing Dynasties was the classic of compass navigation. It uses 8 heavenly stems[2], 12 terrestrial branches, and 4 eight diagrams directions to divide the circumference of the navigation compass into 24 equal parts to indicate the direction with high accuracy. In addition, at that time, the advanced navigation technologies included the log, the depth sounder and other navigation instruments, as well as nautical maps such as the chart and the needle road book.

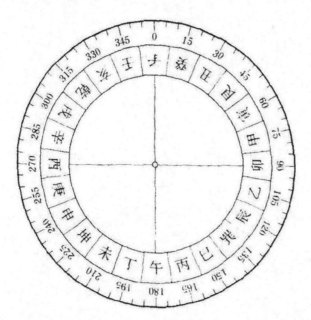

The navigation compass (Image source : *New Compilation of Zheng He's Navigation Atlas*)

---

[1] It is an important military work in Ming Dynasty, which is a comprehensive military book with the largest number of words in ancient China.

[2] 10 heavenly stems minus the 5th and the 6th of the ten heavenly stems.

5. Epilogue

Although Zheng He's voyages to the west didn't realize the historical mission of geographical discovery, there is no doubt that this is a great feat in the history of Chinese navigation. It has constructed the maritime passage of various countries and regions, strengthened the close ties between countries along the routes, and not only has a profound impact on the maritime cause, but also has made outstanding contributions to the development of world civilization.

Zheng He's fleet played an important role in strengthening trade between East and West, and strongly promoted the development of international trade along the maritime Silk Road.

The Direct Road in Qin Dynasty
—The Earliest Expressway in the World

(Image source : Ordos Museum)

On the hilly area of the Loess Plateau, the hundreds-of-kilometers Direct Road has prepared for the urgent needs of the army. The Direct Road in Qin Dynasty is a miracle in the history of world engineering that can be compared with the Great Wall. If the Great Wall is compared to a shield that stopped Xiongnu from encroaching, then the Direct Road is the sword that pierced the hinterland of Xiongnu.

1. A Sword Pierced the Hinterland of Xiongnu

Qin Shi Huang conquered the other six of the Seven Warring States and achieved great unification, the first tyrannic centralized feudal dynasty was established. However, Xiongnu, a minority in northern China, became the biggest threat to Qin State. They had strong folk customs, raised their families as soldiers, lived by water and grass, had excellent riding skills, which made them extremely difficult to defend.

In order to better protect the security of the northern region , Qin Shi

Huang repaired the remains of the Great Wall built in Yan and Zhao times, and connected them with the Qin Great Wall, finally forming the "Great Wall" today.

The Great Wall, which can be attacked and defended, played a very good early warning role, but the Great Wall alone was far from enough. In order to further prevent Xiongnu from encroaching, Qin Shi Huang drafted tens of thousands of elite troops to defend the border. With such a large team stationed here, the monthly consumption of food and fodder is extremely huge, as well as the transportation of strategic materials such as weapons and armor. In order to maximize the role of the Great Wall, it was imperative to build an expressway from the Guanzhong Plain to the northern areas, so as to facilitate the material supply and the infrastructure construction in the northern border areas.

After Qin Shi Huang's unification, he disbanded the original armies of the Six Warring States. However, in such a vast territory, on the one hand, it was necessary to prevent the resurgence of feudal lords, and on the other hand, it was necessary to defend Xiongnu. If the original armies of Qin were assigned for defense, there would be too few armies to dispatch, and once an incident occurred, it would not be enough to respond.

In order to better deal with the "division" and "combination" of military forces, Qin Shi Huang unified the roads of all states, calling it "Highway for the Emperor", and then connected them with each other, creating a highway network centered on Xianyang, the capital city, in this way to reach out and strengthen the connection. The purpose is that no matter where there is war, the army can quickly arrive and respond. Based on this strategic consideration, Qin Shi Huang decided to build a road that could quickly reach the north, namely the Direct Road, which will be extended and developed as this chapter progresses.

In 212 B.C., Qin increasingly levied men to implement a series of constructive activities and started a new round of expansion war, and appointed general Meng Tian as commander in chief, officially starting to build the Direct Road. There is a saying that the road ends in Jiuyuan, which is at the forefront of the border defense line in the northern area; it starts in Ganquan Palace, and there are safe passages closely linked with Xianyang, the capital city.

The Direct Road opened the main artery between Central Plains and the north of the Great Wall, and became a bridge for economic and cultural exchanges between inland and border areas. In the fierce war with Xiongnu from the north for many years, the Direct Road built by Qin Dynasty always played a pivotal role, and the transportation of thousands of tons of military supplies depended on this artery. With the construction of the Direct Road, the connection between Guanzhong area and the northern area is closer, which marks the birth of a miracle in the history of world logistics.

Road traffic is the most important infrastructure in a country as well as an important part of the national defense system. Relying on the road foundation in the old land of Qin and the other Six States, highway network was built quickly. The Direct Road is the shortest road from Xianyang to Yin Mountains in the north, which is generally straight from north to south, and the project was huge, far beyond highway.

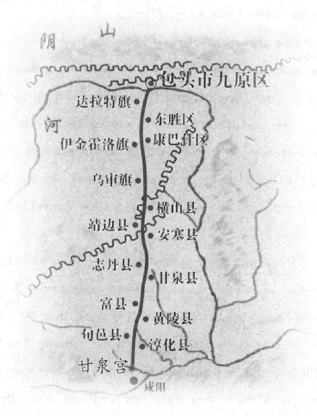

Alignment of the Direct Road（Image source：Ordos Museum）

There is no grass on the Direct Road, which is not only due to frequent use, but also directly related to the construction technology. The soil used is processed after high-temperature treatment, which not only has little water, but also has no plant seeds and other organic matter; when building the pavement, the builder tamped the subgrade, and it is difficult for weeds to take root on it. In the next more than 2000 years, the Direct Road has been the main traffic road, with an extremely high utilization rate. Even if the grass grows occasionally, it would be trodden down by people and cars. In addition, the Qin Dynasty implemented extremely cruel criminal law. In engineering construction, there were supervisors at every level. If there was a problem, they could be held accountable. Moreover, the punishment for mistakes was extremely heavy, which made the quality of the Direct Road beyond criticism.

The pavement of the Direct Road is hard and solid, open and flat. The width is generally 30 meters to 60 meters, and the widest place can even be used as the landing runway for medium-sized aircraft today.

Because the southern half of the Direct Road was built on the Ziwuling Mountain, the builder conquered many difficulties: excavated the mountains, chiseled stone to clear the way, and filled valleys. The project is huge and the construction period is short, which is unprecedented. Its magnificence is unprecedented. According to estimation, if the earth-rock used and moved in the construction of the Direct Road is used to pile up a wall with a width and a height of 1 meter, the length can be more than half a circle around the equator of the earth.

The Direct Road has been around for more than two thousand years. The earliest expressway in the world— the expressway from Bonn to Cologne in Germany was completed in 1931, which is wider than the famous Roman Avenue. It can be called the originator of the world highway. The Direct Road is not only a miracle in the field of highway construction engineering all over the world, but also a feat in the history of material circulation during the war. It is the crystallization of the wisdom of the working people in ancient China, and it also provides an extremely important experience for the design and development of logistics systems in wartime.

2. A Classic Work of Design and Development of Wartime Logistics System

2.1 The Route Selection is a Masterpiece

According to *Records of the Historian:* "Qin Shi Huang intended to travel all over the world, through Jiuyuan to Ganquan Palace, and he sent Meng Tian to open the way for him." From Jiuyuan to Ganquan Palace, there were different landforms along the way, such as grassland, desert, etc. It was extremely difficult to build a road. Besides, it was required that the road be short, flat and wide, and keep smooth, otherwise it would lose the function of building a fast and mobile wartime supply road, which was even more difficult. Therefore, it was necessary to find the shortest feasible route connecting the two points.

The Direct Road in Ganquan County (Photo by Bai Teng)

The route selection of the Direct Road was mainly considered from two dimensions: nature and manpower. The natural dimension is to respect the laws of nature, make rational use of them, and reduce the input of material costs. This thinking played a dominant role in the design and development of the Direct Road. For example, chose to cross the Yellow River in the south near Zhaojun

中国物流故事 STORY 古代辑 汉英对照

Tomb to reach Jiuyuan, because this place is where the Yellow River ferry is wide and gentle, which solved the problems of the Yellow River's shoal, flood season and water cut-off, and ensured that materials could be transported to the front line in time without the influence of seasons and geographical conditions.

For another example, the southern section of the Direct Road is on the ridge of Ziwuling Mountain, which seems incredible, but it is actually the best route choice. This road construction scheme can avoid being cut by the river valley as much as possible. The reason why two adjacent lands are divided into two independent geographical units is that their topography is self-contained and directly reflects different water system structures. There are two independent river systems, Jing River and Luoshui River, which are located in the south of Longdong Plateau and Shanbei Plateau. If you find their watershed, you can find the boundary between the two plateaus, and at the same time, you can find a natural roadbed that is not divided by the river valley. However, not all watersheds can undertake this task, only watersheds whose altitude is not too high can do it. Ziwuling Mountain is the dividing line, which is only 1300 ~ 1800 meters above sea level, the terrain fluctuates slightly and the terrain is relatively flat, which is suitable for building roads, so that the magnificent project of the Direct Road can be realized.

In addition, military security needed to be considered. The forest vegetation coverage rate in Ziwuling Mountain of Qin Dynasty was extremely high, which was beneficial for carrying out covert operations under specific circumstances. Marching along mountain roads could reduce the possibility of troops being ambushed by enemies, which was quite safe and can improve the marching speed of troops. Moreover, the commanding geographical advantage enabled the valley roads on both sides to be controlled by people. These valley avenues had flat terrain and lush vegetation, which was the only way for Xiongnu cavalry to invade. After the opening of the Direct Road, the pressure for Xiongnu to move in valley avenue increased sharply, thus ensuring the safety of the capital city.

The construction of the Direct Road took advantage of the best time and place. In order to ensure the shortest distance, and ensure the road is wide and flat, the builder could only excavate mountains to fill valleys, cut mountains, chisel stones, fill valleys and clear roads in case of forests. Its magnificence is unprecedented. Looking down at the Direct Road from the air, it is like a dragon crawling in the winding mountains and walking silently in the low jungle sometimes.

The whole journey of the Direct Road is more than 700 kilometers. The straight-line distance from Jiuyuan to Xianyang, which is now Baotou to Xi' an, is only about 700 kilometers. In case of backward conditions and insufficient resources, the Qin Dynasty completed such a high-quality project in only two and a half years, which made people awe and admire it.

Sima Qian, a historian, has set foot on the Direct Road. When he stepped into the Direct Road, the offensive and defensive tendencies of Xiongnu in the north and farming nations in the south had already been completely transformed. Han people not only built the Great Wall by virtue of the geographical advantages of Yin Mountains, but also climbed over Yin Mountains and built a large number of walls and beacon towers on the vast grassland and Gobi.

2.2 The Communication System Made Great Contributions

The early warning system, built on the Direct Road and Qin Great Wall, was equivalent to the "radar" in the cold weapon era. Beacon tower was built in a high place. Soldiers on duty could detect the invaders' movements as early as possible, and transmit the key information of their operation to the nearby garrison in the form of smoke or light (smoke during the day and fire at night), and the continuous transmission speed could reach thousands of miles a day. The Direct Road continued to pass the battle report to the military command center at the next higher level until the central government by using beacon tower and post. With this early warning system, the development level of the army has been significantly improved, and the number of soldiers deployed to ensure border security has been greatly reduced. Therefore, the consumption of people, goods and materials was also reduced.

In addition, the early warning system of the Direct Road deployed 300000 Qin troops near Xianyang, not on the Great Wall, so that all the troops could be organically unified and commanded. Only this could reduce the corresponding taxes, military service and hard labor that must be borne when there was no early warning system, and saved a lot of logistics costs.

2.3 Complete "Offensive and Defensive" System

Apart from pavement sites of the Direct Road, many sites related to the Direct Road have been excavated, including checkpoint (the Direct Road site in Fuxian County), post station (Anjiagou site in Ganquan), beacon towers (Dadian Village site in Xunyi, Wulidun site in Huangling County), palace (Renyaozi Palace site in Zhidan), and protection facilities (drainage ditch, slope protection), etc. It is easy to understand that the Direct Road is not only a pavement, but also a sound logistics management system, which has a very good enlightening effect on the network design and development design of modern logistics industry.

2.3.1 The Direct Road and the Great Wall Formed Encirclement— an Arrow Pierced the Heart of the Invaders

The construction of the Direct Road followed the example of the Great Wall, and adhered to the principle of "Building with terrain, and using its steep features to defend the enemy" , thus achieving the effect of "If one man guards the pass, ten thousand cannot get through" . Nomads' horses changed from sharp weapons of military operations to burdens, which not only delayed their encroaching to the Central Plains, but also increased obstacles for the safe withdrawal to grasslands. Military stations along the Direct Road can quickly assemble troops and realize rapid mobility of forces and impedimenta.

Qin Great Wall is a pure national defense security project, while the Direct Road is a transportation line catering to national defense security. After the completion of the Direct Road, it took only three days and three nights for the armored cavalry troops of the Han Dynasty from the station in Shaanxi Province to the foot of Yin Mountains. While in the 1990s, it also took several days by bus from Xi 'an to Yulin. Therefore, under such circumstances, the Direct Road could strengthen the armed forces guarding the Great Wall, and could also introduce some reinforcements to withdraw from other obstacles and immediately bypass the enemy to implement the flanking besiege attach strategy. With the help of reinforcements from the Direct Road, the defenders of the Great Wall turned from defense to attack and carried out the tactics of making dumplings against the enemy who crossed the Great Wall, which made the invaders always face a kind of risk that is difficult to eliminate, thus resulting in a ten-year stable situation of the border that "Meng Tian built the Great Wall in the north to guard the border, which made Xiongnu retreat more than 700 miles, and the Hu people did not dare to go south to graze".

2.3.2 The Direct Road Guarded the Two Rivers and Defeated Nomadic People with Farming Culture

The Direct Road, built in Ordos grassland and main vein of Ziwuling Mountain, has a commanding topographic advantage, especially for the Ziwuling Mountain section, thus has a very significant supervision on the valley avenue of Luo River and Malian River, a tributary of Jing River. Qin Shi Huang made full use of the superior geological resources, and migrated 30000 people to carry out farming activities in the Two Rivers Plain, so that people could cultivate and settle safely, which not only expanded the scope of farming civilization of the Central Plains, but also enhanced the sense of squeezing for nomadic Xiongnu.

With farming, there were food and grass as well as a thriving population. Along the Direct Road, checkpoints, beacon towers, palaces, post stations, and others were built to temporarily store all kinds of wartime materials. In peacetime, the Direct Road was used for trade thus prospering the economy of the Two Rivers continuously; in wartime, the army and the people worked together to complete the rapid assembly and transportation of military materials.

The Direct Road was built according to the terrain, with different widths. Small cars were used on the narrow road, which is flexible. While for pass avenue, big cars were used and small cars were turned back which worked as "porters" for material gathering. The second half of the Direct Road was built in Ordos grassland. The road was very wide, which was convenient for cart transportation and ensured that large numbers of materials reached the Yellow River Ferry.

中国物流故事 STORY 古代辑 汉英对照

The Direct Road Tourism and Cultural Industry Park（Image source：Ordos Museum）

With the Direct Road and the network layout along it, Xiongnu could be deterred strategically, and quick response could be achieved tactically, so that there was the situation "After that, Xiongnu fled to the far north, and there was no Xiongnu wicked court in the south of the desert" "Building fortress and beacon tower, building walls around the Great Wall and sending guarding garrisons, then border settled down gradually."

3. New Era Chapter

History is constantly repeating. When military products or technologies are transformed into civilian-used products or skills, their potential will be more fully displayed.

Especially after Zhaojun's diplomatic mission, the Direct Road changed from the original military route to the civilian commercial route. Tea, silk, utensils in the central region and cattle and sheep in the north as the main products, not only enriched the business activities between the two parties, but also narrowed their distance and enhanced the emotions among different ethnic groups. With the beginning of the era of long-term peaceful coexistence between Han and Xiongnu, the amount of materials transported on the Direct Road has increased exponentially. From then on, areas along the Direct Road became prosperous areas where merchants gathered and trade exchanges continued, and this prosperity continued until the Tang Dynasty.

After Tang Dynasty, with the eastward movement of the political center, the Direct Road played an obvious role in communicating the economy, culture and art in Gansu, Shaanxi, Ningxia, Inner Mongolia and other places. The advanced technology and production tools of the Central Plains were quickly spread to the north of the Great Wall. When the Silk Road was blocked in Hexi Corridor, the Direct Road was also a detour choice for commercial vehicles and goods.

According to *Zhengning County Annals* by Qianlong Emperor: "This road has always been a broad road for north–south traffic, and vehicles can pass through it after being repaired. During the Ming Dynasty, the Direct Road lead to Yinchuan and Ningxia, so that commercial vehicles pass through it. " Thus, until Ming Dynasty, the Direct Road was still an important thoroughfare. According to historical materials, the gradual silence of the Direct Road began in the early Qing Dynasty.

With the steady situation in the northern region, the Direct Road entered a downturn stage. In the Qing Dynasty, Mongolian tribes in the northern region were completely being conquered, and there were no soldiers beyond the Great Wall. In the old crowded downtown area, it was already in a state of "No crowing for thousands of miles" . Wash away the historical splendor, the Direct Road has lost its original charm, and along the hundreds of kilometers stretch, it is sparsely populated and deserted, and there is no complete relic so far.

The protection monument of the Direct Road (Image source : Ordos Museum)

After more than 2000 years of noise, silence, war and integration, the Great Wall still lies under the Yin Mountains, and the Direct Road connects the ups and downs of the Chinese nation's history and social transformation, leaving a heavy imprint in the long history of China.

History is a mirror for our guidance. The influences of the rise and fall of the Direct Road have given important enlightenment to the development of urban transportation along the route. The Direct Road contains profound logistics thought, and its enlightenment to modern logistics can be summarized in four aspects.

First, "Goods circulate around the world", whether in history or in modern times, the logistics transportation network represented by the Silk Road and the Direct Road not only carries the needs of war and trade, but also is a link of geopolitics, regional economy, and culture. Because of this, the level of infrastructure construction in logistics industry is closely related to a country's economic and social development, which must be seriously concerned.

Second, logistics is the organic combination of transportation, storage, loading and unloading, handling, packaging, circulation and processing, distribution, information processing, etc. The core of rapid response of emergency logistics is the effective transmission of information. Nowadays, in case of power failure, network disconnection or even war, it is an effective alternative to follow the think of information transmission in old times and constantly bring forth new ideas.

Third, "The written language is standard, and the size of the vehicle track is standard". Standardization construction is the "quantitative change" for the solving of logistics problems, and the accumulation of logistics technology and theory is the "qualitative change" for the high-quality development of logistics industry, so it is imperative to strengthen education and training and theoretical research of logistics specialty. Nowadays, hundreds of colleges and universities across the country have set up professional courses such as Logistics Management and Logistics Engineering for the subject of logistics, which not only provides the backbone of specialization for China's logistics industry, but also sets up specialized training courses for the actual operation in grass-roots of logistics enterprises, laying the foundation for the orderly development of China's logistics industry.

Fourth, historical experience teaches us that culture should not only be inherited, but also be innovated. Logistics culture plays an indispensable role in promoting the development of logistics technology. Yesterday should be understood, today should be grasped, and tomorrow should be more innovative. The development of logistics industry is the responsibility of every logistics person, and the development of logistics culture is the mission and responsibility of every logistics person.

From the construction of the Great Wall to the Direct Road, such a fast speed of construction came from the working people's efforts and persistence, who created brilliance with hard work. Behind the aura and those touching creations are full of unimaginable hardships of working people.

From Two Bombs and One Satellite to "Chang'e" Lunar Exploration, from the launching of the first submarine to "Jiaolong", from the first generation of supercomputer Galaxy to now Internet big data, the construction speed of the two emergency hospitals Huoshenshan Hospital and Leishenshan Hospital is more praised by people... The speed of China, which has created the miracle of the world, reflects China's indomitable fighting spirit. China's speed and strength shocks the whole world, holds up the people of all ethnic groups' longing for a safe, happy and better life, and drives China to increase its power again and advance at full speed to the great rejuvenation of the Chinese nation.

Pinglu Canal and Quanzhou Canal
—Military Application of Canals

(Photo by UAV)

In the 10th year of Daye of Sui Dynasty (614 A.D.), Yang Guang, Emperor Yang of Sui Dynasty, who failed in his third eastward expedition to Goryeo, returned from the front line of Liaodong. The accompanying personnel and horses were depressed, and the imperial guard had no fighting spirit.

Yang Guang, who was full of ambition, led a million-strong army to attack Goryeo. His army was huge with the vanguard had passed the Liao River, while rear team was still in Zhuo County, the banners and flags were whistling, and the army and horses were large, which was overwhelming. However, the three expeditions failed, which caused hundreds of thousands of people and horses lost, and countless grain, grass and materials discarded, and people lived in poverty thus rebels occurred one after another. All this had dealt a heavy blow to the emperor, whose dream of surpassing the ancient emperors was shattered.

When the emperor drove past Jieshi in the Liaoxi corridor, Yang Guang got out of the carriage and stood for a long time. Under the high cliff where he stepped, the waves surged. This is the place where Cao Cao wrote *The Sea* more than 400 years ago. That year, Cao Cao led his army to the north to conquer Wuhuan[①] and achieved great success. When he passed Jieshi, he was so excited and left this famous poem.

Yang Guang was also a brilliant emperor. He didn't seem to like Cao Cao very much. In his poems, there was almost no praise or even mention of Cao Cao. But, with the same eastern expedition and the same route, more than four hundred years ago, Cao Cao was able to create great achievements, while he could only return home with hatred, which made Yang Guang sigh.

After thousands of years, when people reviewed the failure of Yang Guang's eastward expedition to Goryeo and the success of Cao Cao's northward expedition to Wuhuan, they found that logistics was an important factor in determining the results of the war. The key to Cao Cao's success in that classic battle lies in canal.

1. Disappeared Canals

"Logistics" is an imported word from Japanese, its original meaning is "circulation of things". In human history, water transportation has always been the first choice of large-scale material transshipment because of its large transportation volume and low loss. Therefore, the construction of canals connecting major water systems has become a hot issue in all countries of the world.

In a broad sense, the canal is an artificial waterway used to communicate water transportation between regions or waters, which is usually connected with natural waterways or other canals. In a narrow sense, the canal is a navigable

---

① Wuhuan is also known as Wuwan, which is one of the nations of ancient China.

channel dug by people. In addition to shipping, canals can also be used for irrigation, flood diversion, drainage, water supply, and so on.

China's canal construction has a long history. For example, Xu Stream (also known as Xu River), which was dug in 514 B.C., is the oldest artificial canal in the world, the earliest recorded canal in China as well as the earliest canal dug in the world. It was named Xu River because it was dug by Wu Zixu of Wu State. In 219 B.C., the Ling Canal was excavated to communicate the shipping between Xiang River and Li River. Because it was the first project to communicate the two major water systems, it was written into the history textbook. However, the most famous one is the Beijing-Hangzhou Grand Canal.

In people's minds, most of China's canals are built in the southern region with developed water systems and abundant water flow, while the impression of the northern logistics mode remains in the land transportation. This is not the case. The climate in northern China has been relatively humid for a long time. For example, near the Jiayuguan Great Wall, which was built in the Ming Dynasty, there were traces of water plants in most of rammed earth, which showed that the concept of water shortage in Northwest China is actually biased. Northwest China was humid in ancient times, and the precipitation was greater in North China, which was affected by monsoon climate for a long time. Therefore, in ancient China, there were many rivers, lakes, and swamps in North China.

Today, what we are exploring is an ancient canal that has disappeared for more than 1000 years —Pinglu Canal and Quanzhou Canal.

Is Quanzhou Canal located in now Quanzhou, Fujian? It seems that it doesn't match the scope of Cao Cao's activities in the north. It seems that there are also Ju River and Lu River in modern times. Are they in the same position as in ancient times?

Fortunately, the ancient Chinese were fond of recording, which left foundation to solve these puzzles today.

There are notes in *Records of the Three Kingdoms*: "After Ye City was pacified, Dong Zhao was appointed as a doctor of remonstrance. Yuan Shang defected to Wuwan Ta Dun, Taizu wanted to crusade against them, but it was difficult to transport grain, he drilled the two canals of Pinglu and Quanzhou and connected them to the sea......"

The beautiful Hutuo River (Photo by Ren Peng)

Hutuo River is commonly known as the Hutu River by local people. Hutuo River originates from Wutai Mountain, Shanxi Province, flows eastward to Xian County, Hebei Province, and joins Fuyang River to form Ziya River. Hutuo River is 587 kilometers long, with a drainage area of 27300 square kilometers.

Ju River, which originates from Xinglong County, Hebei Province, flows through Pinggu District in Beijing City and Sanhe City in Hebei Province, enters Baodi District in the southeast and flows into Ji Canal.

Lu River, now known as the North Canal, is one of the tributaries of Hai River. The main stream from Tongzhou District to Tianjin is also the northern section of Beijing-Hangzhou Grand Canal. It is called Wenyu River in the upper reaches north of Tongzhou District. It flows through Xianghe County, Hebei Province, Wuqing District, Tianjin, and meets Yongding River in Tianjin.

Ye, or Ye City, is now Linzhang County, Hebei Province. It is an important city in northern China during the Wei, Jin, Southern and Northern Dynasties.

Ye City, where the Zhang River flows, has long been one of the capitals of the northern regime.

Quanzhou County is the name of an ancient county. Founded in the Western Han Dynasty, which is now southwest of Wuqing District, Tianjin. It was incorporated into Yongnu County in the 7th year of Taiping zhenjun in the Northern Wei Dynasty (446 A.D.).

In this way, a grand and complicated painting by Cao Cao came to life.

The repair of Pinglu Canal and Quanzhou Canal can make ships from Ye City reach beyond the north of the Great Wall. So, how much work did this canal play at that time, and then why did it disappear? Perhaps, looking back at the history of Cao Cao's northern expedition to Wu Huan, this mystery can be revealed.

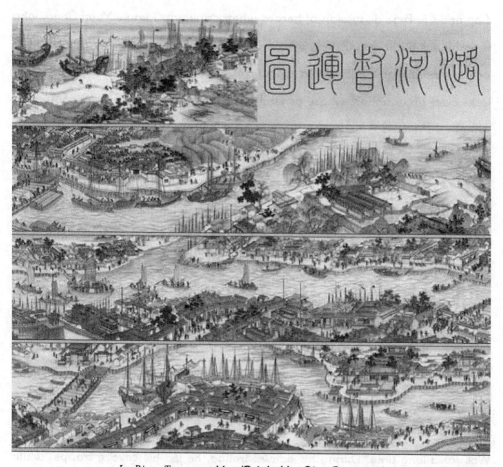

Lu River Transport Map **(Painted by Qing Jangxuan)**

2. All for the War

Because of the wide spread of *Romance of the Three Kingdoms*, today's readers are familiar with the stories of the Three Kingdoms, and even more familiar with the struggle between Cao Cao and Yuan Shao. There is no need to repeat the Chaos of Ten Attendants, Campaign against Dong Zhuo and Guandu Warfare. This story about the canal has to start after the Guandu Warfare.

Yuan Shao was defeated in the Guandu Warfare in the 5th year of Jian'an (200 A.D.) , and returned to his hometown Jizhou to recuperate in order to fight again. But at this time, there were some rebellions in Jizhou, which made Yuan Shao very angry, so he began to quash rebellions.

People's impression of Yuan Shao is mostly based on the words of Cao Cao and Liu Bei's discussion of heroes when drinking: "I know Yuan Shao, who is ambitious but lacks wisdom, who is dignified but timid, who is afraid of other people's intelligence but has no dignity on his own, who has many armies but lacks clear organization, whose general is arrogant but has no unified command. Although the land is wide and there is a lot of food, they are all prepared for me!" Cao Cao's contempt for Yuan Shao was revealed between the lines. However, in *Records of the Three Kingdoms*, his words changed and he showed an objective view of Yuan Shao: "Yuan Shao occupied the north of the Yellow River, and his army was very powerful. I don't think my strength can match with him" .

Therefore, although Yuan Shao was defeated in the Guandu Warfare, Cao Cao did not take any action during the year when Yuan Shao returned to Jizhou to quash rebellions. After all, Yuan Shao was still very powerful after the defeat.

How powerful is Yuan Shao? For example, Yuan Shao once destroyed Gongsun Zan, the warlord who occupied the land of Youyan. Gongsun Zan had the nickname of "white horse silver gun" , and he kept area beyond the Great Wall for a long time. During his administration, he led his cavalry troops "white horse form" to sweep the ethnic minorities such as Wuhuan, Xianbei and Qidan in the area beyond the Great Wall. There was a young general in "white horse form" , who was not prominent under Gongsun Zan, but later became brilliant in the battle of Changbanpo in *Romance of the Three Kingdoms*, that man is Zhao Zilong. Gongsun Zan, whose troops are like clouds and warriors like rain, was still defeated by Yuan Shao.

When Yuan Shao attacked Gongsun Zan, he showed extraordinary military accomplishment. His troops confronted with Gongsun Zan's cavalry, pretended to be defeated and lured Gongsun Zan's cavalry to fight in the swamp where it was not easy for the cavalry to exert their fighting power. Gongsun Zan was defeated by this method many times, then he took the tactics of withdrawal defense and fought for a long time. Gongsun Zan troops dug trenches, built mountains and high-rise buildings, and had sufficient grain and grass. Yuan Shao cut off Gongsun Zan's internal and external contact, eliminated Gongsun Zan's reinforcements and friendly forces by encircling enemy post in order to attack reinforcements coming to its aid and rested and ready to face the attack of the fatigued enemy. After many years of fighting, the general attack was finally launched. Yuan Shao's army dug tunnels to the gates of Gongsun Zan, and finally ignited the wooden pillars used to support the tunnels, causing the city walls to collapse. According to *The Book of Later Han*, "Yuan Shao' s attack is like ghosts and gods, with ladders dancing upstairs and drums sounding in the ground."

Therefore, Cao Cao was able to defeat Yuan Shao in Guandu Warfare, which fully proved his outstanding military strategy. However, Yuan Shao still had a large army and a large number of counselors. Because Yuan Shao was generous and benevolent when he was in charge of Jizhou, the people all admired his kindness. All these factors made Cao Cao suppress his mind of going north to Jizhou.

In the 7th year of Jian 'an (202 A.D.), Yuan Shao died at home due to illness after Jizhou Uprising subsided. Yuan Shao's youngest son, Yuan Shang, inherited Yuan Shao's regime under the support of counselor Shen Pei, which caused dissatisfaction of Yuan Shao's eldest son Yuan Tan, and Yuan Shao' s second son Yuan Xi joined the Yuan Shang camp, and the three men began to fight for power and profit. In order to defeat Yuan Shang, Yuan Tan turned to Cao Cao for help, and finally "led the wolf into the room". Cao Cao stared at the opportunity, entered Hebei in a large scale, quickly defeated Yuan Shang and Yuan Xi, and returned to the army to kill Yuan Tan. In the 10th year of Jian'an (205 A.D.), the brothers Yuan Shang and Yuan Xi fled North in a hurry to seek refuge in the territory of Wuhuan.

Wuhuan was far away from the Central Plains, and the king's tent of Tadun, the leader of Wuhuan, was set up in Liucheng. If Cao Cao wanted to march from Hebei to Liucheng, there would be neither today's highway nor the so-called "post road" at that time. Only the path in the mountain can get there, and it also needed to cross the Great Wall. At that time, only traders ventured to take these paths in order to seek profits. It was difficult for Cao Cao's army to attack Wuhuan.

In ancient times, when the means of transportation were backward, it was not a simple thing to send troops on expeditions, especially the transportation of military provisions. For this reason, Cao Cao had discussed this matter with the civil and military officials many times. Most of them thought that it would be not only difficult to transport military supplies, but also Liu Bei, who was in Jingzhou in the south, would persuade Liu Biao to attack Xudu. They were afraid that they would suffer losses at both ends, so they thought that it was not suitable to go to Wuhuan for the time being.

At this time, Guo Jia, a counselor, proposed for an immediate expedition to Wuhuan: Wuhuan was far away from the Central Plains, and they didn't know Cao's power, so their defense was bound to be lax and careless, and we could take advantage of it by surprise Wuhuan and we will succeed. Moreover, Yuan Shao had always been kind to the Wu Huan. If Yuan Shang and his brother were allowed to make an alliance with Wu Huan, they would surely go south to seize Jizhou after recuperation, and there would be no end of trouble for the future. And Liu Biao, who loves to talk freely, is wary of Liu Bei's talents, so he probably won't listen to Liu Bei's suggestions. Cao Cao accepted Guo Jia's suggestion and decided to continue to pursue victory. Considering that the expedition will take a long time, the transportation of military supplies is the top priority. Therefore, in the 11th year of Jian' an (206 A.D.), Cao Cao ordered Dong Zhao to dig the Pinglu Canal and Quanzhou Canal.

3. The Confidence of Victory

At the same time that Cao Cao ordered people to dig canals, Guo Jia's prophecy came true quickly. In the 11th year of Jian' an, the Wuhuan invaded Youzhou and plundered more than 100000 people, causing social unrest.

Facing the severe situation in the north, Cao Cao accelerated the process of digging canals. Soon, the Pinglu Canal and Quanzhou Canal were successfully excavated. Troops and impedimenta were quickly transported from Ye City, and Cao Cao's army quickly gathered at the north exit of Quanzhou Canal through these two canals.

However, new problems emerged. Cao Cao's military supplies were hoarded in the north mouth of Quanzhou Canal, while the king' s tent of Wuhuan was set up in Daling River basin deep in Yanshan Mountains, so Cao army still faced the dilemma of marching thousands of miles. Therefore, Cao Cao ordered the excavation of an artificial canal named "Xin River" to connect Quanzhou Canal and Ru River (now Luanhe River in Hebei Province), in order to approach Wuhuan as far as possible.

Cao Cao arrived at Wuzhong County in April of the 12th year of Jian' an (207 A.D.). In July, it rained heavily, and many rivers flooded with water. Cao Cao wanted to go to Liaoning Province along the coast, and then turn north to Liucheng, but the river overflowed, and this "coastal road" was blocked.

At this moment, a hermit named Tian Chou suddenly appeared to support Cao Cao. Originally, in order to avoid war, Tian Chou and some people lived in seclusion in the mountains. He didn't want to take care of what happened between Cao Cao and Yuan Shao. However, because Wu Huan plundered the

The Wei River Jun County section of the Grand Canal (Photo by Xie Jingyi)

Han people for a long time, he felt that this was a problem of self-defense, so he went out and volunteered himself to Cao Cao, and acted as a guide for Cao army, leading them through a path called "Lulong Road" , passing through Xifengkou, reaching the west of Liu City, with a total length of more than 500 Li. In fact, this "Lulong Road" was not a small road, it was the main road leading from Lulong Fort to Liu City. However, after Emperor Guangwu in the Eastern Han Dynasty, it was shut down for nearly 200 years and became an unknown road.

Cao army encountered Tadun army in Bailang Mountain near Liu City. After the start of the battle, under the leadership of commander Zhang Liao, the vanguard of Cao army fought bravely and killed the Tadun. Immediately, Cao Cao's main force arrived, accepted the surrender of more than 200000 Hu people and Han people, which won a great victory. Yuan Shang and his brother fled to Gongsun Kang, the prefect of Liaodong, to seek protection. As a result, Gongsun Kang killed them and gave their heads to Cao Cao.

At this point, Cao Cao unified Hebei, brought the whole north of China into his own ruling category, and completed the key step of unifying the world.

After reviewing Cao Cao's conquest of Wuhuan, we found that Cao Cao paid attention to military logistics from beginning to end, and only when the problem of grain and grass supply was solved, would he fight boldly. At the critical moment when he faced thousands of miles of attacks and couldn' t get enough logistical support, he adopted the quick method to defeat his enemy, thus avoiding the dangerous situation of losing logistics in a long—term decisive battle. Four hundred years later, Emperor Yang of Sui Dynasty marched eastward to Goryeo, and the combat distance was farther than that of Cao Cao, but the logistics relied on the transshipment of Zhuo County. No matter how powerful the combat power was, it was discounted, which laid the foundation for failure.

So here comes the new question. Digging canals has always been a time—consuming and laborious task, why did Cao Cao's subordinates use only one year to excavate the Pinglu Canal and Quanzhou Canal, and temporarily dig the Xin River? The answer may be unexpected, because Cao Cao is a veteran in digging canals.

In fact, Pinglu Canal and Quanzhou Canal were not the first time that Cao Cao involved in the excavation of the canal. Cao Cao's original base was small in territory and small in population. "The bones of the dead are exposed everywhere in the wilderness, and chickens can't be heard on the scorched earth for thousands of miles" . Therefore, Cao Cao paid great attention to solving the problems of grain production and transportation. He adopted the method of setting up garrison troops to open up wasteland and grow food grain to solve the problems of production. Digging canals, dredging stagnant and abandoned rivers, and connecting the Yangtze River, Huai River, Yellow River, and Hai River basins were important means to solve the problems of transportation.

After the diversion of the Yellow River, the original old channel of the Yellow River formed the White Ditch due to the need of irrigation. Because of the diversion of the Yellow River, the White Ditch lacked water and was often in a dry state. In the 8th year of Jian' an (203 A.D.), when Cao Cao attacked Ye City, he first commanded the army to attack Liyang, and then led the army to cross the river from Xuchang. In order to solve the problem of military grain transport, Cao

Cao ordered the army to introduce the water from Qi River into White Ditch, which successfully solved the problem of military grain transport.

Cao Cao is not only a veteran in digging canals, but also a master who knows the geography of mountains and rivers. The east—west Hutuo River formed a lot of huge berths in front of the high sand dyke which was formed by the north flow of the Yellow River. Due to the outbreak of mountain torrents, the Hutuo River has been diverted and breached many times, forming numerous ancient rivers crisscrossed like fishing nets on the North China Plain. Cao Cao chose to dig a canal along the old road of the northern branch of the Hutuo River in Raoyang to pass through Gu River to the north, reach Li County, cross Baiyangdian to Yizhou, then go north along Yongding River to You Zhou and take Youzhou back, which is a precisely planned route. In order to reduce the loss, he opened Quanzhou Canal, connecting the transfer route of the army to the sea, because the coastal shortcut could directly reach Wuhuan's base.

Therefore, although Cao Cao finally won the battle of conquering Wuhuan by crossing the Yan Mountains and making a surprise attack, it was the confidence of Cao army to send the grain to the estuary of Xin River, the nearest place to the front line. Logistics supported the army, and the canal contributed to logistics.

4. The Afterglow of History

After Cao Cao conquered Wuhuan, he took the Wuhuan cavalry into his pocket. Since then, Wuhuan fighters have become another army with strong fighting capacity under Cao Cao. After Cao Cao returned to the Central Plains, his strategist Guo Jia died of illness in Yizhou. This battle was remembered by the world because of the widespread of the famous poem *The Sea*, but the canal that made great contributions faded out of people's vision.

Because the north entrance of Pinglu Canal and the south entrance of Quanzhou Canal are connected to the present Hai River, Pinglu Canal and Quanzhou Canal have become the water transport channels running through the Hebei Province and connecting the Yellow River, Hai River and Ji Canal.

Sanchakou in Tianjin Haihe River is the important node of Quanzhou Canal opened by Caocao (Photo by Sun Fanyue)

However, although the Pinglu Canal and the Quanzhou Canal were dug in the same area at the same time, their historical destiny was quite different. Since its opening, Pinglu Canal has become an important channel from Henan to the Hebei Province. Later, it became an important part of White Ditch, Qing River, Yongji Canal in Sui and Tang Dynasties, Yu River in Song and Yuan Dynasties, Wei River in Ming and Qing Dynasties, and the modern South Canal. It plays an important role in transportation. While Quanzhou Canal is totally different. When describing Quanzhou Canal, Li Daoyuan in *Shui Jing Zhu* mentioned: "The upper stream of the old channel of Quanzhou Canal receives the Hutuo River in Quanzhou County, so it is named after Quanzhou." This showed that Quanzhou Canal had become an abandoned relic when Li Daoyuan wrote *Shui Jing Zhu* in the Northern Wei Dynasty.

However, the historical significance of Pinglu Canal and Quanzhou Canal is still strong.

They perfected the canal network in the north. Pinglu Canal and Quanzhou Canal are of great significance in military, economy, geography, engineering, and water conservancy. In terms of canal transportation for expedition to areas beyond the Great Wall, they are hundreds of years earlier than that of Emperor Yang of Sui Dynasty. They are also an important part of the canal network in Northern China. More than 1800 years ago, China had a vast territory, changeable geographical conditions, high land transportation costs while low efficiency, and the sea route had not been opened yet. The inland river shipping became a kind of transportation mode that saved money, time, and labor. The water transportation also promoted grain production, economic exchanges, material transfer, and circulation in the north.

Pinglu Canal and Quanzhou Canal further contributed to the formation of a unified national water system and laid the foundation for the unification of China. Under Cao Cao's rule, the opening of White Ditch, Pinglu Canal, Quanzhou Canal, and Xin River made it possible to successfully connect Zhang River, Luan River, Hutuo River, and other rivers in the north of the Yellow River to Ji River, Huai River, Yangtze River, and Qiantang River. Since then, the water transportation among the rivers and seas has been connected, with Wuyue in the East, Bashu and Hanzhong in the west, Wuling and Zhuhai in the south, and Youzhou and Luan River in the north. People in all regions of China can travel by boat and have close economic and cultural exchanges. These exchanges objectively promoted China's unification and laid the foundation for the formation of the Beijing—Hangzhou Grand Canal in Sui and Tang Dynasties.

Fengtu Charitable Granary

—Logistics Thought of Combining Peacetime with Wartime

(Photo by Shao Rui)

Fengtu Charitable Granary, located in the Grain Station Compound of Chaoyi Town, Dali County, Shaanxi Province, is an ancient private granary which has experienced wind and frost, and it is still well preserved and plays the role of storing national grain and relieving famine. Its ingenious layout shows the Chinese nation's high wisdom and careful and reasonable technology, which has important value and historical significance for the study of China's ancient warehousing management.

1. Confidence and Responsibility

When it comes to Fengtu Charitable Granary, we have to mention Yan

中国物流故事 古代辑 STORY 汉英对照

Statue of Yan Jingming (Photo by Tian Xichao)

Jingming[1]. He had a characteristic when he was an official, no matter where he went, he would place a loom in the government office. He handled official business in the front hall, while his wife was reeling silk and weaving in the back hall. The squeaking sound of the loom always warned him of people's livelihoods, honesty, and diligence.

In the third year of Guangxu in the Qing Dynasty (1877), a huge drought occurred in Shanxi, Henan, and Shaanxi. At this time, Yan Jingming was over 60 years old, suffering from a cough, he was very skinny and needed to walk with a cane. Although he felt that he was ill and could not shoulder the heavy responsibility, he saw that the disaster situation was getting worse and the number of victims was increasing. He felt deeply that he could not stay out of the disaster. He was ordered to go to Shanxi to check the relief work. During that period, he was also ordered to check the relief work in Shaanxi.

Yan Jingming, dressed in plain clothes and with only simple luggage, traveled thousands of miles to reach the disaster area and donated all of the 1000 Liang of silver travel expenses allocated to him by the court for disaster relief. The more places visited, the more severe disasters Yan Jingming saw. He was suffering in his heart, but he was helpless.

Yan Jingming dispatched people to the south to buy rice to meet their urgent need. Until the next year, although he tried his best, he only bought a little grain. At the same time, he asked for help everywhere to raise money and food, and wrote no less than 9 letters for help every day, but the effect was not ideal.

---

[1] Yan Jingming (1817–1892), whose courtesy name was Danchu, was born in Zhaodu Town, Chaoyi County, Shaanxi Province (now Chaoyi Town, Dali County, Shaanxi Province), was a scholar in Daoguang 25th year. He was an incorruptible official with good money management, and was named "precious prime minister".

However, what was more difficult was that even if food was purchased, it could not be delivered to the disaster area in time. Because of the continuous drought, the canal dried up and the grain could not be transported back by water. Therefore, they could only go around by land which was long and rugged. The freight was three times as much as the grain price, which greatly increased the difficulty and the cost of transporting grain.

Although in the Qing Dynasty, the disaster prevention and relief mechanisms were relatively sound, at this time, the Qing government faced the pressure of foreign invasion and domestic peasant uprising, and it was weak. Social economy had not yet recovered from the depression. At the moment, the court also suffered from the border crisis, Zuo Zongtang sent troops to Xinjiang. As the logistic support, the demand for food and grass increased significantly. Yan Jingming repeatedly asked the imperial court to allocate money for grain relief. Although the imperial court transferred grain many times, there was a big gap between the amount and the actual demand.

At the end of the 3rd year of Guangxu, the disaster continued to spread, especially in Shanxi, where corpses of the starved were shocking. Yan Jingming was very distressed and asked the court to transfer 60000 Dan of grain from Jiangsu and Hubei to Shanxi. In the memorial, it was said that "I have been ordered to travel around the disaster area for two or three thousand Li. What I saw was people emaciated from hunger; what I heard was nothing but crying." "Even dead bodies blocked the way, around my carriage, panting for help, looking at the ground and their bodies were stiff. According to statistics, there were more than 1000 people died of hunger every day in a province." At that time, the court realized the severity of the disaster and urgently dispatched rice to Shanxi.

This natural disaster is called "Ding Wu Famine" [1] in history, and even

---

[1] The "Ding Wu Famine", also known as the "Ding Chou Famine", mainly refers to the catastrophic famine that occurred in Ding Chou and Wu Yin (1877—1878). It is one of the largest famines in Chinese history. The disaster is extremely serious, which has a very profound impact on the history of later Qing Dynasty.

reached the level of people eating each other. In the 5th year of Guangxu (1879), the famine was alleviated. According to statistics, the number of people who died of hunger and diseases during the Ding Wu Famine reached tens of millions, and 20 million people were displaced and left home.

"Fengtu Charitable Granary", titled by Yan Jingming, written by Cai Wentian, the supervisor of Chaoyi County (Photo by Tian Xichao)

When he returned to his hometown, where he had been away for a long time, there were full of ruins. Yan Jingming tossed and thought hard and decided to build a granary to make up for possible shortages with a surplus. Only by storing up in fat years to make up for lean years, can he prepare for drought and famine in the long run. He wrote the memorial in detail together with the gentry in the court, and made six requests within five years, urging the court to approve it.

In the 8th year of Guangxu (1882), Charitable Granary was built, which was located on the high slope of the Nanzhaizi Village of Chaoyi County with high terrain and flat surface. It is bordered by the Yellow River beach in the east, connected to the 800 Li Qinchuan in the west, and looking southward to Hua Mountain. In addition, there were abundant loess resources, which could be used locally to burn bricks and make tiles, thus minimizing the loss of manpower and material resources. After the investigation, Yan Jingming decided to make full use of this natural advantage to build granary.

This place was located in the lower part of the west bank of the Yellow River. When the weather was dry, the grain would have a bumper harvest, and when it encountered floods, the grain would have a poor harvest; when the grain gained bumper harvest, it would have a surplus, while it had poor harvest, it would be not enough. The Charitable Granary here can be used as a swap granary, where grain is stored in good years and transferred out in bad years. According to their own actual situation, local households donated food and stored it in the granary. In the famine year, they borrowed food from the granary and returned it in full after the harvest. Repeatedly, they didn't need to pay interest and could solve the problem of food storage.

The Charitable Granary was completed in the 11th year of Guangxu (1885), which lasted for four years and cost more than 30000 Liang of silver. Don't forget hunger and cold when we have enough to eat and wear, don't forget the bad year in the good year, don't forget to save when production increasing, therefore, it was named "Fengtu Charitable Granary" , which means "bumper harvest makes up for poor harvest to serve the people" . Later, it was named "The Number One Granary in the World" by Empress Dowager Cixi.

In fact, this is not the first time that Yan Jingming pondered over this issue. As early as the 11th year of Tongzhi (1872), he advised people to accumulate grain. However, at that time, his opinions were not understood and could only be a dream.

According to *Annals of Dali County*, in the 26th year of Guangxu (1900), another famine occurred in Guanzhong area, with no rain in summer and autumn and poor harvest in autumn. Fengtu Charitable Granary provided relief, distributed grain according to population, and set up porridge factories to save people from the disaster. According to *Annals of Fengtu Charitable Granary*, there was "Recalling the relief in the year of Xin Chou, the number of people saved was incalculable, all thanked to Charitable Granary" .

Since then, for more than one hundred years, Fengtu Charitable Granary has been playing the role of storing food for the people and stabilizing the country. At the end of the Qing Dynasty, most of Charitable Granaries of Shaanxi gradually disappeared, while Fengtu Charitable Granary is still well preserved up to now, basically continuing the original architectural layout, and has been used for grain storage. The granary can store soybean, corn, peanut, wheat, sorghum, rice, and other food crops, especially wheat and corn. Although most of the grain was stored once a year, the wheat in Fengtu Charitable Granary can be stored for up to 10 years.

After the founding of New China, Fengtu Charitable Granary was named by the Shaanxi Provincial Government as the third batch of provincial key cultural relics protection units , and has been protected by the county through the way of "feeding the granary with grain" . It can store and transport more than 20000 tons of grain every year, which is one of the few large granaries in ancient China. It is also the only ancient granary still in use, and one of the granaries with the best grain storage quality in China.

2. City in the City

Fengtu Charitable Granary is built on the old cliff of Nanzhaizi Village on the west bank of the Yellow River in the east of Guanzhong Plain. It is located in Guanzhong Basin where the Yellow River, Wei River, and Luo River meet. It has vast riverbanks and tablelands with unique geological and climatic conditions. Charitable Granary leans on the ancient road of Linjin in the north and the Yellow River in the south, which is very convenient both by land and by water, thus effectively ensuring the bringing in and bringing out of grain.

The main building resembles a heavily fortified city, which integrated grain storage and military defense. The inner granary city can store grain and station troops, the north granary can be used for observation and command, and the inner square can exercise soldiers. Looking at the whole design of granary, its architectural layout was that there were cities in the city. The terrain was high and dry, and it was mighty and magnificent.

Fengtu Charitable Granary fully embodied the comprehensive function of granary, which not only met the needs of grain storage, but also took into account the needs of military defense, its structural design was thorough and scientific.

The vertical view of Fengtu Charitable Granary (Photo by Shao Rui)

The inner granary city faced south. The structure of the wall was of brick surface and soil core, with east and west doors. The granary body was of a single arch structure, with caves instead of large houses. In addition to saving time and materials, this setting also had an important reason, that was, it made the cave keep constant temperature and humidity, warm in winter and cool in summer, which was beneficial to ensure the quality of stored grain, and it was sealed tightly, which was convenient for preventing rats and corrosion. When putting in and putting out grain, there was no interference.

The granary gate was opposite to the square in the city, which saved the time of putting in and fetching out, and was also convenient for adjusting granary and drying grain. The courtyard of inner granary city was set to be long from east to west and wide from north to south, which increased the sun-exposed area and helped keep the grain dry. At the same time, the granary was divided into several small granaries with solid walls to achieve the purpose of separate storage. In this way, in case of fire and other unexpected situations, only one granary would suffer losses, thus avoiding the unexpected risks. There was a spacious courtyard in the granary, and vehicles and horses could pass freely. There was a rectangular courtyard in the middle of the granary gate, which was the place where granary officials worked and lived.

In the 17th year of Guangxu (1891), the outer city walls and moats were built outside the granary. The outer city was closely connected with the river tableland on the west bank of the Yellow River, which was higher than the beach. A deep trench was opened up on the north side of the city, which was the post road from Guanzhong Basin to the ancient ferry of the Yellow River, forming a special terrain with high visibility in the east, south and north, and tableland in the west.

As a high-quality ancient granary, Fengtu Charitable Granary had three unique designs: rammed earth granary wall, suspended granary body and zonal drainage method, which made the granary keep a constant temperature throughout the year, and was conducive to ventilation, and also isolated the hidden danger of rain erosion.

2.1 Rammed Earth Granary Wall

The 58 granaries in Fengtu Charitable Granary were all built on the thick inner city walls, without separate walls, which not only saved the building materials, but also used the thick walls for heat preservation. In order to bear the pressure from 58 granaries, the inner granary city designed the wall as a trapezoid with wide bottom and narrow top, which made the base more stable, greatly improved the bearing capacity of the foundation and reduced the lateral pressure of grain on the wall.

Each granary can store about 2000 Dan of grain. Such a large amount of storage tested the structure and facilities of the granary. In addition to adopting brick kiln structure to increase its temperature and stability, the granary also increased the thickness of the wall. The rammed earth was thick and had good thermal stability, radiating heat in winter and absorbing heat in summer. In addition, the rammed soil had high density and few gaps in the soil, thus well isolating the outdoor temperature and achieving thermal insulation. In this way, the temperature of the granary can be kept relatively constant, and it was about

18 degrees Celsius all year round, which was suitable for long—term preservation of grain. This innovative move of granary storage not only made use of the thick wall, which was convenient for constant grain temperature, but also saved building materials, and was one of the granaries with better comprehensive function utilization.

In addition, the clay brick can withstand the high temperature of 800~900 degrees Celsius, and the water guide partition wall in the granary city had the function of firewall. The wall of granary was of solid brick structure, which can also achieve the function of fire prevention. The fire resistance limit standard of general firewall (0.4~0.5 meters) is 4 hours, and the wall thickness of this granary was 0.8 meters, which far exceeded this standard and can achieve an ideal fire prevention effect.

2.2 Suspended Granary Body

In addition, in order to prevent corrosion and moisture, and further improve the storage conditions, the surface and bottom of each granary were treated with lime soil. The adopted insert—board granary door can be opened according to the grain storage height and climatic conditions, releasing moisture in the granary and keeping the granary dry.

In order to prevent the grain in the granary from getting damp and deteriorating due to the moisture in the ground, there was one granary with one door, and the back wall had an air window, the wooden board of the granary was about 40 centimeters away from the foundation, forming a natural ventilation channel. Exhaust holes were drilled around the wall of granary, which can keep indoor and outdoor air circulation and timely discharge moisture, and meet the "three lows" storage requirements of low temperature, low humidity, and low oxygen of grain.

In addition, the granary surface was paved with pine wood, which had high density, good hardness and wear resistance, and strong insect resistance. It was an ideal preservative wood, and the grain was not easy to mildew and breed worms, thus ensuring the safety of grain storage.

2.3 Zonal Drainage Method

The roof of the granary was paved with blue bricks which were resistant to oxidation, hydration and atmospheric erosion. A large area can also be used for drying grain. It was divided into 12 drainage areas, each of which was high in the periphery and low in the middle, forming a slope from east to west, north to south, and skillfully collecting rainwater in the middle, and then discharged to the outdoor through U-shaped iron casting flumes, so as to avoid accumulated water and seepage caused by scattered rainwater. On the one hand, the design of the water guide wall can avoid the accumulation of water on the roof of the granary, and the rainwater can flow to the square in the granary quickly, on the other hand, it can be used as supporting wall and firewall, which greatly improved the fire prevention ability of granary.

This zoning drainage design can ensure the smooth flow of water, which can be directly discharged to the eaves, and the granary will dry when the rain stops. Since the inner granary square is slightly tilting to the south, the rainwater discharged into the inner granary square will follow the two outlets in the south of the square, pass through the culvert, then pass through the open channel to the outer granary city, flow to the drainage channel outside the city wall, and finally be discharged under the cliff on the east side.

In order to avoid the steep erosion of the cliff on the east side caused by excessive rainfall, a pool was built outside the east gate, which can be used to buffer the water potential and serve as a reservoir for fire fighting.

After a hundred years of journey, the wall foundation has left traces of weathering and corrosion, but it has almost no damage and cracks, and can still be used today, all of which depend on the scientific and strict architectural structure design and effective drainage system of the granary. In fact, after more than one hundred years, Fengtu Charitable Granary has never experienced leakage.

U-shaped iron cast water channel of Fengtu Charitable Granary (Photo by Tian Xichao)

3. Grain Storage and Defense

The granary was often damaged by people during the period of war or famine. When Fengtu Charitable Granary was built, it had the function of military defense and temporary shelter. It can be used to store grain in peacetime. In case of war, it would become the military guard of Chaoyi, guarding the safety of the country.

According to the records of *Annals of Dali County*, Fengtu Charitable Granary was built on the western terrace of Chaoyi city, occupying a strategic commanding height. It faces cliffs in the north and cliffs in the east, which was conducive to concealing, observing and shooting. Coupled with the "nested" design of Fengtu Charitable Granary, it put on layers of defense coats for granary city, and also brought many difficulties to enemy's attack.

Chaoyi was a strategic military location and the gateway to Chang'an. The significance of building Charitable Granary here was also obvious. On the one hand, it can be used as an important food supply station, the construction of Fengtu Charitable Granary could hoard food for the army to prepare for the war, on the other hand, it could also be used as a military fortress, which could keep and attack, move according to the enemy's situation, launch the war, and intercept the enemy to cross the river. In this way, Fengtu Charitable Granary can be said to be a solid backing for the Qing Dynasty's war and the maintenance of its rule.

Whether in the late Qing Dynasty or the Republic of China, Fengtu Charitable Granary made indelible contributions in storing food and resolving famine after war and natural disasters. Even during the period of the War of Resistance Against Japan, Fengtu Charitable Granary played an important role. In 1938, when the Japanese army invaded and shelled Chaoyi, the situation was extremely severe. At that time, the Red Army gave full play to the role of Fengtu Charity Granary as a military fortress, and set up a command post here to command the whole line of operations and ensure military supplies.

There is a saying in *The Mozi* , "City wall is used for self-defense" . There is also a saying in *The Mencius*, "A small city with a radius of three Li has only an outer city with a radius of seven Li. If it is surrounded on all sides, it will not be conquered" . It can be seen that "wall" should have the natural attribute of defense. Almost every important granary in history was built in the manner of "Building wall around the granary" .

Hua Granary, built on a hill with the wall, which can be described as Granary Wall; Ao Granary, building on the mountain and facing the river, is also a mountain city. In addition, the site selection principles of granaries such as Luokou Granary in Sui Dynasty, Huiluo Granary in Sui Dynasty were generally similar. Giving full consideration to factors such as storage, food security and convenience of transportation.

Fengtu Charitable Granary fully realized the functions of defense during peacetime and stationing troops in wartime, which was like the Acropolis.

When Fengtu Charitable Granary was built, the functions of grain storage and defense were fully considered. Whether it was the location of the building or the design of ventilation, moisture-proof, fire-proof, insect-proof, earthquake-proof and so on, they were considered more scientifically and reasonably, which was beneficial to the future use and management of the granary. At the same time, it also has a certain reference and guiding role for the future development of warehousing management. Fengtu Charitable Granary has not been eliminated by the times of development. Its structure and pattern have been used up to now and play an important role. Fengtu Charitable Granary has been rated as a four-no granary for more than 30 years, and has become a major representative of modern warehouse buildings.

Fengtu Charitable Granary embodies the wisdom and foundation of the Chinese nation from the aspects of site selection, layout, architectural design, and technology, and carries the innovative development of warehouse administration, warehousing history, and warehousing culture in China.

4. Food First

In ancient China, agriculture was the foundation of the country. The ancients knew the importance of grain and grass for war. It is the so-called "Prepare food and forage before dispatching the soldiers" . Therefore, in the past dynasties, the importance of grain storage has never been neglected. Hoarding grain is regarded as an important measure of the country, hard work and diligent grain storage have become a good character handed down from generation to generation.

All kinds of granaries perform their own duties. The Zheng Granary and the Military Granary collected taxes and grain from peasants or soldiers, mainly for military supply; Changping Granary implemented buy in low prices and sale with

234

high prices to adjust the market price; through relief and loans, Charitable Granary stabilized people's hearts in case of food shortage; transshipment granary was used for transshipment and storage. Over the past two thousand years, the construction and operation of these granaries have played a positive role in relieving the victims, stabilizing society, and promoting economic development.

Food is the first priority for the people, and the food problem has always been concerned. The idea of "Hong Fan's eight policies, with food as the first policy" reflected the importance of food storage; Fengtu Charitable Granary also embodies the rich technical and management experience of the ancients in grain storage. From groping to familiarity, from pit to intelligence, the millennium deformation record of granary is not only the iteration of technology, but also reflects the sustainable development of grain storage in our country.

As early as the Spring and Autumn Period and the Warring States Period, China had the granary system, which was inherited and developed in the Qin Dynasty, became popular in the Western Han Dynasty, and formed a certain scale in the Sui Dynasty. By the Tang Dynasty, the grain storage management system had further developed and entered a new stage. As the last feudal dynasty into Chinese history, the Qing Dynasty integrated many traditional factors into its grain storage system and built a more perfect system. Abundant grain reserves not only enhance the country's financial strength, but more importantly, enhance the country's ability to resist famine and provide a guarantee for the survival of countless people.

In the construction and operation of social construction and disaster prevention and relief systems, the coordination and linkage between the central and local governments are very important, especially the overall planning and leading of the government, the inheritance of folk poverty relief fashion, the improvement and maintenance of grain storage system, the smooth and convenient transportation and the establishment of big market awareness, all of these should be strengthened, and the cadres who care about people's livelihoods, who are honest and diligent are the key factors in social construction and disaster prevention and relief.

Escort Agency
—The Embryonic Form of Modern Logistics Organization

In the summer of 2018, Duan Tianlin, a folk martial artist in Qi County, Shanxi Province, was instructing his grandson Yu Zhichao to practice the stick technique handed down from his family. It was not as handsome and beautiful as that presented in the film and television dramas. It was just a few simple moves back and forth. Yu Zhichao was going to Taiyuan to participate in the provincial martial arts competition. This set of stick technique was not dazzling at all, so it was difficult for him to stand out.

It was not until one day, in the interaction with other players, that Yu Zhichao hit the key to others by using his stick technique, which could take the other's life. Only then did he discover the subtlety of his stick technique. He told Duan Tianlin how he felt. Duan Tianlin told him that this set of stick technique was born out of Dai Xinyi boxing. More than 100 years ago, Dai Kui, the fourth generation of Dai Xinyi boxing, taught it to Duan Tianlin's ancestors and then it was inherited.

This set of stick technique is extremely ruthless. There is a saying that "If you learn Dai Xinyi boxing well, you can kill people in one year; while it's more difficult to learn Tai Chi, and it's hard to master it if you don't learn it for ten years" in Qi County, which shows its great power. The stick technique derived from Dai Xinyi boxing contains simple and sharp trump. This is a short story about "stick" in the documentary *Eighteen Kinds of Weapons*[1].

Why did Dai's family use such fierce martial arts as a family skill? Because Dai's ancestors run escort agencies.

Qi County, Shanxi Province, where Dai's family lived, was the headquarters of the main ancient Chinese business camp, the Shanxi merchants. Shanxi merchants started with foreign trade, and then involved in the issue of national exchange shops[2]. Brick tea, porcelain, iron pots, silk and cloth transported from the south to Mongolia and Russia would mostly pass through here. The goods were calculated in large quantities, and the gold and silver remitted from ticket banks in the north and south to Shanxi were as much as millions of Liang to ten millions of Liang.

Such a huge flow of materials, money and personnel was bound to give birth to the third-party logistics and security organization, the escort agency. Traffic and safety issues were particularly important. Therefore, escort agencies were blooming everywhere in Shanxi Province, which were quite popular. In order to ensure the smooth journey, the escorts naturally practiced their skills, and had to get a fast, simple martial art that could deter those who covet gold and silk along the way. Martial art, which was quick and vigorous, had become the main practice of the people in the escort agency.

How did the escort agency, the famous organization in history, form, improve and even influence the whole country? It covered a wide range, operated with rules

---

① It premiered on CCTV Science and Education Channel in December 2020. The film focuses on the ancient Chinese weapons to interpret ancient political etiquette, military system, scientific and technological achievements, tactics, and explore the spiritual characteristics of Chinese traditional culture carried in ancient military equipment.

② Old-style credit institutions transformed from commercial capital.

and flexible innovation, which can be called the miracle of Chinese logistics history. What mirror role does it play in the development of modern logistics?

1. Born Out of Demand

There are different opinions about the origin of escort agency. No matter what kind of origin it is, it is believed that the "镖" of the escort agency evolved from the "标".

What is "标"?

The so-called "标" was originally meant to be a logo. Later, because hotels and restaurants used it a lot, it had the meaning of "酒标（logo of the hotel）". The logo of the hotel was the shop sign hung by the restaurant. In *Jiangnan Spring* written by Du Mu, a poet of the Tang Dynasty, it is written that "On the vast south of the Yangtze River, the orioles sing and swallows dart, the peach trees are in bloom and the willows are turning green, spring is evident everywhere. In the villages near the water and the cities near the mountains, there are flags everywhere", the "flag" mentioned here means "标".

Scene of Jinming Pool page by Zhang Zeduan

In the Southern Tang Dynasty, the meaning of "镖" was further extended. As a result of the emergence of the "Dabiaozhouzi" [①], the government awarded the winner of the boat race "colorful silk and silver bowl", giving the meaning of competing for the championship in the dragon boat race, which means "夺标 (winning)". Zhang Zeduan, a painter of the Northern Song Dynasty, created one of China's top ten famous paintings, *Riverside Scene at Qingming Festival*, and another famous painting, *Scene of Jinming Pool*, which has been handed down to the later generations. The "标" here means the prize.

In the Ming Dynasty, the meaning of "标" continued to expand, and had its own interpretation in the business and military circles. Finally, after multiple changes, it came to the meaning of "镖" with pure meaning and clear direction.

In business circles, during the Zhengde period (1506—1521), Songjiangfu (now Shanghai) produced a new type of cotton cloth, which was regarded as the "标布 (standard cloth)" of top quality because of its fine yarn, tight and durable body. Here "标" means standard and superior. Merchants and hawkers who sell these standard cloths from south to north are called "标客 (standard customers)", and organizations composed of standard customers are also called "标行 (standard banks)". In the Ming Dynasty, these people traveled between Beijing, Shandong and the south of the Yangtze River, most of which gathered in Linqing, Shandong and Nangong County of Beizhili (now Nangong City, Hebei Province). The historical records show that in Zhujiajiao Town of Songjiang Prefecture in the Ming Dynasty, "Merchants gathered together, trading cloth". As the standard customers of vendors, because of the high value of the goods they carried, they would also employ some people who had martial arts and were good at boxing to help transport them safely. Most of the employed people were members of the local "Da Hang", and Da Hang was the organization of hatchet men. As time passed, they were also

---

① "Dabiaozhouzi" is the title of the winner.

called the standard customers. The meaning of standard customers turned to logistics transportation and security escort.

In the military circles, there had been a saying of "pacesetters" in the military. During the Jiajing period (1522-1566), because there were Japanese pirates in the south and tartar criminals in the north, the garrison troops guarding the local area were often unable to bear important tasks, so the central government had to send people to organize troops to fight. Usually, when the central police officers act as governors or grand coordinators, they must have a guard force called the central army. The central army was composed of the most powerful soldiers under the command of all generals. These people were highly skilled and powerful. They were regarded as the benchmark of soldiers and also called "镖兵(pacesetters)". Besides guarding the commander-in-chief, the pacesetters also had an important duty, which was escorting and guarding the army's pay and provisions.

At the end of the Ming Dynasty, there were frequent wars. From the governor to the grand coordinator to the general officer, each had his own central army and the pacesetter was greatly expanded. With the decline of national strength, many defeated or scattered pacesetters led a wandering life in poverty. In order to make a living, some of them changed into bandits and started robbery; some of them were engaged in security work and became a protective force for the logistics of merchants from North and South China. In the process of escorting, these groups of pacesetters set up flags, also known as "镖旗 (standard flags)", to expand their influence.

With the passage of time, the standard customers with the background of Da Hang and the pacesetters with the background of soldiers had basically merged. After the establishment of the Qing Dynasty, commodity economy prospered. The radical "金" of Chinese character "镖" symbolized the traditional eighteen weapons. The radical "票" of Chinese character "镖" symbolized money. In this way, "镖" means defending property by force, and "镖局 (escort agency)" is a force organization to protect the security of property.

中国物流 故事 古代辑 汉英对照

The sword of escort (Image source: North China First Escort Agency)

Since then, the "escort agency" has stepped on the stage of history and become a safety protection organization for the transportation of civil long-distance goods. No matter how the escort agency evolved, it can be seen that the appearance of escort agency must have a basic condition: the high prosperity of commodity economy.

The economy in the south of the Yangtze River developed rapidly in the late Ming Dynasty, security was urgently needed for the north-south cargo transportation. The earliest Chinese escort agency appeared during the reign of Qianlong in the Qing Dynasty, with the historical background of the prosperous Kangxi and Qianlong years and the great development of domestic economy.

The first escort agency officially recognized is Xinglong escort agency, which was born in the Qianlong period of the Qing Dynasty. According to *The History of Shanxi Exchange Bank*, Zhang Heiwu, a Shanxi man, was granted the imperial edict to set up Xinglong Escort Agency in Qianmenwai street of Shuntianfu, Beijing.

The Qing Dynasty was a period of unprecedented prosperity for escort agencies. In the middle and late Qing Dynasty, the business coverage of the escort agency gradually expanded. They not only accepted the transportation of ordinary goods and valuable property from private shippers, but also were entrusted by the local government to escort the soldier's pay. After Xinglong Escort Agency, escort agencies all over the country also appeared in the literature. According to statistics, Beijing has the largest number of escort agencies in the country. Shanxi, Hebei, Tianjin and the south of the Yangtze River with developed commodity economy were also popular places for escort agencies. No less than 30 of them were well-known around the world. There were ten escort agencies with wide business coverage and activities spanning the north, south, east and west. According to the geographical division, they were Xinglong Escort Agency, Huiyou Escort Agency and Yuanshun Escort Agency in Beijing, Chengxing Escort Agency, Sanhe Escort Agency and Wantong Escort Agency in Hebei, Tongxinggong Escort Agency in Shanxi, Guangsheng Escort Agency in Henan, Yuyong Escort Agency and Changlong Escort Agency in Jiangsu.

Yuanshun Escort Agency was particularly outstanding. Wang Wu[1], a famous martial artist in the late Qing Dynasty, set up the escort agency in Beijing Banbi Street in 1877. Yuanshun Escort had standardized operation, reasonable pricing, advocating morality and justice, thus attracting endless customers. Its brand had become famous in just a few years. The escort agency ran through the north and south, reaching Shanhaiguan in the north and Qingjiangpu in Huai'an, Jiangsu Province in the south.

In 1898, Wang Wu received a unique "escort", which was responsible for the security work for Tan Sitong, a political reformer who was preparing for

Wang Wu, a famous martial artist in the late Qing Dynasty

---

[1] Wang Wu, whose real name is Wang Zhengyi, is from Cangzhou, Hebei Province. He was good at using a broadsword. Because he ranked fifth in his master's homegate, Jianghu people call him "Broadsword Wang Wu".

the New Deal of the Reform Movement in Beijing. In their contacts, Wang Wu and Tan Sitong, the important promoters of the Reform Movement of 1898 as well as the loyal people full of the passion of saving the country, became close friends.

After Empress Dowager Cixi launched the coup, the Reform Movement of 1898 failed, and Tan Sitong was imprisoned. Wang Wu contacted people in Jianghu to prepare for the breaking into the jail to rescue Tan Sitong. However, Tan Sitong dissuaded Wang Wu on the grounds that he hoped to awaken people with blood[①].

After the death of "Six Gentlemen of the Reform Movement of 1898", Wang Wu cried his eyes out. In 1900, Wang Wu participated in the Boxer Rebellion and was killed by the Eight-power Allied Forces at the age of 56. After Wang Wu was killed, his head was hung above the city gate by the inhuman coalition forces. Huo Yuanjia, a generation of martial arts master, heard about this incident and rushed alone with indignation. He took it down and buried it at night, which made the famous talk of heroes cherishing each other for ages in the history of Chinese martial arts.

Fang Biao, an expert in Beijing history, said that compared with Huiyou Escort Agency, Yuanshun Escort Agency is a small escort agency, with only 40 to 50 people. As the leader of Yuanshun Escort Agency, Wang Wu, who was upright, loyal and patriotic, had brought great shock and influence to the whole escort industry, and he deserved to be called as the "model of escort industry".

2. Rise by Rules

Faced with the environment full of bandits and robbers, people needed an escort agency to ensure the safety of long-distance transportation. However, in the face of gold and silver, the people with job of the escort agency seldom

---

① Tan Sitong said that, all countries' political reforms were all basic on blood, China never heard of bloodshed for political reform at present, and that's the reason why China cannot be prosperous, if there should be, please begin from Sitong.

appeared self—theft for hundreds of years. On the contrary, because they kept their promises, they became the models of chivalry and faithfulness in folklore, martial arts novels and even film and television work. How did the escort agency do this? This had a great relationship with the unique internal management mechanism of the escort agency. In other words, the escort agency had its own unique rules to protect the interests of customers.

An escort agency generally consists of the boss, the chief escort, the escort leader, the escort, the shopkeeper, the accountant, the traveler, and the handyman. In most escort agencies, the head of the chief escort is usually held by the boss. Of course, not all the bosses can be qualified as the chief escorts. Most of the outstanding chief escorts were famous "tycoons" , with powerful kung fu, and had contacts in Jianghu. Generally speaking, the escort agency protected the property or personal safety of the client by force. Therefore, the business of the escort agency can be divided into the "walking escort" of transporting the client's money and goods and the "sitting escort" of guarding the client's home.

According to the classification of transportation objects, there were six kinds of escorts, which were letter escort (sending letters), ticket escort (escorting silver of the exchange bank), silver escort (escorting cash silver), grain escort (escorting grain), goods escort (escorting commodity goods), personal escort (protecting employer's personal safety).

According to the different purposes of protection, sitting escort can be divided into guarding the courtyard (guarding private residence), guarding the shop (protecting the normal operation of the shop from being disturbed), and guarding the night (protecting the property safety of the shop at night). The broadsword Wang Wu mentioned earlier accepted Tan Sitong's escort, which was a sitting escort, mainly performing the duties of guarding private residences.

According to the mode of transportation, walking escort can be divided into land escort and water escort. Land escort was that the escort rode horses

中国物流故事古代辑 汉英对照

or took palanquin to escort on the Guanyi Avenue; water escort was escorted by ships. Escorts engaged in waterway escort must have swimming ability and be protected by ships. The route of walking escort depends on the familiarity of the chief escort and escort of each escort agency with the situation along the road.

As for walking escort, the escort agency usually charged "escort profit" according to the distance of transportation, the value of goods and the difficulty of transportation business. The escort agency and the employer would sign an "escort list" . The escort list would indicate the trade name, name of goods, quantity, place of departure, escort profit and so on. After confirmation by both parties, it would be signed and marked as a voucher. The escorts would deliver the goods in the escort list to the designated place in good condition, and obtain the escort profit after delivery.

Usually, several escorts are led by the chief escort or the escort leader of escort agency branch. They can go on the road with the escort list of goods they receive and the pass issued by the government.

On the way of escorting, the escorts not only had to go through a long journey, but also often encountered robbers during the journey. Therefore, it was necessary for them to shout a song. The song was called the "escort song" in the escort circle. When the escorts yelled, they would respond to each other with cadence and awe. On the one hand, they can build up momentum for the team and frighten ordinary bandits; on the other hand, they can also play the role of self-reporting home and talking with each other.

Of course, there were times when escorts and robbers had a disagreeable conversation. If the two sides can' t talk properly, they would exchange martial art. If the escort wins, the robbers would naturally give way; if the robbers win, the escort team would be robbed. For the escort team, this is "lost escort" . In addition to paying the corresponding amount of compensation to the client, the reputation of the escort agency would also be negatively affected to some extent. That' s why escort agencies were mostly run by famous martial artists, and it's also why all the martial arts handed down by escort agencies hide killing tricks.

An escort agency is a special agency of logistics organization, which has its own unique aspects in operation and management.

2.1 Clear Rights and Responsibilities, High Degree of Organization

In the management and operation of the escort agency, clear industry regulations and standards were formed. A qualified escort should not only have basic skills, but also strictly abide by the code of conduct of the industry. For example, the skill of "three can and one no" includes cooking with a stove, repairing broken shoes, hairdressing, and not washing face. Because the escorts often eat in the wind and sleep in the dew and pass through deserted areas for many times, therefore cooking, repairing shoes and hairdressing were necessary skills. As for not washing face, it is because the dust-covered face can resist the wind and frost and protect the face. The "three rules" of water escort means that escorts can't leave the boat on the way, can't sleep at night, and can't meet women, these three situations might cause the loss of escorting. There were three kinds of "no accommodation" for the land escort, that is, no accommodation for prostitutes, no accommodation for newly opened hotels, and no accommodation for changed owners, these three situations might be risky. When sleeping, there was "three inseparable", that is, weapons, clothing and horses can not leave the visible range.

At the same time, from the perspective of human resources management, the escort agency had a clear division of labor, and each member had their own duties. The boss of escort agency was mainly responsible for building the relationship between escort agency and illegal and legal groups. The shopkeeper should be good at calculation, mainly controlling the daily affairs of the escort agency, such as goods inspection, valuation, and so on. The chief escort, as the movable type signboard of the escort agency, should make a good reputation with outstanding Kung Fu, and also undertake the task of escorting important goods. The escort leader and the escort were the participants and implementers of the goods transportation. Each time, the escort leader and several escorts formed an escort team to escort the goods. The accountant and the handyman belong to the financial and logistics departments of the escort agency and were responsible for the bookkeeping and miscellaneous affairs of the escort agency.

2.2 Formed its own Cultural Characteristics

The development of the escort agency produced its unique culture. Because of the particularity of its industry, it had formed a kind of cultural soft power full of cohesion, creativity, inheritance, and support, which had a subtle influence on everyone in the escort industry. Martial arts culture was the core support of escort agency culture. The martial spirit and integrity values advocated by traditional martial arts were integrated with the benevolence, righteousness, propriety, wisdom, and faith advocated by Confucianism, and had evolved into the core value pursuit of integrity, martial arts, boldness, modesty, justice, and helping others, as well as the behavior standards and principles of respecting teachers and respecting morality, self-examination and self-discipline in the escort agency culture.

2.3 Technological Innovation in Means of Transport

During the development of the escort agency, people, horses, donkeys and vehicles had always been the common means of transportation. With the development of the escort agency, in order to further pursue the safety of transporting goods, the escort cart and box used for transporting goods had been applied. Escort carts can be divided into one-wheeled carts, two-wheeled carts, horse and mule carts, cars, foreign carts, etc. The escort box was used for storing goods made of elm wood by skilled carpenters, and its lock design was more ingenious. It was a kind of secret lock that could only be opened after two unique keys were spliced, and these two keys were held by two shopkeepers respectively, that is to say, the box could only be opened after both of them agreed, which greatly improved the safety of goods in the box and prevented the situation of self-stealing during transportation.

Escort carts and escort boxes (Image source: North China First Escort Agency)

2.4 Information Management of Transportation

The big escort agency had a broad business and a wide range of services. If the escorts returned empty-handed after a long haul, it would be like the current situation of empty trucks, which would lead to a waste of resources and invalid expenses for the escort agency. Therefore, the escort agency would take advantage of its unique information network to accept the next business in advance at the end of the previous business, so that the escorts would not return empty-handed. In order not to return empty-handed, the escorts would even wait for a period of time at the end of the previous business, so that they can receive new business on their return journey and reduce unreasonable transportation.

2.5 Personalized Customization

With the gradual prosperity of the escort agency, many civilians, businessmen and even the imperial court would entrust the escort agency to escort goods. As a result, there were more and more kinds of escorts sent by the escort agency, ranging from a letter, a box of rare treasures to several carts of goods, and even the millions Liang of silver of the imperial court. The escort agency would adopt different modes of transportation and dispatch escorts of corresponding scale and ability according to the different objects to be transported. At the same time, it would set different charging standards according to the value of the goods, the distance to be transported and the difficulty of transportation, so as to obtain escort profits.

2.6 Resource Integration

There were great differences in the routes opened by different-scale escort agencies. When some small-scale escort agencies needed to pass through the routes that they had not yet opened, they needed to rent the routes from larger-scale escort agencies and pay "toll" to them. In the process of transportation, they could plug in the flag of larger-scale escort agencies and could easily reach the destination.

3. Decline and Enlightenment

The escort agency, which had flourished for hundreds of years, entered a declining era. There were several reasons.

First, dignitaries began to deposit a large amount of gold and silver treasures into the more secure banks opened by British and American powers, and their dependence on escort agencies decreased.

Second, with the use of new transportation vehicles such as trains and ships, north-south freight transportation began to enter an era of high efficiency and large quantities, further reducing the demand for escort agencies.

Third, warlords fought in melee, bandits and soldiers armed with guns ran rampant everywhere, the legal and illegal chieftains' flags over the city were always changing[1]. The Jianghu network on which the escort agency relied for communication was destroyed. In the era when guns were prevalent, the danger of escorting increased sharply.

Fourth, the same type of occupation rose. After entering the Republic of China, the rise of police, security and other professions greatly diverted the inherent business

---

[1] From the poem written by Lu Xun, which means that the chieftains' flags over the city are always changing, which refers to that in warlord era, the rulers changed constantly.

scope of the escort agency and replaced the value of its existence.

The time has been shifted to the end of the 20th century. In Tonglu, Zhejiang Province, China started to run express delivery, breaking the inherent state-owned logistics system and forming a vigorous development momentum. With the development of China's economy, logistics industry has become an important industry which affects the national economy and people's livelihoods.

As a special agencies of logistics organization in history, the operation and management of escort agencies have a new inspiration for modern logistics.

Compared with the professional and standardized management system of the escort agency, the modern logistics enterprises need to improve on the problems of unclear division of labor, lack of integrity of organizational structure and serious waste of resources.

The escort agency has established a unique culture for hundreds of years. Modern logistics enterprises can actively absorb and learn from the culture of the escort agency, and build their own corporate culture in combination with the current situation of the industry, so as to enhance the overall competitiveness of the enterprise and the industry.

The escort agency attaches great importance to innovation, especially the front-line escorts have a set of unique methods on how to maximize the use of vehicles, ships and other equipment, save the most money and be the safest. Modern logistics enterprises should make full use of technological innovation to improve efficiency and competitiveness, such as establishing an information platform to maximize the use of resources and maximize benefits.

Modern logistics enterprises can use professional, high-quality and personalized sub-escorting models for different customers and implement special customized services.

Referencing the resource restructuring of large and small escort agencies and implementing the measures of benefit sharing, the government and modern logistics enterprises should unite to make relevant merger and reorganization policies after an in-depth investigation, integrate existing logistics resources, improve efficiency, reduce costs and expand profits.

Ancient Customs
— From Military Town to Trade Passage

"Jinhai New Pass" plaque (Currently housed in the China Customs Museum)

One day in the early winter of the 3ʳᵈ year of the reign of Tang Zhenguan (629 A.D.), there was a hubbub outside the Yumen Pass, the important place of the Western fortress. A wanted notice signed and issued by Li Daliang, the governor of Liangzhou in the Tang Dynasty, was posted on the wall of Yumen Pass.

Onlookers and businessmen were discussing the contents of the notice, it turned out that, a monk named Xuanzang, regardless of the imperial court's ban on border blockade, infiltrated the refugees and traveled westward from Chang'an. Now he has crossed the Hexi Corridor and was about to leave the border of the Tang Dynasty. In order to enforce the law, the governor issued the wanted order for monk Xuanzang, and demanded to search him carefully at all passes along the way.

Beside the Hulu River outside Yumen Pass, a 27-year-old young monk Xuanzang, was resting in the reeds, accompanied by a Hu people from the Western Regions named Shipantuo. They had just finished discussing how to

中
国
物
流
故事
STORY
古代辑
汉英对照

bypass Yumen Pass and continue westward. They did not expect that their journey to the west would be written by a man named Wu Chengen in more than 900 years later. Based on their experiences and combined with folklore, Wu wrote the immortal Chinese classic *Journey to the West*. Monk Xuanzang became the prototype of Tang monk, while Shipantuo became the prototype of Monkey King.

As the night fell, Bangbang beat came from city, and the vigilance of the patrol soldiers began to decrease. Monk Xuanzang got up, packed his luggage in the horse, nodded with Shipanto, and then began to send out on the journey following the source of Hulu River. After about ten Li, they found a place to cross the river. The surface of water was more than one Zhang wide. Shipantuo cut down trees to make a bridge, paved grass and filled sand on it. Finally, they crossed the river safely.

Riding on a horse, Xuanzang couldn' t help looking back at Yumen Pass, which represented the psychological boundary of the Han nationality, the lights were flashing and shining in the dark night. He left Yumen Pass, which means from then on, he really became a wandering monk in a foreign country. After passing the Yumen Pass, there was the vast desert stretching for hundreds of miles in front of him. Xuanzang fastened the reins, on his face writing words "proceed without hesitation" .

Time flies like a shuttle. In the autumn of the 18th year of Zhenguan (644 A.D.), after many years of studying Buddhism in the west, Xuanzang, who had already been an eminent monk, carried the Buddhist scriptures obtained from Tianzhu under the protection of

Special stamps to commemorate Xuanzang's journey to the west issued by China Post

the countries in the Western Regions along the way, and marched on the road of Dunhuang. Xuanzang's name had spread all over the Western Regions in recent years. The Tang Dynasty also knew how important Xuanzang was as a sage monk, so they no longer investigated Xuanzang's sneaking across the border. Li Shimin, Emperor Taizong of the Tang Dynasty, thought that it was a great event for Xuanzang to travel westward to learn from the classics and spread the knowledge in the Central Plains. He ordered the pass along the way to open the door to welcome the sage monk.

On the way back, Xuanzang did not choose to go through Yumen Pass, instead he chose Yangguan Pass, maybe he could not bear to recall what happened outside Yumen Pass. At that time, after successfully crossing the Hulu River, Shipantuo repented and did not want to follow Xuanzang to the west. He even wanted to murder Xuanzang for a time. When Xuanzang found out, he immediately agreed with Shipan Tuo's idea of going back and let him go. Although his safety was guaranteed, it was a blow to him.

Fifty kilometers south of Yumen Pass is Yang Pass. At this time, almost half of the Western Regions had been incorporated into the territory of the Tang Dynasty, and Yumen Pass and Yang Pass had become inland. But they were still the critical pass. What's different was that they were more likely to be the Guan Market to collect the tax on business travel and goods.

Looking at the bustling caravan passing through Yang Pass one after another, Xuanzang could not help but be proud of the prosperity of his motherland and was pleased with the prospect of peace between the east and the west. It is said that "There will be no old friends out of the west of Yang Pass", the pass represented bid farewell but at this time, the pass had become one of the pronouns of wealth collection place, and eventually evolved into the custom that people are familiar with today.

What kind of evolution had it experienced from the precipitous pass to the commercial customs? How many interesting stories are there?

中国物流
故事
STORY
古代辑
汉英对照

1. The Earliest "Pass" Did Not Collect Taxes

Every Chinese, more or less, can recite a few verses about "pass", such as "The Moon and the wall has not changed from dynasty to dynasty, but nobody has returned from the crusade" "I invite you to drink a cup of wine again, no more friends will be seen out of the west of the Yang pass"; or can talk a few allegorical sayings about the pass, for instance, "Wu Zixu passed Shao Pass, he was too worried that his hair turned white overnight" "Force five passes and slay six captains" and so on. So, what is the pass? How did it evolve into today's customs?

The original meaning of the word "Guan" was the latch, and later extended to "close the door". Then, it was extended to the dangerous place of mountains and rivers, that was, the pass. There were many passes in ancient times, such as the Jianmen Pass "If one man guards the pass, ten thousand men are unable to get through it", the prestigious Hangu Pass "How majesty the Hangu Pass is, that many historical affairs happened here". Once upon a time, in the Warring States Period, outside Hangu Pass, pennons and banners of the five coalition forces were fluttered. But in the end, because of their different intentions, Qin army crushed them one by one. Finally, they were bloody and defeated, which made the great reputation of the Qin Empire. At the end of the Eastern Han Dynasty, the heroes rose together. Before Hulao Pass, Liu Bei, Guan Yu, and Zhang Fei fought against Lv Bu, Dong Zhuo's subordinate, which staging the eternal talk of "The Battle of Three Heroes and Lv Bu".

However, gradually, people found that in addition to military use, the pass has another function, that is, it can also manage foreign trade, especially tax collection.

As early as Zhou Dynasty, the emperor of Zhou set up an official post called "Si Guan", to take charge of the inspection of border checkpoints and issue passports for goods entering and leaving the country legally. According to the records, the important purpose of pass is to "hold prohibition to check", that is, according to the official regulations, inspecting the envoys, officials and businessmen who enter and leave the country and the goods they carry. "If the goods are not going through customs, they would be lifted and the owner would also be punished." And the "pass" is a kind of official certificate to allow goods to enter and leave the country.

In the Western Zhou Dynasty, they did not collect tax at the checkpoint. In the Eastern Zhou Dynasty, the function of tax collection began to be added. In the classical books of the Spring and Autumn Period, the written records of "levy of pass and market" began to appear. The so-called "levy of pass and market" referred to the "pass" of goods passing through the border stipulated by the state and the domestic "market" (the meaning of the market, at that time, was its original meaning, that was the place where goods were traded), which must be inspected and taxed.

Zang Wenzhong, a senior official of Lu state in the Spring and Autumn Period, was regarded as a typical figure who initiated the tax collection at the checkpoint. At that time, Zang Wenzhong was aware of the financial inadequacy and began to enrich the national treasury. He found that there were many "passes" in the Lu state. These "passes" were the gateway of the state and the bearing of the appearance, as well as the necessary places for the communication between the princes. However, most importantly, they were channels for people to travel and the gateway for the circulation of goods. If tax passes were set up in these places, the benefits of tax collection would be considerable. Without delay, Zang Wenzhong set up 16 tax collection "passes" in Lu state. For a time, the taxes flowed into the state treasury.

However, later in *Zuo Zhuan*, Confucius, who advocated benevolent government, criticized Zang Wenzhong's works. He said that Zang Wenzhong was "three non-benevolent practices, and three unwise aspects". The reason was that Zang Wenzhong's practice of tax collection was to compete for profits with the people, which was not a benevolent government.

What you dream is light, what you see is night. Many countries had not

中国物流故事古代辑 汉英对照 STORY

adopted the views that Confucius called for, which is not to compete for the benefit of the people, on the contrary, because tariffs could increase fiscal revenue, which made governments at all levels set up checkpoints and fortresses crazily, and constantly strengthen collection and supervision. Especially during the period of war, people's tariff burden was heavier. Even the states of Qi and Jin, which had always been light in levying tariffs, went astray in levying tariffs heavily and accumulating taxes excessively.

In the Spring and Autumn Period and the Warring States Period, the most legendary story about "pass" was the allusion of Laozi's leaving Hangu Pass to the west. Laozi is the founder of Taoism (his real name is Li Er). When Taoism was well developed, the current political situation in the Central Plains was more turbulent than before, which was contrary to his idea of governing by doing nothing. He left Luoyang disappointedly, where he had lived for decades, riding a green ox, and was ready to spread his thoughts to the west. When he arrived at Hangu Pass, he met Yin Xi, the officer who guarding Hangu Pass. Yin Xi was responsible for inspecting passers-by and appreciated Laozi's writings and thoughts. Yin Xi strongly asked Laozi to leave his ideological achievements for later generations before he returned to seclusion, so Laozi wrote the previous and next chapters of the book, which said more than 5000 words about morality, which was called *Tao Te Ching* then he left. For thousands of years, many Taoists at home and abroad have made pilgrimages to Hangu Pass.

The "pass" eaves tile used in Hangu Pass gatehouse in the Western Han Dynasty (Image source: the China Customs Museum)

The story of Yin Xi and Laozi witnessed how the earliest "pass" operated in China. Combined with the story of customs system and Zang Wenzhong, we can also see that the rudiment of "Customs" was gradually taking shape.

2. The Silk Road is a "Tariff" Road

Qin Shi Huang, who had great talent and bold vision, unified the six countries. However, the political laws of the Qin Dynasty were strict, the people were frequently accused, and were imposed with heavy corvee. In the end, in just over ten years, the Qin Dynasty was submerged in the flames of the peasant uprising.

After the establishment of the Han Dynasty, Liu Bang abolished the harsh laws of the Qin Dynasty in the face of the decline of the people, adopted the way of Huang and Lao, and implemented non-interference "rest with the people". In the early years of the Western Han Dynasty, in order to communicate the wealth and goods, activate the market and promote economic development, there was no tariff. In the reign of Emperor Wen of the Han Dynasty, the checkpoints of the Central Plains were removed. During the reign of Emperor Jing of the Han Dynasty, there was "rebellion of seven countries" , then the central government restored the passes of the Qin Dynasty, but did not levy tariffs.

However, in the 3rd year of Yuan Shuo (126 B.C.), when Zhang Qian returned from the Western regions after traveling for many years, the bilateral trade between Han Dynasty and Western regions began to flourish rapidly. Booming business activities and massive material exchanges had made wealth accumulate rapidly. Emperor Wu of the Han Dynasty changed the rule of inaction of the previous emperors and began to conquer lands on a large scale. These great deeds urgently needed a lot of money to support. One of the important financial sources of the Western Han Dynasty was to use the checkpoint to collect taxes.

The Western Han Dynasty set up many passes in the inland and border areas, and began to levy tariffs. In particular, Yumen Pass and Yang Pass had become important tax gates in the Hexi Corridor from Chang' an to the Western Regions.

According to *Records of the Historian*, the Han Dynasty appointed Pass Captain to manage the goods from the Western Regions. Pass Captain inspected business travel and customs clearance documents at major points along the Silk Road and collected tariff and market rent (market transaction tax). The name of Yumen Pass was the witness of a large-scale customs tax collection activity. Yumen Pass was first set up when Emperor Wu of Han Dynasty opened roads to Western Regions and set up four counties in Hexi. It was named "Yumen Pass" because it was the place where jade was imported from Western Regions. Later, in order to prevent the merchants from evading the customs duties and the invaders from besieging Yumen Pass, a new pass was set up near Yumen Pass in the Han Dynasty. This pass was in the south of Yumen Pass. The ancients said that "the south of the mountain and the north of the river are the 'yang' ", so this pass in the south of Yumen Pass was called Yang Pass. From then on, Yumen Pass and Yang Pass could not only echo each other, but also guarded the pass to the maximum extent and prevented business travelers from tax evasion by bypassing. At the same time, both Yumen Pass and Yang Pass served as Pass Captain' s government equipping with massive forces. The Central Plains and the Western Regions all need to pass these two passes.

Since the Han Dynasty set tax collection customs, there would be corresponding tax collection standards. Han Dynasty set the central administrative organizations responsible for the collection of customs duties. They monopolized foreign trade by the government. According to "Fu" and "Zhuan" , they permit goods to enter and leave the Customs. If somebody traded with foreign businessmen without authorization, he would be punished, the heaviest punishment was sentenced to death.

The Han Dynasty established two ways to calculate and collect tariffs: quantity based and ad valorem based. The quantity based mainly used for physical goods which were divisible and storable, such as silk, grain, tea, metal, etc. Based on the quantity or weight of goods to impose the tariff. If there was a merchant who took a load of silk to go through the customs, the tariff object he had to pay was the silk. For those living animals, leather, medicinal materials and other inseparable commodities, they were taxed in currency according to the market value of the goods, this is ad valorem based. In addition to tariffs, the Han Dynasty also collected market rent for export goods. The tariff rate was generally about 10%. The market rent was calculated on the basis of transaction volume, with the market rent rate at about 2%.

However, for some special commodities, the tax rate was very high, and a progressive tax rate was implemented. For example, grain was strictly controlled to outflow by the state. If someone left the customs with rice, the tariff rates on rice were one seventh, one fifth and one third respectively when they passed the Han Dynasty's internal, central and foreign customs clearance. The progressive tariff rate after the three customs clearance of the rice was the sum of the three customs tariff rates, reaching 68%. Ironware, crossbows, and horses were listed as contraband and were not allowed to go through the customs.

Quantity based and ad valorem based are still in use today and have become the basis of China's modern tariff collection.

3. New Customs Appearance

One day in the 7th year of Yixi reign of the Eastern Jin Dynasty (411 A.D.), in a temple in the Simhala (now Sri Lanka), Faxian, an eminent monk from China, was told by the Zhike monk that a treasure had just been consecrated in the temple, and the believers were flocking to watch it. Faxian could not help but look at the Buddha. When he saw the treasure, he burst into tears. This wasn't a Buddha, it was a white silk fan from the native land of the Central Plains. Many local people had never seen such exquisite textile, so they regarded it as treasure. At that moment, white silk fan suddenly awakened Faxian's homesickness, and he decided to return to China.

Faxian, the first monk to arrive in India in Chinese history, was also the first who went by land and returned by sea. It was more than 200 years earlier than Xuanzang's journey to the west in Tang Dynasty. In addition, an important factor for later Xuanzang's westward journey was his admiration for the feat of Faxian. Faxian compiled what he saw and heard in the travel into the book of *The Kingdom of Buddha*, which left important historical materials of Western Regions and South Asia for later generations.

Faxian chose to walk to India by land. He and several monks, starting from capital city— Chang'an, went through the vast desert, and after all hardships, they finally reached their destination. In India, he studied Buddhism extensively for several years, and later, he came to the Simhala to continue to promote Dharma, two years later, he saw the white silk fan.

Faxian didn't want to cross the yellow sand, which was not only dangerous, but also time-consuming. He was eager to return, and finally found out that it took only a few months for the ships of the merchants of India to reach Guangzhou directly. He was overjoyed and contacted the merchant ship. When he was promised, his eyes filled with tears.

The planned route was recorded in *The Book of Buddha*: from the mouth of Heng River of India, through Sri Lanka to the Indian Ocean, through the Malacca Strait, then from Malacca Strait to Java Sea, from Java Sea to South China Sea, and finally to Guangzhou. The full journey was completed in two to three months.

However, it was very difficult for him to return. After crossing the Strait of Malacca, the merchant ship was damaged, so they stayed in Yevati for five months, and then changed a ship and continued to Guangzhou. Suddenly, they encountered gale weather, the ship deviated from the channel. After driving to the northeast for several decades, they finally saw the land. After Faxian landed, he found that he had arrived at Laoshan, Changguang County, Qingzhou (now Laoshan, Qingdao, Shandong).

After all kinds of hardships, Faxian finally returned to the Central Plains. This passage, which he described in *The Book of Buddha*, became the earliest record of studying China's maritime trade with India, Iran and other countries.

With the gradual development of maritime trade, in the Tang Dynasty, this route was called "Road from Guangzhou to Haiyi" .The merchant ships first set out in Guangzhou, drove southward to Tunmen port at the mouth of the Pearl River, passed through the Qizhou ocean in the northeast of Hainan Island, passed through the southeast sea of Vietnam, and then passed through the Singapore Strait to Sumatra island, sailed southeast through Java Sea, then sailed out of the Malacca Strait, finally arrived at Obola Port and Basra port in the Persian Gulf. This route, with a total length of 14000 kilometers, was the longest route in the world at that time, and the prosperity of Guangzhou came from it.

In 661 A.D., the imperial court set up the official post of "Shi Bo Shi" in Guangzhou. The duties of the Shi Bo Shi were to collect customs duties on the ships coming to trade, purchase a certain amount of imported goods on behalf of the court, manage the goods that the merchants paid tribute to the emperor, and supervise and manage the Shi Bo trade. To some extent, Shi Bo Shi can be regarded as the earliest "Customs" commissioner in China. However, the real person who held the post of Shi Bo Shi, which firstly recorded in the second year of Kaiyuan (714 A.D.), was Zhou Qingli, who was appointed as Shi Bo Shi of Annan city.

The tariff imposed by the Tang Dynasty government on foreign merchants was called "Bo Jiao" , and it was also called "anchorage tax" because it was levied when foreign ships landed. The Tang Dynasty stipulated that foreign businessmen could trade freely within the territory after paying the Bo Jiao. At that time, in addition to collecting the Bo Jiao in Guangzhou, the Tang government also set up tax collection places in Yangzhou and other places, and the tax rate was set by local officials. At that time, the tax rate was relatively heavy, and Cui Rong, a famous official of Tang Dynasty, demanded that the functional management of "Customs" and "market" should be divided on this basis, making it one of the early theories to distinguish customs tax from other taxes. "The market was complex and sophisticated, and the pass went to the end of the road" "The pass was the place of imperial violence, and the place where people gathered was the market" . But at the same time, Cui Rong opposed to levying pedestrian tariffs, saying that tariffs hinder the circulation of goods and were not conducive to social stability. "If the tax is levied on the pass, the country will prosper ...If one pass is uneasy, all passes of the whole world will be concerned" .

After the Anshi Rebellion in Tang Dynasty, the situation of separate government became more serious, and the phenomenon of setting up checkpoints and collecting taxes was more and more serious. At the time of Emperor Xianzong of the Tang Dynasty, foreign businessmen came by boat, in addition to paying the Bo Jiao, they also had to pay the "anchorage tax" . Therefore, foreign businessmen often bribed and entertained officials at all levels below the military commissioner, in order to reduce their business costs. The government of Tang Dynasty also realized that the burden of foreign businessmen was heavy, so it ordered that no more money should be collected. According to the records in *The Entire Donovan*, it was said that the South Sea sailboat originally came out of naturalization and admiration ...the fan tourists in Lingnan, Fujian and Yangzhou should be appointed to save time, and observe the envoys often have doubts. Except for the Bojiao, closing and tribute, they should be allowed to make their own transactions and should not increase the rate of tax.

4. Open the Sea, Ban the Sea, and Build Customs

In today' s Quanzhou City, Fujian Province, there is a stone tablet engraved with the words "Quanzhou Shi Bo Si site in Song Dynasty" , which is also the only existing ancient customs site.

The customs mentioned here are the foreign trade management organization established in the Song Dynasty and flourished in the three Dynasties — Shi Bo Si.

In the Tang Dynasty, Shi Bo Shi was only an official post, while in the Song Dynasty, Shi Bo Si was set up as a special organization to manage foreign trade. In the Song Dynasty, Shi Bo Si was set in Guangzhou, Hangzhou, Mingzhou, Quanzhou, Mizhou, etc, which was almost the same as today' s customs.

The establishment of Shi Bo Si also confirmed the prosperity of water trade in Song and Yuan Dynasties.

In Song Dynasty, *Shi Bo Tiao*, the policy and regulations for the management of foreign trade were formulated. The key responsibilities of the Shi Bo Si are as follows. According to the goods applied by the businessmen, the amount of personnel on the ship and their destination, send the public certificate, namely the sailing permit certificate; send people to board the ship to provide maintenance services and avoid bringing weapons, copper coins, women, escaped soldiers and so on; go over the ships returning

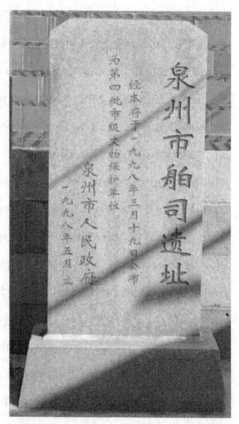

Site of Quanzhou Shi Bo Si in Song Dynasty (Photo by Lin Jie)

to the port; implemented system of sampling, that was the goods imported and exported were divided into thick and thin parts, the government took a certain proportion of the goods, which was actually a kind of physical Shi Bo tax; the goods drawn shall be removed to the capital of the country (extraction), and purchase some goods from the vessel at the prescribed price (purchase), when after the extraction and purchase, sent the public certificate to the remaining goods according to the specifications of the municipal shipping department, and then they can be transported to other places for sale. This was a very mature form of customs management, which was almost the same as the main work of customs today.

The income of the Shi Bo was a main source of the revenue for the state treasury in Song Dynasty. In the middle of the Northern Song Dynasty, the income of the Shi Bo reached about 420000 Min (Guan). In the early Southern

Song Dynasty, the ruling crisis of the Song Dynasty was deep, and the influence of Shi Bo revenue in the Financial Bureau was more critical. During the Southern Song Dynasty, the annual revenue was only 10 million Min, while Shi Bo revenue reached 1.5 million Min, which supported the national treasury to a certain extent. Zhao Gou, the emperor of Song Dynasty, once said, "the benefits of the Shi Bo are helpful to the country" "the benefits of the Shi Bo are thick, if the settings are prosperous, the income will be millions" . In the1ˢᵗ, the 7ᵗʰ and the 10ᵗʰ years of Shaoxing, the Shi Bo revenue was more than 1 million Min, and reached 2 million Min in the 29ᵗʰ year of Shaoxing.

Public certificate, also known as public credential and public inspection, was the certification materials sent by the Shi Bo Si of Song Dynasty to the foreign traders. There is a replica of Li Chong's public evidence on display in the China Customs Museum. Li Chong's public evidence is the most complete trade voucher in Song Dynasty, the original script is now in Japan. In the first year of Chongning (1102), Li Chong along with some people went to Japan for business, and returned to China two years later. And in 1105, Li Chong and others went to Japan again, and submitted Chinese public evidence to the Japanese government of Dazai for trade. At that time, because Quanzhou did not set up a Shi Bo Si, the merchant ships had to go to Mingzhou (today's Ningbo, Zhejiang Province) to go through the exit formalities. The Shi Bo Si of East Zhejiang and West Zhejiang issued the public evidence to them and then sailed to Japan. This kind of public evidence is actually equivalent to now passport visa.

After the establishment of the Ming Dynasty, there were Mongol attacks in the north and Japanese pirates rampant on the sea. Zhu Yuanzhang ordered the implementation of the policy of sea ban, stipulating that no board is allowed to go into the sea. Although there was a brief resplendence of Zheng He's voyages to the west during Zhu Di's reign, the policy of sea ban was still the mainstream. There was only one foreign trade port in China, namely Guangzhou. The sea ban led to the unsmooth trade exchange of non-governmental materials, which eventually became the main cause of the enemy's chaos in coastal areas in the middle Ming Dynasty. Until the first year of Longqing (1567), Emperor Mu Zong of Ming Dynasty announced eliminating the policy of sea ban, adjusting the policy of foreign trade, and allowing the people to carry out foreign trade. The non-governmental foreign trade in coastal areas had entered a new trend, and an all-round opening-up situation appeared in Ming Dynasty.

After the ban was lifted in Longqing, the Yuegang port in Zhangzhou city of Fujian Province became a key trading port. The Ming government also established institutions here to improve the tax system. At that time, the government departments of Ming Dynasty required that the ships entering and leaving the harbor must go for the record, and report in detail the size of the ships, the country of origin, the country they went to, and the type and total number of their goods. The government departments would collect "tax", "land rate" and "water rates" from them. The Ming Dynasty also set up a professional tax management organization— "the governor's pay hall". Every year, the government departments selected a senior official to the harbor to manage taxes in turn. This kind of tax reform immediately endangered the management of the government departments in Guangzhou and Macao.

After the collapse of Ming Dynasty, the following Qing Dynasty continued to implement the strict policy of sea ban and abolished the Shi Bo Si. In the early Qing Dynasty, Zheng Chenggong's family was in a stalemate with Qing government in the Taiwan Strait, while in the middle and late time, the coastal region was invaded by western colonists. In this context, the rulers of Qing Dynasty chose the policy of sea ban and closing the door of the country. At the end of Ming Dynasty and the beginning of Qing Dynasty, the "order of moving from the sea" was issued. The coastal residents had to retreat to inland areas for dozens of miles, foreign trade and fishing were prohibited. In the middle and late Qing Dynasty, the policy clearly defined that those who went out to do business— if they did not return within 2 years, they would be abandoned by the Qing Dynasty and would never be allowed to return home.

However, the huge trade activities between China and the west could not be interrupted, and the Qing government also needed to collect sufficient taxes through sino-foreign trade to supply the operation of the country. Therefore, in the 23rd year of Kangxi (1684), the Qing government issued an edict and decided to open customs in Guangzhou City, Zhangzhou City, Ningbo City and the south of the Yangtze River, and declared that they were called Yue customs, Min customs, Zhe customs and Jiang customs. The government established the method of selecting senior officials from the government of the internal affairs, which was called customs supervision. Hao Yulin, the governor of Fujian Province at that time, once said: "There are about 30, 28 or 29 foreign cargo ships in Fujian Province in one year. The value of each ship varies from about 60000 to 100000. Every year, Fujian foreign cargo ships get about 2~3 million silver to return to the country. The profit of loan interest replenished the deficiency of hard work."

The "customs" began to form at that time. But from the system point of view, it was the continuation of the Shi Bo system. In 1757, the original coastal customs were abolished by Emperor Qianlong, and only the Yuehai Pass in Guangdong was reserved for foreign trade. As a foreign trade organization under the Guangdong Customs, Guangzhou ShiSanHang was also the only legal foreign trade zone in the Qing Dynasty. All the trade between China and overseas countries gathered here until the Opium War. As a result, this foreign goods company monopolized China's foreign trade for more than 80 years. The important reason why Guangzhou ShiSanHang was able to do his own business was that the emperor regarded it as a private coffer, which was called "the south coffer of the emperor" at that time.

A brief history of ancient Chinese customs reflected the historical trend of Chinese people moving from land to sea and returning from sea to land. In the era of openness and inclusiveness, the customs system was constantly innovating, leading the country to continue to open to the outside world; in the era of seclusion, the customs were trapped in a corner and became a place to satisfy the rulers' selfish desires.

The real customs system in modern China was established after the Opium War, during the Shanghai Small Sword Society Uprising, the Western powers exploited it and seized the right of customs administration, and was established in about half a century after the British Lord Hurd was in charge of the Chinese customs.

Every drink and every peck is the cause. How many things have happened to the customs in the past are all in the laughs of today's people.

Grain Transport

— Inland River Transport Matters the Safety of the Country

Part of *Qingming Shanghe Tu* by Zhang Zeduan (Currently housed in the Palace Museum)

In the long feudal era of China, grain transport was an important economic system under the centralized government. The system of grain transport was a major political system in China, which had been attached great importance in all dynasties. According to *Shuo Wen Jie Zi*, the Chinese word "漕" means transporting grain through a waterway, and there are three modes of transportation: river transportation, land and water transportation and sea transportation. In China's ancient agricultural society with underdeveloped infrastructure, the basis of state operation was the collection of taxes. The materials collected such as taxes and grain needed to be transported to the capital, frontier and other places. Water transportation had certain advantages, thus grain transport rose. As for grain transport, it refers to all water transport in a broad sense. In a narrow sense, it is the name of water transport (sometimes including part of land transport) in which local governments transported the grain collected to the capital or other designated places in the past dynasties as mentioned in *Cihai*.

Grain transport has a history of thousands of years in China. It not only played the role of balancing economy and ensuring supply, but also was closely related to political stability, national defense security, and disaster relief. A lot of manpower, material and financial resources will inevitably be consumed in the long journey of grain transport. In addition, grain transport was closely related to the storage facilities arranged in various places, including the management of grain transport, river course and storage personnel, as well as the participation of transporters, sailors and boat trackers along the way.

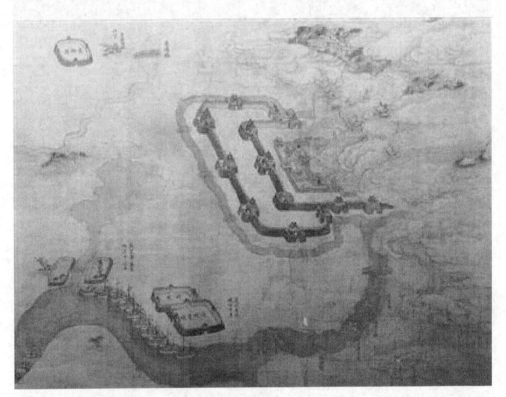

Part of *The Grain Transport Map* during the Qianlong period of the Qing Dynasty (Author unknown, currently collected at the Tianjin Museum)

The prosperity of grain transport promoted the development of trade, and the "Four Big Cities of Grain Transport" (Yangzhou, Suzhou, Hangzhou, and Huai'an) emerged as times require. On the one hand, grain transport promoted the development of economy, the water transportation and trade also flourished; on the other hand, it ensured the balance of supply and demand in the grain market, and alleviated the pressure of regional and seasonal imbalance of grain market through grain transport, which is of positive significance to regulating the market and stabilizing prices. In addition, grain transport objectively changed the regional social and economic pattern, and the canal economic belt sprouted.

1. Evolution and Change

The origin of grain transport was very early. In the Spring and Autumn Period, the state of Jin suffered from famine. Duke Hui of Jin borrowed grain from the state of Qin. From the capital of Qin to the capital of Jin, the mighty grain ships connected end to end on the road, transporting grain to the state of Jin, which was called the "Battle of the Boat".

In the pre Qin period, most wars were related to the control of land and population, so the demand for military logistics supply was increasing. Land transportation could not meet the increasing needs, at this time, the role of water transport was increasing because of its advantages of large scale and high economic benefits. In the Qin and Han Dynasties, the system of grain transport formed gradually, laying a solid foundation for the later development. The core of the grain transport system established in the Qin Dynasty was the storage management. During this period, many large granaries were built, mostly in the capital or waterway hub, to meet the needs of transportation and storage. At the same time, they also actively dug channels to dredge the way of water transport.

Efficient transportation capacity is the guarantee of the implementation of military strategy. For example, when Qin destroyed the state of Chu, General Wang Jian led 600000 troops to the army. The total amount of daily rations was 66667 Dan, which was estimated to need more than 2600 vehicles to transport. The shortage of land transportation must be supplemented by Jianghan water transportation.

The ancients said that grain transport was responsible for national and military demands. First, it needed to facilitate the efficient tax collection and transportation network of water transport organization to ensure the realization of resource concentration and serve the maintenance of national financial operation; second, it should meet the needs of national defense and military affairs.

In the Spring and Autumn Period, the states of Wu and Yue were the first to build canals to carry out military activities. They were located in the south of the Yangtze River and were good at using geographical conditions to carry out water transportation. As for the origin and route of Han Ditch, Du Yu proved that "build city in Han River and connect the ditch, which leads to Sheyang Lake in the northeast, ending at the northwest and flowing to Huai River, and connects the channel for grain transport". In 486 B.C., Fu Chai, the king of Wu, built the Han Ditch to go north to attack the State of Qi. After Han Ditch was opened, Wu opened up He River in the area between Shang State and Lu State, which connected Yi River and ancient Ji River, and a new canal was opened for navigation.

After the unification of the six countries in Qin Dynasty, due to the formation of unified centralized power, the three water systems of the Yellow River, Huai River, and Yangtze River were connected. The channel of grain transport from the north and south was formed, the capacity of grain transport was further improved, and the system of grain transport gradually improved.

The Tongji Canal and Yongji Canal were excavated in Sui Dynasty, and the Han Ditch and Jiangnan Canal were repaired closely linking the Central Plains, Hebei Plain and Jianghuai area, forming a major traffic artery connecting the north and the south. Later, Guangtong Canal was built, and the Grand Canal connected the Yangtze River, Yellow River, Huai River, Hai River, and Qiantang River, forming a complete system of water transportation across the country. In the Tang Dynasty, the emphasis on grain transport was gradually placed on the south, and the grain transport routes presented southeast and northwest changes. In the middle and late Tang Dynasty, the prime minister was in charge of the grain transport administration.

By the Song Dynasty, the southern economy developed and became the main source of material supply for the imperial court, especially in the south of the Yangtze River, which became the main area for supplying grain. In the Northern Song Dynasty, the three ministers of the central government were in charge of the administration of grain transport, and the transshipment department (grain department) responsible for collecting grain and the shipping department responsible for transporting grain were set up in each department. With each performing their respective duties, the grain transport became more specialized and efficient, and the canal conditions were further improved, the annual transportation volume of grain transport during the period of Zhenzong and Renzong could reach 8 million Dan. By the Southern Song Dynasty, the grain transport system had made important adjustments, with Lin' an (now Hangzhou, Zhejiang Province) as the center, the Yangtze River and Jiangnan Canal as the transportation backbone, and formed a new mode of grain transport with official transport as the mainstay and commercial transport as the supplement.

In the Yuan Dynasty, the sea transportation was developed, and the grain transport began to take the sea transportation as the main and the inland river transportation as the auxiliary. During the Yuan, Ming and Qing Dynasties, the political center continued to move to the Northeast, while the economic center was more and more clearly established in the south, especially in the middle and lower reaches of the Yangtze River. The grain transport changed to the north–south direction. The political center and economic center were separated from north and south, which lasted for a long time, and much grain was transported from south to north. Therefore, fundamentally speaking, the transfer of political and economic centers determines the renewal and change of grain transport routes. The state has formulated various measures to ensure that grain collected from the people can be transported to the capital smoothly.

With the changes of the times, the grain transportation was continuously reformed, and it was not basically perfected until the Ming Dynasty. At the beginning of Ming Dynasty, the grain transport of Yuan Dynasty was mainly by sea, supplemented by river and land transport. The organization and management of grain transport were becoming more and more mature with the combination of branch transportation method, exchange transportation method and modified exchange transportation method. The grain supply from the south is called south grain, and the grain supply from the north is called north grain.

In the Qing Dynasty, the excavation of the Middle Canal completely ended the era of using the Yellow River for transportation, and built the junction of the Yellow River, Huai River and canal to ease the water surface gradient, reduce the turbidity flow for irrigation and transportation, and improve the grain transport conditions. In the Qing Dynasty, the "Cao Biao" were responsible for the collection and transportation of grain. According to statistics, during Yongzheng period, the grain transport can supply more than 4 million Dan of grain to the capital every year. In the late Qing Dynasty, the canal transportation gradually declined due to the influence of Opium War, Taiping Heavenly Kingdom and the diversion of the Yellow River. By 1901, the grain transport was suspended.

2. Check and Balance

Direct transportation and transshipment are two basic forms of ancient grain transport. If the waterway was unobstructed, the water transport would go smoothly. If there was any obstruction, the grain would be stocked waiting for allocation at the right time.

After the transportation of grain from south to north, the route of grain transport was becoming longer and longer, and the transportation of grain had become a huge project, and had a closer connection with the regional society in a larger space. The imperial court gradually realized the significance and value of grain transport to local regulation and began to make use of it. As the grain transport route connecting the north and the south was gradually fixed, the process of grain collection, distribution, and transportation was relatively stable, which provided conditions for the imperial court to use grain transport to solve political problems.

Since the Song Dynasty, the social function of grain transport was gradually recognized by the imperial court. One is buying and selling grain[①], the other is relief. To buy and sell grain is to balance the market supply and demand by buying and selling grain, so as to stabilize the price of grain. In Song Dynasty, the Hedi method[②] was carried out. Every year, there was a quota task of grain transport. In case of famine, some areas could not complete the task of grain payment, so they could use money to pay the same value, and then the government purchased grain from the rich areas in the south of the Yangtze River, thus ensuring the completion of the task. The Hedi method gradually developed, and it evolved into the Daifa system in Renzong period of Song Dynasty. The shipping department in charge of collecting and transporting grain had a certain amount of purchasing funds. They could adjust the grain strategy in time according to the harvest situation of each region. When the harvest was good, they could buy rice and reserve it. If there was a shortage of grain in the region, they could supply it with the stored grain, then the grain and freight would be converted into money and handed in. "If the grain was cheap, the government would buy it, and the peasants would not be hurt. If people were hungry and had poor harvests, they would accept money. The people thought it was convenient. The capital would increase year by year, and the army would have a food surplus", this method not only ensured the completion of the task of grain, but also maintained the market balance, stabilized the grain price, alleviated the grain pressure in grain shortage areas, and was conducive to disaster relief.

Compared with Song Dynasty, the market regulation function of grain transport in Ming and Qing Dynasties was more flexible. In order to deal with the unexpected situation in the grain market, the government could intercept and allocate the grain in transportation at any time. Generally speaking, the Ming

---

① In Chinese, "Di" means buying grain, "Tiao" means selling grain, when putting them together, it means buying and selling grain.

② A method of national management of food supply, in which the government and the people bargain to buy national grain.

and Qing Dynasties changed the Song Dynasty's "buying mainly" to "selling mainly".

The interception and allocation of grain referred to the rearrangement and allocation of grain before or in the course of transportation due to temporary needs (storage, military pay or disaster relief, etc). It was the main way for the government to sell or provide relief.

Qing Dynasty made full use of the spatial advantages and convenience of grain transport, as well as the characteristics of route mobility, without increasing the cost, realized its social functions such as enriching storage, stabilizing grain prices, disaster relief and so on, so as to maintain social stability. Once the regional help occurs, it can be transferred in time to realize the social functions of grain interception and relief quickly, conveniently and efficiently.

With the development of grain transport, the related system of grain transport became more and more advanced and mature. The compilation of *Complete Book of Grain Transport of Hubu*[①] began during the period of Yongzheng reign, and it was required to be updated every ten years. The contents of the book included collection amount of grain, collection cases, exchange transportation cases, grain transport ships, supervising transportation duties, selecting and supplementing officials, grain collection by officials, planning and warehousing, channels for grain transport, grain storage in Beijing, interception and allocation cases, purchase and transportation, sales and examination, etc. Each major system also included various sub-items, which completely covered all aspects of water transport affairs and fully reflected the comprehensiveness and strictness of the grain transport system in Qing Dynasty.

3 . Canal Economic Belt

In the Northern Song Dynasty, Kaifeng was the capital, and the grain transport mainly went through the Bian River and then the Jiangnan Canal,

---

① It is a comprehensive record of grain transport system in Qing Dynasty.

and the transported materials were mostly southern materials. In the Yuan Dynasty, the capital was established in Dadu, and the canal could not reach the capital directly. Grain transport was mainly carried by sea, but the pattern of the canal connecting the north and the south was formally formed, which was of self-evident significance to the transportation of goods. In the Ming and Qing Dynasties, Beijing was the capital, and the Grand Canal carried the responsibility of transporting grain from the south to the the north, and made it the most dynamic and influential area in this period. The exchange of goods and materials between the north and the south, the development of the economy along the canal, the rise and prosperity of towns along the canal, the directional gathering of businessmen and the long-distance development of trade and so on, these economic phenomena began to attract people's attention. With the change in history, the interaction between grain transport and regional economic pattern has formed a distinctive regional economic development model, and the canal economic belt has gradually taken shape.

The canal economic belt refers to a relatively systematic, flowing, divergent and radiating economic belt formed by the canal waterway, while carrying grain transport, it communicates a huge amount of material exchanges between the north and the south, continuously promoting more economic activities and contacts, connecting more regions, towns, materials, industries and people.

Urban development is closely related to transportation. In ancient times, waterway was the main traffic channel, and convenient waterway transportation was the basic guarantee of economic development at that time. Along with the development of grain transport, every town and city along the line would form a central hub city with developed economy. These cities gradually evolved into transport hubs and distribution centers of grain transport routes, where businessmen gather and commodities flow, thus promoting the development of economy. Repeatedly, the canal city formed by the radiation of canal economic belt has high economic level and rapid development.

During the Ming and Qing Dynasties, the canal cities such as Suzhou,

中国物流
故事
STORY
古代辑
汉英对照

Yangzhou, Huai'an, Jining, Liaocheng, Linqing, Dezhou, and other towns such as Jiujiang, Wuhu, Hankou constituted the canal economic belt in that period. Most of the coming and going grain ships stopped at these stations. Whether the purchase of local specialties, the exchange of goods among merchants, or the business with troops, sailors, and escort officials, most of their activities are underway here. Merchants, tourists, and citizens gathered at the wharf, forming distinctive trade activities. The wharf culture gradually formed and greatly promoted the development of local economy. Every year in the grain transport time, the grain transport ships berthed back and forth, with a lot of ships and goods.

The docks and ports where these boats berthed had become the distribution center of goods and the gathering place for merchants to carry out trade activities. According to *She Zhi*, the large capitals at that time were Dongjing, Xijing, Jiangsu, Zhejiang, Fujian, and Guangdong Province, followed by Suzhou, Songjiang, Huai'an, and Yangzhou Mansion, Lin Qing and Ji Ning Zhou, Yizhen and Wuhu County, Guazhou and Jingde Town.

So-called born and prospered by grain transport, the prosperity of grain transport not only promoted the commodity circulation and economic development in the north and the south, but also formed an economic belt with radiating effects, driving the prosperity of one side. Taking Huai'an, the capital of grain transport, as an example, convenient traffic conditions, frequent trade activities and businessmen and officials provided favorable conditions for the development of Huai'an, and both the city's appearance and the level of economic development had been significantly improved. Huai'an had the same reputation as Yangzhou, Suzhou, and Hangzhou these three great capitals at that time. In the Qing Dynasty, the governor of grain transport[1] was set, which was in vogue at that time.

Taking 1840 as the demarcation point, the grain transport in Qing Dynasty

---

[1] The senior officials in Ming and Qing Dynasty to manage the grain transport.

began to decline, the main reason was the decline of national power in Qing Dynasty, and the shipping rights of inland river and territorial sea were opened by the great powers. Coupled with the destruction of the Taiping Heavenly Kingdom Movement, the inland-waterway grain transport of the whole Qing Dynasty was destroyed. The grain transport economy gradually withdrew from the historical stage, and coastal cities also declined.

The department of the governor of the grain transport in Huai' an (Photo by Jiang Yi)

4. Relying on Water Area for Living

Where there are boats, there are Jianghu. For thousands of years, all kinds of people who have relied on grain transport to "earn a living" are undoubtedly an important part of the history of grain transport.

During grain transport every year, troops were selected to undertake transportation tasks. Troops and grain ships in various places transport grain with gang[1] as the unit.

---

[1] The number of ships under the jurisdiction of each gang varied from 20 to 80. The grain transport team is known as the Cao Gang and the Boat Gang.

中国物流故事 古代辑 汉英对照
S T O R Y

The work of grain transport was very hard, but the treatment of sailors was very poor. In the long canal navigation, they often encountered the situations such as retrograde, stranded, through the gate, through the dam. The sailors had to use the rope to drag the ship. For example, the Song poetry says: "Only hundreds of boat trackers working together can help the ship pass, and when the water is shallow and the ship is huge, the date of pass is unpredictable." Most sailors had no official native place, eating wherever they arrived, did not have families to be concerned with, with weak concept of law and discipline, often changed ships they served and even left temporarily on an impulse. The part-time sailors were more irregular.

Sailors towing a boat in *Qingming Shanghe Tu* by Zhang Zeduan (Currently housed in the Palace Museum)

In the past dynasties, the canal network centered on the capital city relied on large and small rivers and lakes such as the Yellow River, the Yangtze River, and the Huai River. In the situation such as flood season, sudden changes in weather, and siltation of rivers, there were considerable risks in navigation. For example, many sailors died in Sanmenxia dangerous section of the Yellow River.

As the economic lifeline of the country, grain transport involved hundreds of thousands of people in the links of grain collection, ship transportation and grain storage. Whether it was the grain transport troops and sailors, the river gate officials, the guard and escort officials, or the local officials and grain farmers along the way, all had direct or indirect contact with water transport, which would affect the overall situation of the grain transport.

In order to ensure the normal operation of grain transport, all dynasties adopted various methods to organize transport teams. In general, before the Ming Dynasty, the feudal government solved the problem of transportation personnel mainly by means of recruiting civil servants and organizing professional transportation soldiers. For example, the civilian households serving in the Han, Tang and early Song Dynasties and the transportation army in the Song and Ming Dynasties undertook the transportation task under the strict control of the government. But the phenomenon of fleeing was quite common.

In the early Qing Dynasty, the army transportation system was inherited from Ming Dynasty, the flag troop[①] transportation team was organized in each area. However, it was difficult to maintain transportation due to lack of transportation troops. After Kangxi period, with the implementation of the "Tan Din Ru Mu" system in Qing Dynasty, the traditional registered residence control policy also loosened, and people had greater freedom of migration. The large number of unemployed peasants and handicraftsmen could freely change and choose the way out than before. Some of them turned to grain transport.

In the Qing Dynasty, hiring sailors to lead the transportation team also brought many problems to the management of the Qing government. In the past, households took turns to serve, and they did not make a living by transportation. After the task was completed, they could go home to engage in production. Troops could receive monthly wages and had certain living security. However, the sailors hired in Qing Dynasty had to consider wages to earn their living, and they were unemployed every year during the ship shutdown. Most of them were bachelors, and they could change careers at any time, so it was difficult for the court to effectively manage them. Moreover, the composition of boatmen

① Soldiers transporting grain in Qing Dynasty.

in Qing Dynasty was extremely complex, including not only a large number of unemployed farmers, but also unemployed people and beggars in cities and towns, and even local ruffians, hooligans and criminals who had nowhere to go. At that time, there were many descriptions in the vernacular novels. For example, in *The Biography of Ge Xianweng*, it was written a story that a rogue went to the canal wharf to pull a towline after failed cheating.

After a large number of exiles turned into sailors, although they often quarreled and fought because of competition, they gradually formed the consciousness and atmosphere of mutual rescue and assistance. Over time, some gangs and secret organizations were formed. The old sailors, who were old and fighting, naturally became the leaders.

In the process of grain transport, internal contradictions would also be aroused due to the great disparity of power and uneven distribution of interests among transporters. Because the sailors were recruited, the troops who led the boat were the owners in name, so the sailors asked to raise their employment value constantly. In the early Qing Dynasty, each sailor was supposed to pay one Liang a year, but after Jiaqing, it gradually increased to dozens of Liang. In addition, when the ship was heavy and difficult to sail, the sailor asked for more money, which was called "lair money"; in case of shallow water, the sailor would ask to increase the foot fee, which was called "life money"; when the grain ship passed through the gate against the current, they also asked to increase the money of "Jiaoguan" [①]. In order to cope with the situation that the income could not make ends meet, on the one hand, the troops demanded money when they exchanged the grain, on the other hand, on the way of transporting grain, they bullied people and merchant ships, even plundered property, and often fought with other boat gangs.

In view of illegal acts, the Qing government always attached great importance to it, and took many measures to rectify the order of shippers several

---

① When conducting a hydrographic survey, they needed to lay ropes across the river. The Jiaoguan was used to straighten the ropes.

times, strengthened all the restrictive measures and punished the sailors who had caused trouble. However, due to the fact that there were more than 100000 sailors and porters, stretching thousands of miles from the north to the south of the canal, many systems had become written documents, which could not be thoroughly implemented. These punishments can only become a formality, and can not fundamentally solve the problem. Large-scale fighting between sailors and gangs had occurred constantly, resulting in social unrest. At the end of the Qing Dynasty, when the canal was cut off and grain transport stopped, a large number of sailors joined the peasant armed forces such as the Taiping Heavenly Kingdom, Nien army and Boxer Rebellion, which accelerated the decline of the Qing Dynasty.

5. Conclusion

The cost of grain transport was high, however, the imperial court did not have a mature accounting system for this matter. Huang Mengwei estimated the cost of transporting grain to Beijing in the Qing Dynasty as follows in his *Ting Cao Lun*: "Overall planning, we can't transport one Dan of rice to Beijing without forty gold" . It was estimated that the imperial court transported four million Dan of grain by water every year, which cost an astonishing amount of money.

In the late Qing Dynasty, grain transport declined for many reasons. Not only did the water transport system not work well, but the diversion of the Yellow River and the war of the Taiping Heavenly Kingdom had a negative impact, while the new means of transportation and the invasion of Western colonial forces were changing the original economic and geographical pattern and weakening the strategic function of the Grand Canal.

In addition, every link of grain transport was full of corruption and dereliction of duty of officials, and the money and power transaction had evolved into an irreversible chronic disease. Although the Qing government made strategic adjustments, minor repairs and minor supplements could only quell the crisis but could not get rid of the malady. In this case, the whole grain transport mechanism appeared the trend of slack. The grain transport system, like other systems, showed signs of being rigid and corrupt.

Moreover, China was facing unprecedented historical changes, and the manifestation of geopolitical activities had also changed greatly, which further weakened the function of grain transport. The social and economic form had changed greatly, and the economic structure dominated by self-sufficiency agriculture had been broken. The decline of grain transport was manifested in the decrease of the function of transport, that was, the material cost and time cost of grain transport were improved, and the transportation efficiency was reduced instead. The siltation of the river course and the deterioration of navigation conditions were also important reasons for the decline of grain transport. It is inevitable that grain transport will be eliminated by the development of history.

In the past thousands of years, after the transformation of multiple identities such as a military pivot road, a transportation route and a cultural link, accompanied by the exhaustion of river channels and the impact of modern modes of transportation, the once prosperous grain transport gradually declined in the Qing Dynasty, and the era of grain transport, as an important communication road between the north and the south, finally ended.

Forbidden City

—Logistics Miracle of Palace Buildings in the World

Panorama of the Forbidden City (Image source: the Palace Museum)

In June of the 4th year of the Ming Dynasty (1402), Zhu Di, the prince who fought from Peiping for the battle, led a great army into Nanjing, the capital city. The fire broke out in the imperial city, and Emperor Jianwen Zhu Yunwen disappeared. Since then, it has become a historical mystery.

Zhu Di released the news that Emperor Jianwen died of self-immolation. He became the emperor in a voice of criticism, and changed the title to Yongle the next year, he became the famous Emperor Yongle in history.

Although Zhu Di responded to all the questions with bloody killing, it did not make him feel at ease. Coupled with the aggravation of the Northern Yuan Dynasty's invasion to the Northern Regions at that time, Zhu Di put forward the idea of "the emperor guarding the country's gate", and decided to move the capital to Peiping, where he dispatched troops.

The move not only created a magnificent city, but also left behind the world's great palace complex — the Forbidden City. "Great" is not only because it is the largest existing palace in the world, moreover, every plant, every brick and every tile in this solemn palace is a combination of ingenuity. It carries the memory of history and reflects the dream and imagination of history and the endless wisdom of the Chinese people.

The portrait axis of Zhu Di,the founder of Ming Dynasty (Copied by Yang Lingfu, now collected in the Palace Museum)

It took about 15 years to build such a grand capital, but there are different versions of historical records. Why?

According to *Mingdian Hui*, "In the 4th year of Yongle (1406), in leap July, the Duke of Qi, Qiu Fu and others were asked to build a palace in Beijing to prepare for a tour." According to *the Record of Ming Chengzu*, in November, the 14th year of Yongle (1416), "Convening the officials again to discuss the building of Beijing city… it was started in June in the 15th year of Yongle (1417) and was completed in the winter of the 18th year (1420)". From these historical materials, we can see that the construction of the Forbidden City took 15 years from 1406 to 1420, and the actual construction time in these 15 years was only about three and a half years (1417-1420). Did the construction of the Forbidden City stop for more than ten years?

As a matter of fact, in the more than ten years' time (1406-1417), the main task of the construction of the Forbidden City was the preparation of labor and materials. In other words, in the more than ten years' time, in order to build this miracle in the history of world architecture, the whole Central Plains Dynasty

1. Prelude: Migrants

Before the city was renamed Peiping, it was once Yanjing of Liao State, Zhongdu of Jin State and Dadu of Yuan Dynasty. Especially during the period of Dadu of Yuan Dynasty, the scale of the city reached 50 square kilometers, and it was the most prosperous city in the world at that time. Marco Polo, a legendary Italian traveler, described Dadu of Yuan Dynasty that, "foreign expensive materials and department stores were imported here, and cities in the world can't compare with here".

In the first year of Hongwu in the Ming Dynasty (1368), Xu Da, a general of the Ming Dynasty, led the northern expedition army to encircle Dadu. The Royal relatives and nobles of the Yuan Dynasty fled with gold, silver and jewelry. The garrison was insufficient, and the Dadu city was soon conquered by the Ming army. Then they destroyed the prosperous city with fire. In order to commemorate pacifying the northern region, Zhu Yuanzhang, Emperor Taizu of the Ming Dynasty, renamed Dadu of Yuan Dynasty as Peiping.

Later, when Zhu Di, the fourth son of Zhu Yuanzhang and the king of Yan, came to Peiping, the land for his dragon rising in future, but now had become a desolate and remote city in the north. It was not only sparsely populated, but also deficient in resources and extremely weak in infrastructure. Therefore, many years later, when Zhu Di, who sat on the throne, was ready to move to Peiping, the most important problem he faced was that the construction of palaces and the development of cities which required a large number of laborers and permanent residents.

In the first year of Yongle (1403), Zhu Di renamed Peiping as "Beijing" and upgraded its status to "Xingzai" [1]. This year, he also ordered to move 20000 households from nine Fu in Shanxi and 4000 wealthy households from Zhili,

---

[1] The place where the emperor stays temporarily.

Jiangsu and Zhejiang to Beijing to increase the population of the capital. These people were generally rich, and they soon started their previous business in Beijing. In addition, in the suburbs of Beijing, many farmers gradually cultivated land, and large-scale immigration projects have gradually developed since then.

In the 3rd year of Yongle (1405), Zhu Di sent the third prince, Zhu Gaosui, the king of Zhao, to be responsible for the military affairs of Beijing, and ordered Shuntian mansion and the neighboring two governments to be exempted from land tax for two years, so as to attract personnel to move to Beijing.

In the 5th year of Yongle (1407), Emperor Chengzu of the Ming Dynasty recruited a group of crack troops, consisting of craftsmen, soldiers and general labor force, to go to Peiping, including more than 7000 Annan craftsmen captured and escorted to Beijing. At the same time, Zhu Di ordered to choose able-bodied men and soliders from Henan, Shandong, Shanxi, Shaanxi, and Zhongdu (now Fengyang, Anhui) to arrive in Beijing in the following year to start construction. The number of the labor force should be as high as several hundred thousand.

At this point, the huge construction of Beijing's Forbidden City has opened a prelude. At that time, a difficult problem was placed in front of this group of builders. Where did the bricks, stones and timber urgently needed by engineering buildings come from?

This problem had been left to Song Li, the minister of public works, who was in charge of all construction matters for the country. Which way would Song Li open up the situation.

2. Opening: Dredging the Canal

The construction scale and specifications of the Forbidden City required a lot of top-level building materials. In the imperial edict, when it was decided to build the Beijing Palace, Emperor Yongle appointed Song Li, Minister of the Ministry of industry, Shi Kui, right Minister of the Ministry of official personnel affairs, and Gu Pu, left minister of the ministry of revenue, to go all over the country to purchase various materials. In the end, they carefully selected and determined the origin of the building materials for the Forbidden City: stone came from Fangshan, Beijing, Quyang, Hebei; brick came from Suzhou; lime came from Yizhou, Hebei; five-color tiger skin stone came from Panshan, Hebei; fine masonry used for the temple foundation came from Linqing, Shandong; pine mostly came from the Northeast China; while Phoebe mostly came from Sichuan, Yunnan, Guizhou, Jiangsu and Zhejiang.

The origin of materials in Beijing and Hebei were not far from the Forbidden City construction site, and the progress can be barely guaranteed by means of human pulling and horse carrying. However, the construction materials in Jiangsu, Zhejiang, Sichuan, Yunnan, and Guizhou, which were hundreds of miles away or even thousands of miles away, would inevitably need to be transferred for many times to reach Beijing, and water transportation had become the most convenient and efficient way of logistics. From the Southern Regions to the Northern Regions, the Beijing-Hangzhou Grand Canal had a large freight volume. What was the situation of the Beijing-Hangzhou Grand Canal at that time?

At first, the Grand Canal was dug in the Spring and Autumn Period and the Warring States Period for the crusade against Zhao, and was greatly expanded and repaired in Sui Dynasty. Since Yang Guang, Emperor Yang of Sui Dynasty, opened the Grand Canal connecting Luoyang in the west, Zhuo County in the north and Yuhang in the south, the transportation of materials from north to south was on the fast lane. The Grand Canal flourished during the Tang and Song Dynasties. However, with the change of dynasties, the destruction of war and the flooding of the Yellow River, only part of the canal was in operation by Yuan Dynasty. After Yuan Shizu Kublai Khan unified all parts of the country, in order to make the South-to-North Grain Diversion more convenient, he decided to straighten the Grand Canal, that is, to build the horizontal Grand Canal with Luoyang as the center into a vertical Grand Canal with Dadu as the center and leading to Hangzhou. He ordered the excavation of Jizhou River, Huitong River, Tonghui River and others. Since then, the Grand Canal did not need to detour to

Henan Province, but only needed to go from Huai 'an, via Suqian and Xuzhou to Shandong and then arrived at Beijing. At this point, the Beijing-Hangzhou Grand Canal is the same as today. The new Beijing-Hangzhou Grand Canal was more than 900 kilometers shorter than the Grand Canal bypassing Luoyang.

At the end of the Yuan Dynasty, the Yellow River changed its course again, and the Shandong section of the Beijing-Hangzhou Grand Canal was affected by the Yellow River sediment and began to clog. After Zhu Yuanzhang founded the Ming Dynasty, Nanjing, the political center, had been located in the rich south of the Yangtze River. The requirement of connecting the north and the south was not as urgent as that of the Yuan Dynasty, and the role of the Grand Canal had been reduced. At the end of Hongwu, the Yellow River flooded again, and some sections of the canal were blocked again. When Zhu Di decided to move the capital to Beijing and build the Forbidden City, reconstructing the north-south traffic became the most important policy direction of the imperial court. The court found that the Shandong section of the Beijing-Hangzhou Grand Canal, especially the Huitong River section, was basically silted up by the Yellow River, thus losing the value of fast transportation. To solve this problem, it was necessary to desilt quickly and make Huitong River play its role again.

Archaeological site of the Fenshui Longwang Temple excavated at the Nanwang hub of the Grand Canal (Photo by Xu Suhui)

In the ninth year of Yongle (1411), Ming Chengzu ordered the Minister of Industry, Song Li, and the Governor of Water Transport, Chen Jue, to dredge the canal which had been silted up for many years. Song Li focused his attention on the Huitong River from Linqing, Shandong Province to Anshan, Xucheng (now Dongping, Shandong Province). This section was located in a hilly area, with high terrain and insufficient water source, so most of the river reaches were narrow and shallow, and could not pass heavy-duty ships. In Yuan Dynasty, when the sluice dam was built, the water diversion point was chosen in Rencheng, which was not the highest point, resulting in more water in the south and less water in the north. Song Li's trip was called dredging the river course, but in fact, it was necessary to reorganize the river course, arrange the water source height more scientifically, and promote the use of large ships by both the north and south canals.

Song Li was well versed in the ancient saying that wisdom is in the folk. He often went to the countryside in an incognito way, inspected the river system and terrain along the river, and asked the local people for advice with humility when he encountered problems he did not understand. When visiting Baijiadian Village in the Wenshang County, someone in the village recommended folk Baiying to him, and the villagers told Song Li that Baiying was a water conservancy expert hidden in the folk.

Bai Ying used to be a small foreman of the canal civilian worker. When he was young, he took a team of more than ten people and traveled on the canal. He was very familiar with the terrain and water conditions of the Grand Canal and the vicinity in Shandong, and accumulated rich experience in sailing and harnessing the river. Bai Ying was upright and did not admire fame and wealth. He regarded the officials as fools, and the common people affectionately called him a hermit gentleman.

At first, Bai Ying had a bad impression of Song Li, thinking that he was also a superior official who knew nothing. When he heard that Song Li was upright and saw his frank attitude toward the common people, he finally understood that Song Li was different from other officials. Therefore, when Song Li came to him,

中国物流故事古代辑 STORY 汉英对照

Bai Ying immediately discussed with Song Li the river management strategy he had been thinking about for more than 10 years.

Bai Ying's canal dredging plan was as follows: damming the Dawen River and the Daqing River, raising the water level, excavating the Xiaowen River, leading the Dawen River into the Grand Canal through the Xiaowen River, higher than Nanwang (the highest point of the Huitong River), so as to ensure that the water source of Nanwang, the "ridge of the canal", is sufficient.

According to the topography and rainfall of Huitong River, Bai Ying clearly put forward ways of harnessing the river. With Wenshui as the water source, construct the diversion canal, inject it into the highest place Nanwang in the west, and then separate from the north to the south. Six of them flow northward to Linqing and connect to Wei River, establishing 17 sluices in the middle; four sluices flow south to Jining, and then go down to Si and Huai Rivers, building 21 sluices in the middle, which deal with the difficulty of insufficient water source of Huitong River from the source.

Song Li listened to Bai Ying's proposal and arranged the construction according to the engineering drawings of Bai Ying's design scheme. Song Li recruited more than tens of thousands of migrant workers to start this arduous and huge project. After nine years of hard work, they finally dredged the river and excavated the canal from Wenshang to Jining, which connected the river with the canal, connected the canal with the lake, and formed a huge water system.

The dredging project of Huitong River made the Grand Canal glow again and generate new vitality. Southern materials can be safely and quickly transported to the capital, and can solve the material transportation problem of the Forbidden City under construction.

Two hundred years later, Matteo Ricci, a missionary who came to China during the Wanli Period of the Ming Dynasty, wrote in *Matteo Ricci's Notes on China*: When they entered the imperial city through the canal, they brought a large number of timber, columns and slabs for the palace building... the bricks used for the palace may have been shipped from about 2414 kilometers away by large ships. Just for this purpose, many ships were used, which kept running day and night. A large number of building materials can be seen along the way, which is not only enough to build a palace, but also to build an entire village and town.

Natives of Beijing love to say "our Beijing city is floating through the canal". It can be seen that the role of this north-south waterway is so great.

3. Climax: Material Transportation

At the same time of the arduous dredging of the Grand Canal, the building materials for the Forbidden City are also being prepared.

There were many bricks used in the imperial city. The bricks used in the city wall and the ground were different. Some of the ground had to be paved with three layers of bricks. According to statistics, the whole imperial city needed 80 million bricks.

The ancient city walls and official halls were mostly made of Linqing bricks. Linqing brick is famous for its production in Linqing, Shandong Province. The official kiln of Linqing brick was specially set up for the construction of the Forbidden City in the Yongle period of Ming Dynasty. In the Ming and Qing Dynasties, about 384 brick kilns were built in Linqing.

The manufacturing process of Linqing brick was complicated and strict. After taking soil from the local area, the craftsmen first sifted it with large and small sieves, then filtered it with water and stored it in a pool. After the soil is settled, add water to step the soil, and keep stepping evenly before stripping. When stripping, first lay a layer of cloth in the brick, then take a piece of mud head weighing about 30000 grams, roll it back and forth on the ground into a ball, then lift it hard and fall into the brick mold accurately. The size of the thrown mud should be properly controlled. A bricklayer can only throw 300 bricks a day, and even a strong man can only throw about 400 bricks a day at most.

After the bricks enter the kiln, they need more than 40 tons of cottonwood and wheat straw, which can be burned for half a month and be baked for half a month before they become bricks. Therefore, a brick kiln can produce at most 12 Yao of bricks a year. If the annual output of bricks per kiln is 30000, 384 brick kilns can produce about 11.52 million bricks a year.

Golden Bricks (Image source: *Hall of Supreme Harmony* by Zhou Qian)

Linqing bricks used to build the Forbidden City were extremely demanding. Each brick must be one Chi and five Cun long, three Chi and six Fen thick, with an angular appearance, smooth and straight on six sides, and crisp knocking sound, otherwise, it must not be wrapped in yellow paper. After being delivered to Tongzhou, the officials of the Ministry of Industry and Trade will have to conduct a strict knock-on inspection before being transported into Beijing for use. Because the production process of Linqing brick was complicated and the inspection was strict, the cost of each brick was relatively expensive.

Laying on the ground of several key palaces, there were usually more golden bricks. This kind of brick was about two Chi wide. Because of its hard texture, glossy surface and metallic sound when knocking, it is said that the cost of one piece of brick was one Liang of gold, so it is called gold brick. It was a special brick for imperial palaces in Ming and Qing Dynasties. The production of gold brick needed six steps, which were soil sampling, billet making, firing, kiln out, grinding and oil soaking. The production time was as long as two years. When the Forbidden City was built, the Lumu brick kiln was recommended by the craftsmen of Suzhou Xiangshan Group, and it was decided by the Ministry of Industry and Trade that "the bricks were made in Suzhou, and it was responsible for serving 63 kiln households in Changzhou".

Suzhou's golden bricks and Linqing's tribute bricks were both close to the Grand Canal, so they can quickly use the convenience of the Grand Canal and supply them to Beijing on a large scale. However, the collection and transportation of stone was another scene.

The usage of stone was also great in palace buildings. The abutment under the building, the railings around the abutment, the stone bridge and the main pavement in the imperial city were all built with stone.

In order to reduce transportation difficulties, stones, especially those stone carvings with large volume, such as stone lion and Huabiao stone pillar in front of Tiananmen Square, were taken from Fangshan and Quyang near the Forbidden City as much as possible. Among them, the biggest stone is the Danbi stone on the north side of Baohe Hall in the Forbidden City. It was 16 meters long, 3.17 meters wide and weighed more than 200 tons. This referred to the weight after processing. If calculated according to the original wool, the weight was much heavier.

Whether it is from Fangshan or Quyang, the transportation of stone to Beijing can only be carried by land. There were four ways of road transportation: manpower, animal power, dry boat, and ice boat. Among them, manpower and animal power could only transport materials or products with smaller weights. When the material reached ton level, they needed the other two ways.

Dry boat transportation is to put round rolling wood under large goods and pull them forward by manpower or animal force, which requires a very flat road; ice boat is to use the way of splashing water into ice to reduce the friction of the road to facilitate transportation. The most creative thing here was the transportation of the Danbi stone. This Danbi stone was collected from Fangshan, 70 kilometers away from the center of Beijing. In order to transport stone to the Forbidden City, tens of thousands of laborers built roads and filled pits on both sides of the transportation road, digging a well every other Li or so. In the cold winter, water was poured from the well and frozen on the ground into an ice road. It took about 20000 migrant workers and more than 1000 mules taking 28 days to deliver the stone to the palace. This big stone, which was painstakingly transported to the Forbidden City in Beijing, was placed on the imperial road on the central axis of the Forbidden City.

However, it was the collection and transportation of timber in the Forbidden City that was the most difficult, complicated and time-consuming. Even in many cases, the speed of the construction of the Forbidden City depended on the speed of timber transportation.

The pillars, beams, doors, and windows of the Forbidden City palace buildings were all made of wood, which was not only in great demand, but also in high quality. Among them, the most precious was the golden Phoebe produced in Sichuan, which was an extremely high-grade wood. Its beautiful and elegant color, hard and dense material, beautiful and even texture, warm and soft texture, small shrinkage, fire-resistant, unbreakable, moisture resistant and non-rotten, and delicate fragrance made it a superior material for ancient wood architecture. These monsters, which grew in the primitive forest, were transported to Beijing. Decorated with gold, powder and dragon decoration, they became 72 pillars supporting the hall of supreme harmony. The largest one was more than one meter in diameter.

It was very difficult to exploit timber. The golden Phoebe grows mostly in the mountains in the south, where tigers, leopards, snakes and pythons often haunt, and the difficulty of logging was abnormal. Due to the complex and changeable terrain conditions, and the capricious weather, the felling and transportation were often accompanied by dangerous and uncertain factors. In addition, some of the wood production places were in the remote countryside, which further increased the difficulty of harvesting and transportation. Descendants describe it as "with 1000 people entering the mountain, only 500 people can leave the mountain" . In the 13th year of Yongle (1415), because the cutting progress was not as expected, Zhu Di ordered Song Li to go to Sichuan to supervise the cutting of timber. Song Li worked with local officials and craftsmen to discuss problems and explore solutions, and finally completed the work. Under the hard work of the lumberjack, the timber finally came out of the mountain and finally piled up in Beijing.

Water-land combined transport had become the key method of timber transportation. After the Phoebe was cut down, it was thrown from the high mountain and rolled into the valley, where it was tied into a raft. This process was fraught with dangers. Wang Shixing of the Ming Dynasty said, wood was not difficult to find, but it was difficult to cut, and it was difficult to transport it out...up and down the mountain, there were deep pits in the big stream, and the roots were very long and difficult to rotate, in case of pits, they must use other wood to catch the eagle frame and make it flush with the mountain before they can transport it out, carrying a tree down the mountain often loses several lives. These rafts stayed in the valley until flash floods brought them into the river. The raft then reached the Yangtze River along the vertical and horizontal waterway, which was connected with the Grand Canal. After the timber entered the canal, it was pulled all the way to Beijing with the help of the tracker. Officials were on duty at every station along the road. After the timber was transported to Beijing, it was packed and waiting to be used, which gave birth to many related place names, such as Taiji Factory and Huangmu Factory. These rare timbers drifted for more than 1000 kilometers after being cut down, and it took as short as two years and as long as four years to float to Beijing.

Although this process was not as dangerous as the mountain haulage, due to the long distance and the uneven water potential, not all the timber could reach the capital smoothly. During the reign of Tianqi in the Ming Dynasty, more than 1000 Phoebe were found in the reed marshes near the entrance to the sea of Tianjin.

4. End: Glory of Later Generations

After the completion of the dredging project of Huitong River, the main artery of materials between the north and the south was completely opened, and a continuous stream of bricks, stones, and timber were transported to the construction site of the Forbidden City through this waterway. The construction speed of the Forbidden City was significantly accelerated, and finally completed in the 18th year of Yongle (1420).

With the completion of the Forbidden City just around the corner, Song Li put down his supervision and came to the Grand Canal to meet his partner Bai Ying, hoping to receive rewards in Beijing together. Bai Ying had been overworked for many years. When the team arrived at Sangyuan in Dezhou, Bai Ying died of hematemesis at the age of 56 years old. Song Li had no choice but to return to Beijing alone.

In the 19th year of Yongle (1421), less than four months after the completion of the Forbidden City, the three main halls of Fengtian, Huagai and Jinshen were on fire due to lightning strike. The fire was raging and irresistible. They were burned to ashes. More than ten years of construction efforts were burned to the ground.

Lately, a new round of construction has started. At this time, Song Li had been sick, often lying in bed, and was unable to visit the site in person. But he has chosen an excellent deputy in the construction of the Forbidden City for many years, that was Kuai Xiang, the Minister of Industry. Kuai Xiang was a master of architectural design of a generation. He was praised as the chief designer of the Forbidden City by later generations. Of course, this is another legend.

In the 20th year of Yongle (1422), Song Li went to Sichuan again to look for the giant wood, because there was still a big gap in the construction of the Forbidden City. In July of the same year, Song Li died in office at the age of 62.

Axis of Wanguo Laichao (Currently collected in the Palace Museum)

Song Li dredged the canal, changed the water transportation, cut down imperial trees, and led the construction of the Forbidden City, all of which were projects that cost money like running water. However, he was very upright. "One hundred million trillion yuan was used by him, but he never embezzled anything." *The Ming History* concluded that "On the day of his death, there was no surplus money at home" .

The news of Song Li's death spread to Shandong, and the people on both sides of the canal mourned. They spontaneously built an ancestral temple for Song Li to offer sacrifices, and cordially honored him as the "god of river" .

In the 5th year of Ming Zhengtong (1440), the three halls of Fengtian, Huagai, Jinshen and Qianqing Palace were rebuilt. Since then, after four generations of Yongle, Hongxi, Xuande and Zhengtong, the Forbidden City had finally been repaired as new, and it was presented to the world with its majestic splendor.

The Forbidden City has condensed the wisdom of the working people, the hard work of the craftsmen, and the dedication and even sacrifice of their lives, which has made such a unique luxury palace! In order to build the Forbidden City, the logistics level of the whole ancient China had also improved unprecedentedly and achieved a qualitative leap. The logistics cause behind the construction of the Forbidden City has written a glorious page for the history of Chinese logistics, which can be called a miracle in the history of human logistics and is worth spreading forever.

参考文献

京杭大运河——人水互动文明的巅峰之作

[1] 彭伟．大运河文化的影像构建与叙事策略研究——以申遗纪录片《中国大运河》为例 [J]. 常州工学院学报 (社科版)，2019，37(4):8–12+26.

[2] 霍艳虹．基于"文化基因"视角的京杭大运河水文化遗产保护研究 [D]. 天津：天津大学，2018.

[3] 胡梦飞．明清京杭大运河留给外国人的印象 [J]. 珠江水运，2016(22):49–51.

[4] 卢向阳．北宋东京水运体系研究 [D]. 武汉：华中师范大学，2016.

[5] 杨凤阁．论唐代刘晏漕运改革的始末及影响 [J]. 兰台世界，2013(27):57–58.

[6] 马文波，宫肖愿．南水北调东线工程与运河文化遗产保护 [J]. 东岳论丛，2007(1):199–200.

[7] 木杉．京杭大运河 流动着的文化遗产 [J]. 城乡建设，2006(7):77–79.

丝绸之路——东西方文明交汇的千年之约

[1] 孔旭荣．"仰皇风而悦化"：中国三世纪文学中的丝绸之路 [J]. 铜仁学院学报，2018，20(5):10–14.

[2] 张晓红，詹小美．"一带一路"生成发展的历史逻辑 [J]. 广西社会科学，2017(10):149–154.

[3] 孙启忠，柳茜，陶雅，等．汉代首蓿传入我国的时间考述 [J]. 草业学报，2016，25(12):194–205.

[4] 夏吉金．浅析骆驼城遗址及其在丝绸之路上的重要地位 [J]. 丝绸之路，2016(24):14–15.

[5] 柳菁，王成勇．西北地区丝绸之路经济带协同发展的理论与实践探讨——西北地区党校系统丝绸之路经济带协同发展理论研讨会会议综述 [J]. 甘肃理论学

刊，2015(6):116–120+2.

[6] 王娜，薛阿敏. 试论网络恐怖主义及其应对之策——以中亚地区为视角 [J].
山东警察学院学报，2015，27(2):12–20.

[7] 张以俭. 运河与丝绸 [J]. 江苏蚕业，2014，36(4):41–42.

含嘉仓——天下第一粮仓

[1] 张婷瑜. 隋唐洛阳含嘉仓遗址复原研究 [D]. 西安：西安建筑科技大学，
2018.

[2] 姚佳威. "天下第一粮仓"增产之忧 [J]. 决策探索 (上半月)，
2010(7):44–46.

[3] 安其乐. "建鼓"一词考 [J]. 内蒙古社会科学 (汉文版)，2009，30(3):119–
121.

[4] 亓文香. 汉语典故词语研究 [D]. 济南：山东大学，2009.

[5] 李亚明. 汉语双音并列词语的传承方式——从《连文释义》和《现代汉语
词典》的比较看 [J]. 励耘学刊 (语言卷)，2006(2):54–78.

[6] 於忠祥，鲍春生. 井田制拾遗 [J]. 中国农史，2001(1):11–15.

"车同轨"——践行千年的物流标准化

[1] 李伟. 未来交通运输是综合和智慧的——以《"十三五"现代综合交通运
输体系发展规划》及相关研究为参考 [J]. 中国公路，2018(5):72–74.

[2] 向晓炜. 深化标准化改革形势下我国物流标准现状与建议 [J]. 物流工程与
管理，2017，39(9):7–9.

[3] 刘智洋，高燕，邵姗姗. 实施国家标准化战略　推动中国标准走出去 [J].
中国标准化，2017(11):56–61.

[4] 新华社第 39 届国际标准化组织 (ISO) 大会召开　习近平致贺信 [J]. 标准生
活，2016(9):7.

[5] 王梦恕. 铁道轨距背后的历史 [J]. 大陆桥视野，2014(11):54–55.

[6] 张书源. 国际货物运输业的发展趋势研究 [J]. 交通世界 (运输·车辆)，
2007(10):84–85.

[7] 朱丹，申彩芬. 物流标准化的若干思考 [J]. 地质技术经济管理，

郑和下西洋——大航海时代人类文明的里程碑

[1] 章忠民，胡林梅. 明清海上丝绸之路经略与海权渐失 [J]. 社会科学，2016(1):34-41.

[2] 青舟，顾菁，李钧. 江苏港口城市沿"一带一路"交汇的历史渊源与前瞻 [J]. 城市观察，2015(1):40-47.

[3] 王丽明. 论中国古代航海文化底蕴——以郑和下西洋的泉州元素为视点 [J]. 东方论坛，2011(3):54-58.

[4] 卢良志. 中国第一部航海地图集:《郑和航海图》[J]. 国土资源，2008(7):56-59.

[5] 陈敬根. 郑和精神与中国航运强国发展战略 [J]. 珠江水运，2006(S1):25-29.

[6] 谈谭. 郑和下西洋动因新探 [J]. 世界宗教研究，2005(2):95-103.

秦直道——世界上最早的高速公路

[1] 王跃春，华南，李娜，等. 追溯物流文化之源 [J]. 中华儿女，2016(22):46-47.

[2] 王龙. 鄂尔多斯行政区划朝代更迭简述 [J]. 语文学刊，2015(2):80-82+109.

[3] 康清莲. 秦驰道直道考议 [J]. 晋阳学刊，2011(4):136-138.

[4] 崔德华. 论爱自然教育的主要内容 [J]. 海南师范大学学报 (社会科学版)，2009，22(3):148-152.

[5] 郝诚之. 秦代直道的和平功能与昭君出塞的旅游价值 [J]. 阴山学刊，2006(1):59-64.

[6] 张志俊. 我国物流产业统计指标体系与统计方法研究 [D]. 西安: 长安大学，2006.

平虏渠与泉州渠——运河在军事上的应用

[1] 彭兆荣. 万般景观　在水伊方 : 河流、流域与乡土社会 [J]. 百色学院学报，2019，32(3):33-40.

[2] 蔡茂. 古代官场同僚相互争斗的根源及鉴戒 [J]. 领导科学，2019(7):99-

101.

[3] 哈建强，张倩 . 滹沱河献县张村左右埝间断面过水能力分析 [J]. 海河水利，2018(1):17-18.

[4] 吴季松 . 以协同论指导京津冀协同创新 [J]. 经济与管理，2014，28(5):8-12.

[5] 刘青 . 美丽枯河的前身与消失 [J]. 河南水利与南水北调，2013(1):25-26.

[6] 张兴兆 . 魏晋南北朝时期河北平原内河航运 [J]. 河北师范大学学报 (哲学社会科学版)，2008(6):114-118.

[7] 尤秞 . 中国古代运河工程 (十)[J]. 交通与运输，2001(2):44-45.

丰图义仓——平战结合的物流思想

[1] 成雅莉 . 天下第一仓——丰图义仓——《朝邑丰图义仓记》解读 [J]. 陕西档案，2020(3):18-20.

[2] 石英，王雪 . 清代关中粮仓建筑设计研究——以丰图义仓为例 [J]. 西安建筑科技大学学报 (自然科学版)，2018，50(6):872-877.

[3] 叶玲 . 浅析丰图义仓的建筑特点及保护与利用 [J]. 兰台世界，2014(20):62-63.

[4] 杨宇峤 . "百年仓廪 邑城屏藩"——解读清代丰图义仓建筑 [J]. 同济大学学报 (社会科学版)，2007(3):47-52.

[5] 庞博 . 天下第一仓 [J]. 西部大开发，2006(9):28-30.

[6] 王芳 . 天下第一仓丰图义仓简介 [J]. 农业发展与金融，2004(12):49.

[7] 张建军 . 中国古代粮仓的建筑典范——丰图义仓 [J]. 西部粮油科技，2003(6):58.

[8] 杨宇峤 . 清代丰图义仓建筑研究 [D]. 西安：西安建筑科技大学，2004.

镖局——现代物流组织的雏形

[1] 卢巧舒 . 镖局兴衰的历史分析对我国现代物流运作管理启示 [J]. 物流工程与管理，2017，39(10):23-26.

[2] 杨津涛 . 古代镖局如何 "送快递" [J]. 农村·农业·农民 (A 版)，2016(7):50-52.

[3] 吕如香 . 华中第一镖局 [J]. 档案管理，2010(2):70-71.

[4] 成志芬，张宝秀.大刀王五与源顺镖局 [J]. 文史知识，2008(10):132–136.

[5] 易茗.古代镖局规矩多 [J]. 新闻世界 (社会生活)，2008(1):49.

[6] 彭志忠，柳进.明清民俗与物流发展探究 [J]. 民俗研究，2007(2):215–218.

古代海关——从军事重镇到贸易通道

[1] 邹伟宏.那些行走在古诗中的地名 [J]. 小雪花 (初中高分作文)，2016(9):35–37.

[2] 郭永泉.中国古代海关思想述评 [J]. 海关与经贸研究，2015，36(4):10–18+28.

[3] 黄剑华.汉唐时期的西行取经与佛典汉译 [J]. 地方文化研究，2015(3):9–29+80.

[4] 范柯柯，赵琨.探析旅游景区景观设计——以函谷关景区景观设计为例 [J]. 林业科技情报，2014，46(1):87–89.

[5] 潘清.元代东南沿海外来人口的形成与分布 [J]. 中国社会经济史研究，2005(4):52–58.

[6] 陶艳平.古今词义的沟通与辨析——兼论同义发展规律对中学文言文教学的指导作用 [J]. 达县师范高等专科学校学报，2001(3):99–103.

漕运——内河运输关系社稷安危

[1] 曹娟，吴艳.浅谈漕运文化的传承与弘扬 [J]. 中国水运，2018(4):73–74.

[2] 吴琦.南漕北运：中国古代漕运转向及其意义 [J]. 华中师范大学学报 (人文社会科学版)，2016，55(6):117–128.

[3] 高元杰.20 世纪 80 年代以来漕运史研究综述 [J]. 中国社会经济史研究，2015(1):93–107.

[4] 吴琦.国家事务与地方社会秩序——以清代漕粮征运为基点的考察 [J]. 中国社会经济史研究，2012(2):37–44.

[5] 李德楠.从海洋走向运河：明代漕运方式的嬗变 [J]. 聊城大学学报 (社会科学版)，2012(1):6–10.

[6] 王明德.论中国古代漕运体系发展的几个阶段 [J]. 聊城大学学报 (社会科学版)，2008(3):8–12.

[7] 王伟 . 论明清时期漕运兵丁 [D]. 聊城：聊城大学，2008.

紫禁城——世界宫廷建筑群的物流奇迹

[1] 陈晨心 . 梦回大运河 [J]. 科学家，2014(8):90–94.

[2] 纪维建 . 着力打造新型农村社区文化 [J]. 理论学习，2012(9):35–37.

[3] 杨春雨 . 浅述越南人阮安在营建明朝北京城中的作用 [J]. 兰台世界，2011(19):22–23.

[4] 云妍 . 紫禁城营建采木述略 [J]. 东岳论丛，2006(6):167–172.

[5] 李志坚 . 明代皇木采办的形式 [J]. 安庆师范学院学报 (社会科学版)，2006(6):44–47.